SAN DIEGO

D0687752

AI and the Eye

AI and the Eye

Edited by

Andrew Blake
University of Oxford, UK

and

Tom Troscianko
University of Bristol, UK

NATIONAL UNIVERSITY
LIBRARY SAN DIEGO *e* 1

JOHN WILEY & SONS
Chichester · New York · Brisbane · Toronto · Singapore

Copyright © 1990 by John Wiley & Sons Ltd.
Baffins Lane, Chichester
West Sussex PO19 1UD, England

All rights reserved.

No part of this book may be reproduced by any means,
or transmitted, or translated into a machine language
without the written permission of the publisher.

Other Wiley Editorial Offices

John Wiley & Sons, Inc., 605 Third Avenue,
New York, NY 10158–0012, USA

Jacaranda Wiley Ltd, G.P.O. Box 859, Brisbane,
Queensland 4001, Australia

John Wiley & Sons (Canada) Ltd, 22 Worcester Road,
Rexdale, Ontario M9W 1L1, Canada

John Wiley & Sons (SEA) Pte Ltd, 37 Jalan Pemimpin 05–04
Block B, Union Industrial Building, Singapore 2057

Library of Congress Cataloging-in-Publication Data:
AI and the eye / edited by Andrew Blake and Tom Troscianko.
        p.   cm.
     Proceedings of the 11th European Conference on Visual Perception,
held in Bristol, UK in the summer of 1988.
     Includes bibliographical references.
     ISBN 0 471 92194 7
     1. Vision—Computer simulation—Congresses. 2. Computer vision—
Congresses. 3. Visual perception—Congresses. 4. Artificial
intelligence—Congresses. I. Blake, Andrew. II. Troscianko, Tom.
III. European Conference on Visual Perception (11th: 1988 :
Bristol, England)
QP474.A4   1990   90–11926
612.8′4′0113—dc20   CIP

British Library Cataloguing in Publication Data:
AI and the eye.
   1. Man. Binocular vision. Analysis. Applications of
computer systems
   I. Blake, Andrew   II. Troscianko, Tom
   612.840285

   ISBN 0 471 92194 7

Typeset by APS Ltd., Salisbury, Wiltshire.
Printed and bound in Great Britain by Courier International Ltd. Tiptree, Essex

Contents

List of Contributors

Stuart Anstis

Department of Psychology, York University, North York, Ontario, Canada

H. Harlyn Baker

Artificial Intelligence Center, SRI International, 333 Ravenswood Avenue, Menlo Park, CA 94025, USA

Phil J. Benson

Psychological Laboratory, University of St Andrews, Fife KY16 9JU, UK

Andrew Blake

Robotics Research Group, Department of Engineering Science, University of Oxford, 19 Parks Road, Oxford OX1 3PJ, UK

Heinrich H. Bülthoff

Center for Biological Information Processing, Massachusetts Institute of Technology, Cambridge, MA, USA, but now at Department of Cognitive and Linguistic Sciences, Brown University, Box 1978, Providence, RI 02912, USA

Kyle R. Cave

Department of Brain and Cognitive Sciences, Massachusetts Institute of Technology, Cambridge, MA 02139, USA

Andrew J. Chitty

Psychological Laboratory, University of St Andrews, Fife KY16 9JU, UK

David A. Forsyth

Robotics Research Group, Department of Engineering Science, University of Oxford, Oxford OX1 3PJ, UK

Richard Gregory

Perceptual Systems Research Centre, Department of Psychology, University of Bristol, 8–10 Berkeley Square, Bristol BS8 1HH, UK

Mark H. Harries

Psychological Laboratory, University of St Andrews, Fife KY16 9JU, UK

Bela Julesz

AT & T Bell Laboratories, Murray Hill, NJ 07974, USA and California Institute of Technology, Pasadena, CA 91125, USA, but presently at Psychology Department, Rutgers University, New Brunswick, NJ 08903, USA

David G. Lowe

Computer Science Department, University of British Columbia, Vancouver, BC, Canada V6T 1W5

Hanspeter A. Mallot

Institut für Zoologie III, Johannes Gutenberg-Universität, Mainz, FRG

Amanda J. Mistlin

Psychological Laboratory, University of St Andrews, Fife KY16 9JU, UK

David I. Perrett

Psychological Laboratory, University of St Andrews, Fife KY16 9JU, UK

Vilianur S. Ramachandran

Psychology Department, University of California, San Diego, La Jolla, CA 92093, USA

Tom Troscianko

Perceptual Systems Research Centre, Department of Psychology, University of Bristol, 8–10 Berkeley Square, Bristol BS8 1HH, UK

Roger J. Watt

Centre for Cognitive and Computational Neuroscience and Department of Psychology, Stirling University, Stirling FK9 4LA, UK

Jeremy Wolfe

Department of Brain and Cognitive Sciences, Massachusetts Institute of Technology, Cambridge, MA 02139, USA

Preface

In the summer of 1988 the 11th European Conference on Visual Perception (ECVP) was held in Bristol, UK. The conference is traditionally concerned with studies of biological vision, but the organizers may broaden the subject-matter if they feel that something may be gained by this. In this case, we felt that a dialogue between researchers working on biological vision and their colleagues from the field of machine vision could lead to some new thinking about what is essentially the same subject: how information may be extracted from images.

Various attempts have been made in the past to bring the two sets of researchers together. In spite (or perhaps because) of this, the two fields are largely separate, as anyone can verify by looking at references at the end of most papers: there is usually little reference to papers in "the other camp". Perhaps this is just a natural result of the high degree of specialization in today's science. It is hard to imagine that Newton or Helmholtz would restrict themselves to just biological vision if machine vision were around hundreds of years ago.

There may be quite mundane obstacles to greater cross-communication between biological and machine vision research. One of these is sure to be language. In machine vision, the language of theory is mathematics and the implementation is a computer program. This is often not accessible to psychologists and physiologists. So the first rule of our symposium, and of this book, is that everyone had to speak English as far as possible. Contributors had to explain any mathematics in a simple way, using examples and images as much as possible to illustrate their approach.

Another possible reason for the lack of communication in the past might be that biological vision research is overly concerned with understanding a particular hardware implementation (the brain) rather than the nature of the problem to be solved (how to extract useful information from an image). One can happily study, say, the filter characteristics of a visual channel for years without ever knowing how this channel fits into the general scheme of things. So we asked all our biological vision contributors to stress the general relevance of their work.

Our third criterion was that (with a few notable exceptions) the contributors should be young researchers: people who actually do the nitty-gritty work rather than grand directors of laboratories. That's like a wine-drinker buying vigorous young wines *en primeur* rather than going for the famous makes and vintages. We invited people who, in our opinion, were in the process of making a large impact on their part of the subject.

This book gives some of the latest thinking in perception and computational vision research, with the emphasis on a functional description of the problem. We therefore hope that it will be of interest to anyone who tries to understand vision.

Andrew Blake
Tom Troscianko

Acknowledgements

The "AI and the Eye" symposium was held in honour of Richard Gregory, in recognition of his many stimulating contributions to the theory of visual perception, on the occasion of his retirement from the Chair of Neuropsychology at the University of Bristol.

We would like to thank the following institutions for their generous financial support for the symposium:

British Aerospace plc
British Council
Cardiff Visual Systems
Essilor Ltd
Experimental Psychology Society
Gatsby Foundation
Harveys of Bristol
IBM United Kingdom Academic Fund

IO Research Ltd
Lawrence Erlbaum Associates Ltd
Merck, Sharp and Dohme
Millipede Electronic Graphics Ltd
Pion Ltd
Royal Society of London
US Air Force EOARD
Wisepress

We are grateful to Sue Blackmore and Diana Currant for help in preparing this book. Tom Troscianko was funded by the Medical Research Council (UK) and received support from IBM United Kingdom Scientific Centre.

Introduction

This book is a coming together of people with individual commitment and a shared interest in explaining visual brain function in terms of computing. This implies a philosophical assumption: that the brain does carry out some kind of computing, to make sense of its sensory data. A particular assumption is that many visual processes are, like computers, following mathematically definable rules—algorithms—and that once these are known, we have basic understanding of how we see. That is, how the brain recognizes objects, estimates sizes, distances, slopes and curvatures of surfaces, movements, colours and so on.

There is a temptation (and not all temptations are misleading) to say that the physics, or physiology, of the brain is unimportant compared with its algorithms. But perhaps all the writers in this book (following David Marr) hold that at least the physiology sets *restraints* which are functionally important. But if these are restraints necessary for carrying out algorithms, then algorithms still hold the torch. It is, however, possible to argue that the investigator or theoretician uses algorithms to describe what may in the visual brain be not digital computing but perhaps algorithmic. To take an example outside brains, indeed an unearthly example: consider the moon going round the earth. We may use algorithms, based on Kepler's and Newton's Laws, to *describe* the moon's motion in its orbit; but no way do we want to say that the moon is *carrying out* algorithms. Kepler and Newton were mathematicians—but the moon is not a mathematician. So, by clear analogy, we must be very careful to see whether it is being supposed that the brain carries out algorithms for perceiving the world, or whether *it* does not, but *we* do for describing and explaining it. A bunch of filters and analogue modules, for example, might be said to process information, but without employing algorithms. We, however, might use algorithms (based on filter theory and so on) to describe what such a non-algovistic system does, or how it works. This distinction between kinds or procedures of explanations, and the kind of thing and its procedures that are being explained is surely vital. But it may be difficult to decide whether digital computer-like computations are actually carried out by the brain for vision. My guess is that the first stages are not processing by algovistic computations; although further on algorithms may be employed—if only to select analogue modules appropriately.

One might argue (and this might be right) that even if algorithms are *not* being carried out at all as a digital computer would carry them out, yet it is useful to

develop digital computer models with algorithms for describing functional characteristics of the system. Here we may return to the moon going round the earth. A
mathematical model with algorithms is useful for describing and predicting (and
explaining?) the moon's motions—although the moon is not a mathematician and
does not do it with algorithms. Now consider a digital computer moon simulator.
This works by computing its position, step by step, with algorithms. Does this
simulator, with its algorithms, help us to understand the real non-algovistic moon?
Perhaps it does, perhaps it doesn't. But certainly it would be misleading to say that,
because the simulator works as it does with digital algorithms, so the moon is a
digital computer. This is philosophical danger for Artificial Intelligence (AI)
accounts of brain and mind. But I am sure the writers (and no doubt the readers) of
this book are far too sophisticated to fall into such a trap.

Nevertheless, such issues do necessarily come to the surface when we think about
the hyphen in physiological-psychology. And such issues are central for thinking—of all things!—about consciousness. Is conscious awareness (which we all
believe is part of perception although impossibly mysterious) associated with
algorithms? Or with the physiological *hardware* ("squishyware") of the brain—or
what? Suppose it is associated not exactly with the stream of processing, but rather
with *discrepancies*, or failures of prediction. When driving my car I am most aware
when something not quite predicted turns up, such as a pedestrian jumping out, or
I take a wrong turning. Is this increase of awareness with surprise associated with
selecting different algorithms (or perhaps new analogue modules), as needed to
cope with the emergency or the new situation? If so, are there algorithms for
selecting algorithms? And if so, why should these algorithms for selecting
algorithms be particularly associated with consciousness?

Or, is consciousness straightforwardly associated with the amount or rate of
information being processed? Given that information (in its technical sense)
increases as prior probability decreases, this notion must be on the cards. We
should not be surprised that we are aware of surprise, if consciousness is associated
with rate of information being processed.

Yet it seems too absurd to say that surprise (or improbability) *per se* would be
conscious. It also seems absurd to say that algorithms, (or for that matter non-
algorithmic analogue processors) could *per se* be conscious. This would lead to
activist groups publicly objecting to switching computers off!

Such, perhaps science fiction, considerations serve to suggest that the thinking of
several decades ago in cybernetics and information theory was not a waste of time,
though neither are fashionable today. These issues and theories, discussed a
generation or more ago, are still apposite and still have a lot to say. What has
changed, so dramatically it was not predicted, is the availability and power of
electronic digital computers. So now mathematical models can actually be tried
out, and compared against human and animal perception. How do they compare?
Well, my word processor can find typing errors, and search for words, inhumanly
fast. On the other hand, we or even quite simple animals can recognize objects
incomparably better and faster than any computer system. Is this because the
hardware of computers is still far behind physiological brain performance? Or is it
because we do not yet have the right mathematical models (perhaps necessarily

involving a lot of parallel processing which is still hard to do) to replicate the brain's "squishyware" software? In any case, we have moved away from armchair philosophy to physiological experiments probing brain function quite directly, and to computing operating systems which begin to achieve something of what the brain can do, though perhaps by different means. So we have moved a little into *experimental* philosophy. Let's hope it's not like the alchemists, who got almost nowhere, with two thousand years of setting up rules and experimenting—as they had inappropriate basic ideas.

Whatever the answers, I am sure this book is a significant step towards understanding what goes on in our heads when we open our eyes. And the alchemists' dream did come true, though for the wrong reasons, for we can now transmute elements into gold. Perhaps we will come to transmute silicon into mind.

Richard L. Gregory

1 AI and the Eye?

Andrew Blake[1] and Tom Troscianko[2]

[1]*Robotics Research Group, Department of Engineering Science, University of Oxford, 19 Parks Road, Oxford OX1 3PJ, UK, and* [2]*Perceptual Systems Research Centre, Department of Psychology, University of Bristol, 8–10 Berkeley Square, Bristol BS8 1HH, UK*

The aim of the 11th European Conference on Visual Perception (ECVP), and of this book, is to highlight research of mutual relevance to studies of machine and biological vision. It seems to us that each of those two fields have some special challenges for the other.

1. Biological vision is robust. Infinite varieties of shape, texture and illumination conditions are encountered in the natural world. In human vision, stereopsis, motion and shading analysis and pattern recognition processes seem to cope remarkably well with these variations (see Chapters 2–5).
2. Given a psychophysical theory, it can be tested in detail if it is couched in computational terms, so that "simulations" can be run, either on a computer or as "armchair" experiments. Predictions arising from simulation may be surprising, and lead to experimental hypotheses.
3. There are AI (artificial intelligence) vision systems that are aimed at some of the tasks that have been researched by psychophysicists. Both their successes and weaknesses are interesting. They have shown a measure of competence at processes like object recognition (Brooks, 1981; and see Lowe's Chapter 11), computation of egomotion (for example, Baker's Chapter 10) and stereopsis (Marr & Poggio, 1979; Mayhew & Frisby, 1981). AI vision systems typically perform poorly when their design assumptions are violated—assumptions such as planarity in object recognition, rigidity in egomotion computation and opacity in stereopsis. Biological systems are more robust. Is that simply a matter of degree, or because they are built on radically different principles?

AI and the Eye   Edited by A. Blake and T. Troscianko
© 1990 John Wiley & Sons Ltd.

COMPUTATIONAL THEORIES

The new generation of vision researchers has been handed an immensely powerful framework—the mathematical framework of computational theory—with which to describe, debate and test models of intelligent processes. The significance of this heritage has been expressed in different contexts by Mackay (1969), Dennett (1978), Marr (1982) and Longuet-Higgins (1987), and strongly opposed by Searle (1984). The previous generation of psychophysicists and physiologists had something similar, but on a very much smaller scale. The metaphor of the spatial frequency "channel" came directly from Fourier theory, via engineering practice in the representation of linear systems. Now the methodology of computational theory has developed sufficiently to deserve inclusion in the psychophysicist's toolbox. Note that computational theory does not mean the "theory of computer science" but the practice of expression models of information processing in *precise mathematical and algorithmic notation*. Examples of computational theories include both physical models (for instance imaging geometry) and also others (grammars, for example) that are naturally expressed in terms of symbol-manipulation, something which AI progamming languages (LISP, POP, PROLOG) are particularly suited for. Longuet-Higgins (1987) explains the power of computational modelling as follows:

> The particular contribution that Artificial Intelligence can make to psychology is the concept of a procedure for the performance of a cognitive task.... if one is able to discover an effective procedure for the accomplishment of a given task, then one can check whether or not it really is effective by translating it into a suitable programming language and running the program on a computer.

Mackay (1969), Gregory (1975) and Marr (1982) make much of the distinction between mechanism and computational procedure. Ullman (1979) expounds Marr's philosophy on this point:

> An immediate consequence ... is the distinction that can be drawn between the physical embodiment of the symbols manipulated by the system on the one hand, and the meaning of the symbols on the other. One can study, in other words, the *computation* performed by the system almost independently of the physical *mechanisms* supporting the computation.

A major part of a computational theory is the description of a *problem* whereas an algorithm is a description of a particular *solution*. Marr (1982) uses the example of bird flight: "trying to understand perception by studying only neurons is like trying to understand bird flight by studying only feathers. It just cannot be done ... we have to understand aerodynamics." A computational theory, in Marr's sense, is not so much about computational processes as about the "abstract analysis of a task" facing a psychological system (Boden, 1988).

Will psychologists and physiologists import the new-generation theory? Many are already doing so (Julesz, 1971; Marr & Poggio, 1979; Ullman, 1979; Mayhew & Frisby, 1981; Hildreth, 1984; Yuille & Grzywacz, 1988). This book contains some outstanding recent examples of work in a similar vein—see Chapter 6 by Bülthoff and Mallot, and Chapter 7 by Watt. Perrett *et al.* (Chapter 8), whilst not dealing directly in computational models, also profess to be strongly influenced by computational ideas (moving coordinate frames) in their choice of hypotheses for experimental neurophysiology.

But there is serious opposition to this creed. The philosopher John Searle (1984) devotes three chapters to it. Here is a extract from one of his arguments.

> Well, suppose we were going to design a computer that recognises faces as we do. It would carry out quite a computational task, involving a lot of calculating of geometrical and topological features. But is there any evidence that the way we do it involves computing?

Principally, of course, his book concerns larger problems of philosophy of mind which are outside the scope of this book. But he does suggest that there are negative implications for "cognitivism"—the study of thinking as computational manipulation of symbols:

> The computer is probably no better and no worse as a metaphor for the brain than earlier mechanical metaphors. We learn as much about the brain by saying it's a computer as by saying it's a telephone switchboard, a telegraph system, a water pump or a steam engine.

Ramachandran (Chapter 3) invokes Searle's support when he argues strongly that Nature's evolved solution to vision is not a computational one but a "bag of tricks". Searle and Ramachandran are actually arguing rather different points. Ramachandran says that visual perception is not the product of a *single* computational theory: there are many different processes in that bag. He accepts the possibility that each process has its own computational theory. Searle goes much further, diminishing altogether the relevance of computational theory to perception. However, the existence of perceptual tasks for which there is well-specified computational theory and relevant "hardware" knowledge challenges his pessimism about cognitivist research. Consider, for example, the Reichardt motion detector (Reichardt, 1961). It is a simple model of retinal motion computation, well supported by psychophysical and physiological data (Borst & Bahde, 1986; Troscianko & Fahle, 1988). Thus, we have a computational theory, albeit a simple one, explaining a certain perceptual task, and giving strong predictions for behaviour which would otherwise be ill understood. What holds true for these low-level tasks may possibly be applied to more complex tasks such as face recognition, especially as evidence emerges (see Chapter 8 by Perrett *et al.*) that these "higher" tasks may also be performed by dedicated areas of the brain.

Our claim is that computational theories tell you something about how perception can be done by any system, no matter what are the details of its implementation. It is like the difference between expounding the laws of thermodynamics and building an efficient refrigerator. If you are in the business, it may well be useful to take apart the competition's refrigerator to see how they did it. But the theory tells you, in a strong sense, about all refrigerators that ever have or ever will be built. There are fundamental limits on how efficient a refrigerator can be.

So there are two distinct studies—first, the computational study of intelligence, what it is and how to stimulate it; second, how biological systems implement it. The second is seriously hampered without the first, because the theory is needed in order to make the right hypotheses. Describing a "bag of tricks" is one thing but how are the tricks done?

ROBUST VISION

What objections might the sceptical psychophysicist have? A criticism that is often levelled at AI vision theories (point number 3 at the beginning) is that they cannot deal with noise or other departures from their assumptions. As an example, Todd (1985) points out that AI vision theories of the perception of structure from motion do not account for all the experimental facts. He shows that the human visual system is able to perceive rigid motion even when masked by "noisy" motion of random dots. The situation as a whole is non-rigid because of the dot noise, but human vision is robust to such a disturbance. Todd is right in that analysis of such motion is indeed an unsolved problem, beyond—but perhaps not too far beyond—the leading edge of AI vision. That does not mean that the computational approach is *inapplicable* to the problem. Quite the reverse. It is the rigorous formulation in computational terms that highlighted the importance of rigidity in the first place. Now, because computer programs based on the rigidity assumption explain some but not all of motion interpretation, it has become clear that the assumption of rigidity must be broadened to allow noise, flexure and multiple independent motions. As and when good models of this broader kind are found they will surely be articulated as computational theories.

PARALLELISM?

Another objection that a psychophysicist might raise runs something like this. A program designed to run on a machine with a serial architecture is quite different from one for a machine with parallel architecture. The computational theory may be identical initially, but would evolve into something quite different in each of the two cases. The theory depends on the machine.

Insistence on the earlier distinction between computational theory and algorithm will be helpful here. Questions of architecture, parallelism, etc., belong strictly to the *algorithm* level. The programmer, exercising his parallel machine, does *not* change his computational theory, because that dealt with what information was or was not present in his data, not with how, in detail, to extract that information. However, his algorithmic style undoubtedly will be affected by the machine. Consider shape-from-shading (see also Chapter 6 by Bülthoff and Mallot and Chapter 3 by Ramachandran). Computational theory says that convex/concave reversals can occur because, as a matter of theoretical truth, image intensity patterns are invariant (under certain circumstances) to such surface reversals. This is true no matter how surface shape might actually be computed, whether serially using "characteristic strips" or in a parallel network computation (Ikeuchi & Horn, 1981; Horn, 1986). The sharpness of the distinction between algorithm and computational theory also bears on Ramachandran's "bag of tricks". Biological systems may not have evolved as mathematically planned procedures—that says a lot about the algorithms used and how they were built. (Mind you, large software systems often evolve piecemeal too!) But they are still subject to the analytical scrutiny of computational theory. Computational theory tells you about constraints that *any* algorithm must obey, because of the intrinsic nature of the information processing problem. It is only via computational theory that we can understand, sufficiently precisely, what the tasks are.

CONNECTIONISM

Another important objection could be raised to the "AI and the Eye" paradigm. Why not abandon the computational viewpoint and concentrate on connectionist architectures that may be taken to resemble neural machinery?

In reply, one might first point out that connectionist models still lack much of the important structure that real neurones have, especially the richness of connections. Leaving that aside, the important point is that connectionist architectures are *architectures*—operating at the bottom two Marr levels, algorithm and hardware. For example, a lot has been discovered recently about how cooperative networks can serve as associative, fault-tolerant memories or pattern recognizers (Hopfield, 1982; Gardner, 1988; Lehky & Sejnowski, 1988; Mitchison & Durbin, 1989). In vision, especially, the power of parallel networks has been demonstrated for certain well-defined tasks such as feature recognition (Ballard, 1981; Hinton, 1981) and image filtering (Horn, 1974; Ikeuchi & Horn, 1981; Grimson, 1981; Terzopoulos, 1983; Blake & Zisserman, 1987). Connectionist architectures certainly have their place as implementation models for particular computations. However, these mechanisms are specific to certain computational tasks. In no sense can they be regarded as general machines with "emergent" intelligence. Certainly they can "learn" to recognize new patterns and even to do motor control. But they have not demonstrated competence to learn complex structured skills such as analysis of language, matching of 3D models to visual data, understanding of qualitative physics, or 3D analysis of motion, all tasks that have been extensively penetrated by computational theories.

Even supposing superior connectionist visual processing machines *were* developed, what theoretical advance in knowledge would result? How could the evolution and final state of the machine be described? If another similar machine failed to perform as well, it would be difficult to understand why.

The chapters in this book make strong technical contributions—summarized in Table 1. They also address, we believe, the following general question. One may

Table 1

General issue	Chapter/author	Specific issue
1. Biological vision is robust	2. Julesz	Cyclopean perception
	3. Ramachandran	"Utilitarian theory" of perception
	4. Wolfe & Cave	Visual attention
	5. Anstis	Motion: aperture problem
2. Computational theory in biological vision	6. Bülthoff & Mallot	Integration of stereopsis, shading and texture
	7. Watt	Symbolic model of the primal sketch
	8. Perrett *et al.*	Neurophysiology: 3D vision
3. Computational theory in AI vision	9. Forsyth	Colour constancy
	10. Baker	Motion: spatiotemporal analysis
	11. Lowe	Perceptual grouping for object recognition

accept that the computer is a much more sophisticated metaphor for the brain than its predecessors the switchboard, telegraph, pump and steam engine. Is that going to lead to a deeper scientific understanding of the mind?

REFERENCES

Ballard, D. H. (1981). Generalizing the Hough transformation to detect arbitrary shapes. *Pattern Recognition*, **13**, 111–122.

Blake, A. & Zisserman, A. (1987). *Visual Reconstruction*. MIT Press, Cambridge, MA.

Boden, M. A. (1988). *Computer Models of Mind*. Cambridge University Press, Cambridge.

Borst, A. & Bahde, S. (1986). What kind of movement detector is triggering the landing response of the housefly? *Biological Cybernetics*, **55**, 59–69.

Brooks, R. A. (1981). Symbolic reasoning among 3-D models and 2-D images. *AI Journal*, **17**, 285–348.

Dennett, D. (1978). *Brainstorms*. Harvester Press, Brighton.

Gardner, E. (1988). The pace of interactions in neural network models. *J. Phys. A Mat. Gen.*, **21**, 257–270.

Gregory, R. (1975). Do we need cognitive concepts. In M. S. Gazzaniga & C. Blakemore, (Eds) *Handbook of Psychobiology*, pp. 607–628. Academic Press, New York.

Grimson, W. E. L. (1981). *From Images to Surfaces*. MIT Press, Cambridge, MA.

Hildreth, E. C. (1984). Computations underlying the measurement of visual motion. *Artificial Intelligence Journal*, **23**, 309–354.

Hinton, G. E. (1981). Shape representation in parallel systems. *Proc. 7th IJCAI*, Vancouver, Canada, pp. 1088–1096.

Hopfield, J. J. (1982). Neural networks and physical systems with emergent collective computational abilities. *Proceedings of the National Acadamy of Science, USA*, **79**, 2554–2558.

Horn, B. K. P. (1974). Determining lightness from an image. *Computer Graphics and Image Processing*, **3**, 277–299.

Horn, B. K. P. (1986). *Robot Vision*. MIT Press, Cambridge, MA.

Ikeuchi, K. & Horn, B. K. P. (1981), Numerical shape from shading and occluding boundaries. In J. M. Brady (Ed.) *Computer Vision*, pp. 141–184.

Julesz, B. (1971). *Foundations of Cyclopean Perception*.

Lehky, S. R. & Sejinowski, T. J. (1988). Network model of shape-from-shading: neural function arises from both receptive and projective fields. *Nature*, **333**, 452–454.

Longuet-Higgins, H. C. (1987). *Mental Processes*. MIT Press, Cambridge, MA.

Mackay, D. (1969). *Information, Mechanism and Meaning*. MIT Press, Cambridge, MA.

Marr, D. & Poggio, T. (1979). A computational theory of human stereo vision. *Proceedings of the Royal Society (London), Series B*, **204**, 301–328.

Marr, D. (1982). *Vision*. Freeman, San Francisco.

Mayhew, J. E. W. & Frisby, J. P. (1981). Towards a computational and psychophysical theory of stereopsis. *AI Journal*, **17**, 349–385.

Mitchison, G. J. & Durbin, R. M. (1989). Bounds on the learning capacity of some multi-layer networks. *Biological Cybernetics*, **60**, 345–356.

Reichardt, W. (1961). Autocorrelation, a principle for the evaluation of sensory information by the central nervous system. In W. A. Rosenbluth (Ed.) *Sensory Coding*. John Wiley, New York.

Searle, J. (1984). *Minds Brains and Science*. The 1984 Reith Lectures, British Broadcasting Corporation, London.

Terzopoulos, D. (1983). Multilevel computational processes for visual surface reconstruction. *Computer Vision Graphics and Image Processing*, **24**, 52–96.

Todd, J. T. (1985). Perception of structure from motion: is projective correspondence of moving elements a necessary condition? *Journal of Experimental Psychology*, **11**, 689–710.

Troscianko, T. & Fahle, M. (1988). Why do isoluminant stimuli appear slower? *Journal of the Optical Society of America*, **A5**, 871–880.

Ullman, S. (1979). *The Interpretation of Visual Motion*. MIT Press, Cambridge, MA.

Yuille, A. L. & Grzywacz, N. M. (1988). A computational theory for the perception of coherent visual motion. *Nature*, **333**, 71–74.

2 AI and Early Vision—Part I*

Bela Julesz

AT & T Bell Laboratories, Murray Hill, NJ 07974, USA† and *California Institute of Technology, Pasadena, CA 91125, USA*

A quarter of a century ago I introduced two paradigms into psychology which in the intervening years have had a direct impact on the psychobiology of early vision and an indirect one on artificial intelligence (AI or machine vision). The first, the computer-generated random-dot stereogram (RDS) paradigm (Julesz, 1960) at its very inception posed a strategic question for both AI and neurophysiology. The finding that stereoscopic depth perception (stereopsis) is possible without the many enigmatic cues of monocular form recognition—as assumed previously—demonstrated that stereopsis with its basic problem of finding matches between corresponding random aggregates of dots in the left and right visual fields became ripe for modeling. Indeed, the binocular matching problem of stereopsis opened up an entire field of study, eventually leading to the computational models of Marr (1982) and his coworkers. The fusion of RDS had an even greater impact on neurophysiologists—including Hubel and Wiesel (1962)—who realized that stereopsis must occur at an early stage, and can be studied more easily than form perception. This insight recently culminated in the studies by Poggio (1984) who found binocular-disparity-tuned neurons in the input stage to the visual cortex (layer IVB in VI) in the monkey that were selectively triggered by dynamic RDS. Thus the first paradigm led to a strategic insight: that where there is stereoscopic vision there is no camouflage, and it was therefore advantageous for our primate ancestors to evolve the cortical machinery of stereoscopic vision to capture camouflaged prey (insects) at a standstill. Amazingly, although stereopsis evolved relatively late in primates, it captured the very input stages of the visual cortex. (For a detailed review, see Julesz, 1986a.)

---

* See p. 19.

† Presently at Psychology Department, Rutgers University, New Brunswick, NJ 08903, USA.

AI and the Eye   Edited by A. Blake and T. Troscianko
©1990 John Wiley & Sons Ltd.

The second paradigm was the effortless (preattentive) texture discrimination of computer-generated texture pairs with identical second-order statistics (Julesz, 1962). This finding led to many psychophysical and theoretical insights, but at present is far from the definitive conclusions of the first paradigm. Perhaps the most important insight is the realization that preattentive texture segregation does not depend upon the global constraints of second- and higher-order statistics (and hence, of power spectra) but, instead, rests on quasi-local conspicuous features, which I called textons (Julesz, 1981, 1986b). Much of the spatial information (phase) is lost. Indeed, discrimination depends principally on the density of elongated blobs with specific width, length, spatial frequency, color, orientation, binocular disparity, velocity, flicker rate, etc. Of particular interest are those texture pairs whose elements as isolated pairs yield strong discrimination, yet as textures cannot be segregated. Such texture pairs limit the validity of models that are based on the dissimilarity between the isolated texture elements. Besides elongated blobs (e.g. Gabor patches) there appears also to be some hidden textonal properties, related somehow to "closure" and "corner" that cannot be described adequately by "terminators" and "crossings", and cannot be modeled by Laplacian spatial filters followed by squaring. Such problems have led to arguments between Bergen & Adelson (1988), Voorhees & Poggio (1988) and Julesz & Kröse (1988). It is interesting that the insensitivity to position of texture discrimination by foveal vision seems to hold even for shapes in peripheral vision, where so much of the predictions of the texton theory seem to apply (Saarinen, 1987). It seems that the secrets of preattentive texture discrimination are not yet solved, but are ripe for a breakthrough. In summary, the first paradigm led to the insight that contrary to common belief stereopsis is a global process, while the second paradigm unexpectedly showed that preattentive texture discrimination is not a statistical (global) process, but essentially quasi-local.

ON STYLE AND CONTENT

It is a truism in the arts that style and content are inseparable. On the other hand, in mathematics, say, one often finds the first proof of a theorem in a rather awkward form to be replaced later by a more "elegant" proof. Whether the elegant proof yields a deeper understanding of the theorem is an open question, which explains why the credit usually goes to the first mathematician who proved it. What about scientific discoveries? Does the content of the discovery depend on the style (methodology)? Here I define "scientific style" as methodology, which consists of an ensemble of tools and techniques (tricks) of how to use these tools, and the restriction of problems to a subset for which the tools work.

It seems that scientific discoveries are intimately linked to scientific techniques. As a matter of fact, the introduction of a methodological innovation or a new tool usually raises new questions and results in discoveries. Here I do not wish to dwell on microscopes, telescopes, thermometers and their impact on biology, astronomy, thermodynamics, etc. Instead, I will concentrate on the state of the psychobiology of vision as I experienced it when I entered the field thirty years ago and how that field has changed ever since, and how my own researches with my coworkers contributed to these changes.

My arrival at Bell Laboratories in 1956 and my first years there were accompanied by the arrival of the first large digital computers. These were used mainly for data crunching, although some of us used them to simulate complex systems. Because of my interest in encoding TV signals to "fool the human visual system", by reducing the amount of information without visual detriment, I joined a group with similar interests. I was particularly interested in a scheme where only the extremes of the TV signals were transmitted, and the receiver linearly interpolated between these samples. In essence, one would transmit the position of contours (i.e. sudden luminance gradients). This capitalized on two properties of the human visual system. First, that it could not determine the exact shape of an abrupt luminance change (whether convex, concave or linear). Second, that for very gradual changes (long shadows) the visual system was also quite insensitive for detecting accurate luminance changes. However, the visual system was quite sensitive to the location of the contours. Because implementation looked for extrema in one dimension, one would get jagged vertical edges for grainy (noisy) images. In order to reduce this jitter, one had to determine the positions of the extrema quite accurately, that in turn reduced the information saving (Julesz, 1959). It occurred to me then to search for two-dimensional contours, and try to interpolate two-dimensional minimal luminance surfaces between these extrema (much as soap bubbles fill in minimal surfaces between wire meshes). However, I was not sure of how to extract two-dimensional contours from images. The Laplacian operator was an obvious first choice, but it seemed rather limited to me, since it could not segregate areas of different textures, nor similar textures at different depths. It seemed that in order to find contours in two dimensions, one would have to "know" what objects were—a formidable problem of semantics. So my interest in searching for two-dimensional contours led me into problems of depth and texture perception.

Indeed, my first idea was to track the real three-dimensional scene with a stereo camera to determine the depth relief and then extract two-dimensional contours at places where the depth gradient was above a given threshold. I was stunned to learn that according to prevailing belief (e.g. Ogle, 1964) stereopsis (stereoscopic depth perception) was based on the monocular recognition of contours and forms, just those entities I wanted to extract. It was believed that in order to determine binocular disparity between corresponding features (forms) in the left and right images, one would first have to recognize these features (forms) separately in the two views. As a former radar engineer I knew—what workers in psychobiology apparently were not aware of—that there is no camouflage in three dimensions. Camouflaged objects, which are hidden in one eye's view, jump out in vivid depth when stereoscopically fused. This insight made me aware of the fact that stereopsis does not need semantics, the familiarity with the many billions of cues and relationships between objects on which form recognition is based, but must be a much simpler process, based on a binocular correlation process.

Of course, in real life we have no ideal camouflage, and in 1960 I used the digital computer to generate random-dot stereograms, as shown in Figure 1, that, indeed,

Figure 1. Computer-generated random-dot stereogram where the left and right arrays are always composed of black and white elements selected at random. When binocularly fused, the correlation between the arrays is perceived and a center square jumps out in vivid depth from the background (Julesz, 1971).

are just aggregates of black and white pixels in the left and right image, respectively (Julesz, 1960).

Yet, when stereoscopically fused, by the viewer crossing his or her eyes (or using a prism over one eye), a hidden square (with a binocular disparity different from its surroundings) appears to hover over the background.

Obviously, without having to perform monocular form recognition, the binocular matching process could eliminate the $N^2/2 - N$ false targets and arrive at the N correct localizations, as shown in Figure 2 (Julesz, 1971).

How this binocular matching process works has been the preoccupation of many model-builders ever since and became a pet project of workers in artificial intelligence (see, e.g., Marr, 1982). I will return to this problem in the section on "Luminance versus cyclopean channels of motion".

Here I want to emphasize that in the case of adequate resolution (when the surfaces of the objects are richly covered with textures) stereo pairs contain adequate information to permit the reconstruction of the three-dimensional world without complex familiarity cues. Thus "early vision" can operate with minimal memory; for stereopsis it is enough to "know" that physical objects are usually continuous, and their surfaces are at most places smooth, and except for transparent or ambiguous surfaces (see "Mental holography" in Julesz, 1971) are unique. Obviously, many other depth cues from shading to motion are important. These are processed modularly in the early visual system and are combined together at some rather early stage. We will return to this problem later.

Going back to the initial questions of style and content, I think my research style can be described as using computers to generate visual environments with controlled geometrical and statistical properties, and to study which of these parameters the visual system can extract (process) in the total absence of familiarity cues.

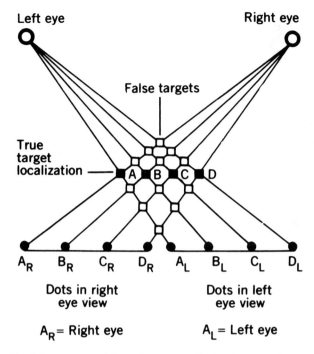

Figure 2.   The false target problem of stereoscopic depth perception (Julesz, 1971).

Since textured surfaces play a dominant role for random-dot stereograms, in my youth I became interested in texture perception as well. It was obvious to me that the canonic textures are three dimensional (like the bark of a tree) whose two-dimensional projections on the retina, with their shadows cast, constitute the real-life textures. Nevertheless, to simplify matters, I embarked on a study of two-dimensional artificial textures with controlled geometrical and statistical properties. I was interested in finding out the level of complexity of effortless (preattentive) texture discrimination, in particular what order of statistics the visual system could utilize. The technical problems of integral geometry to generate texture pairs with identical Nth-order, but different $(N + 1)$th-order statistics were formidable, and preoccupied my mathematically gifted colleagues and me for over a quarter of a century. For details, I refer the reader to Julesz (1981, 1984).

Naively, one might have assumed that the first-order statistics were to control tonal quality (the shades of gray, or color) while second-order statistics were to describe granularity. However, even this assumption does not hold in general. We were able to generate many texture pairs with different second-order statistics (hence different power spectra) that were indiscriminable, as well as many pairs which could be effortlessly segregated. Furthermore, we generated texture pairs with *identical* second-order (even *identical* third-order) statistics that yielded strong discrimination. Figure 3 shows an iso-second-order texture pair that cannot be told apart, while the iso-second-order texture pair in Figure 4 is strongly discriminable.

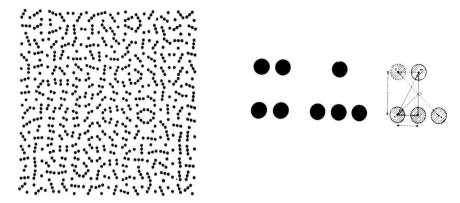

Figure 3. Preattentively indistinguishable iso-second-order texture pair generated by the four-disk method (Julesz *et al.*, 1973).

Such examples clearly show that statistical (global) parameters are not describing preattentive (effortless) texture segregation, but instead some quasi-local features seem to have perceptual significance. For instance, both Figure 3 and Figure 4 were generated using the "four-disk method" (Julesz *et al.*, 1973), yet in Figure 4 the four disks in one of the texture pairs form quasi-collinear structures —absent in the other texture—which appear as conspicuous features and yield texture segmentation. I called these conspicuous features in discriminable iso-

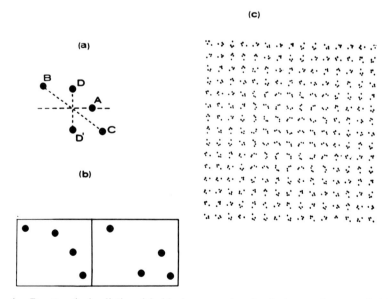

Figure 4. Preattentively distinguishable iso-second-order texture pair generated by the four-disk method. Discrimination is based on quasi-collinearity (Julesz, 1981).

second-(third)-order texture pairs "textons" (Julesz, 1981). Besides quasi-collinear line segments, elongated blobs of certain color, width, length, orientation, movement, binocular disparity, flicker rate, etc., behave as textons. Whether crossings of line segments and their ends-of-lines (terminators) behave as textons too, are interesting questions and have initiated some debate, which will be reviewed.

While preattentive texture segmentation of texture pairs so far did not yield the same insight as research with random-dot stereograms (and cinematograms) did, both fields of research are characterized by the same research style and content. Both use controlled geometrical and mathematical visual stimuli—which can be done only with powerful computers—and both fields show that only relatively simple stimulus parameters, such as binocular disparity or texton density, can be extracted by the human visual system. The underlying "semantics" is rather simple. Continuity and smoothness of surfaces, quasi-collinear texture elements, etc., are the built-in knowledge of "early vision". It is thus a simple—yet quite important —system that precedes the higher perceptual and cognitive visual systems. Because of its relative simplicity, it is quite obvious why model-builders and workers of artificial intelligence use early vision as their "model system".

After this brief note on "style and content", I turn now to the problem of content. In the next two sections I will summarize the main results obtained by my two paradigms, respectively, with some new, hitherto unpublished, results.

CYCLOPEAN PERCEPTION

The field of cyclopean perception, that is the study of visual perception using random-dot stereograms, correlograms and cinematograms originates with the introduction of computer-generated random-dot stereograms (RDS) into psychology (Julesz, 1960) and was formulated as a paradigm in my monograph (Julesz, 1971). After a quarter of a century it had become an elaborate field of scientific study as reviewed in the Silver Jubilee Issue of *Vision Research* (Julesz, 1986). Since it would be a crime to repeat this recent review article of mine with almost a hundred references, I concentrate here on some insights gained since that publication and on a recent discovery by Jih Jie Chang, a close associate of mine, on the effect of luminance channels on global stereopsis. For a detailed history of the field the interested reader is referred to my review article.

When stereoscopically fusing Figure 1, the reader can immediately notice that certain correlated areas jump out in vivid depth, although when monocularly viewed they appear as a uniformly random texture. Thus without monocular form recognition the early visual system can match the binocularly correlated areas in the left and right eye's view. There is no consensus as to how that matching is done, but obviously one does not have to evoke monocular form recognition of corresponding areas that are horizontally shifted in the two eyes' views. Later we will discuss several models of binocular target matching. At the moment we concentrate on the fact that stereopsis of RDS, which I also call "global stereopsis", is a simpler process than assumed previously.

Indeed, it had been assumed previously (e.g. Ogle, 1964) that monocularly recognizable shapes (particularly contours) would be matched monocularly and used to achieve stereopsis. Years after the discovery of RDS Ogle still believed (Ogle and Wakefield, 1967) that RDS were fused because as a result of the shift of certain randomly dotted areas some of the dots would be *cut*, giving rise to faint, but visible, monocular contours. Somehow, he missed the essence of *computer-generated* RDS that the disparity is always an integer multiple of the dot (pixel) width, and therefore these dots *are never cut*!

Of course, the binocular matching problem—with the elimination of the many false localizations—raises many interesting problems, particularly for workers in AI. The basic problem is the *complexity* of features underlying binocular matching. Let us generalize RDS and instead of random dots (pixels) let us use random elements, say, line segments of certain brightness (color), orientation, length and width to portray the left and right aways. Now, the essence of a random-element stereogram is to select the elements in the two eyes' views such that the local tokens (features) that fall within Panum's fusional area should give rise to the maximum number of false matches. For instance, if we select line segments of equal width, length, brightness (contrast and color) and of only two orientations (e.g. $\pm 45°$ arc), then in a small neighborhood several line segments in the left and right images can be matched, yielding many false targets.

Obviously, in order to disambiguate binocular matching one has to seek *global* matching, searching for matches in ever-increasing neighborhood sizes. That is why I called stereopsis of RDS "global stereopsis" (Julesz, 1971, 1978). There are several ways globality can be introduced. An easy way is to take some "Mexican-hat" shaped channels tuned optimally to a given line segment of specified width, orientation, etc., and responding best to a certain binocular disparity (Poggio and Fisher, 1977) and pool a few dozen adjacent ones by *probability summation*. A somewhat more sophisticated way to combine local detectors into a global detector is by *cooperativity*. The reader interested in several robust cooperative phenomena of global stereopsis—including hysteresis effects—might consult my monograph (Julesz, 1971). The same reference describes a spring-coupled-magnetic-dipole model of global stereopsis that gives excellent insight into the workings of cooperative and plastic phenomena of stereopsis that remain hidden in the many computer models, except for a potential-energy model by Sperling (1970).

Because one can show with spatial-frequency (SF)-filtered RDS that channels tuned to different spatial frequencies can independently carry stereo information (Julesz and Miller, 1975), such channels permit another way to introduce globality in the binocular matching process. The lower the SF channel's range, the wider the width of the channel is in the space domain. A "Mexican-hat" function receptive field can be closely approximated by a Laplacian of a Gaussian or by a DOG function (see, e.g., the excellent book by Marr, 1982). Gabor functions also emulate the DOG functions. The important fact is that low-spatial-frequency-tuned receptive fields have spatially wide excitatory and inhibitory regions, thus exhibiting global neighborhoods. Marr & Poggio (1979) proposed an interesting non-cooperative model of stereopsis based on a hierarchy of SF-tuned channels to eliminate the false target problem. It rests on the fact that there is only one zero crossing in the lowest spatial frequency filter with the same gradient slope in the corresponding left and right representations. If one assumes in accordance with Logan's theorem that for one octave filtered signals the zero crossings uniquely determine the signal (provided the DC pedestals obey some common-sense rules), then matching zero crossings in the left and right SF-tuned channels (band-pass filters) will eliminate false matching as long as the disparity is less than half the wavelength. Marr and Poggio further assumed that the lowest SF-tuned channels would become matched first, this in turn would initiate convergence eye movements, and would bring into correspondence the finer SF-tuned channels with less and less disparities. With finer and finer spatial resolution, elements of greater and greater spatial detail would be matched (localized) avoiding at each scale the false matches.

Unfortunately this ingenious scheme suffers from one problem—it is not used by the human visual system. Among others, Mayhew & Frisby (1979) and Mowforth *et al.* (1981) have shown that high SF RDS, with low and medium SF filtered out, can still elicit large disparity convergence eye movements and yield fusion even when presented in a brief flash. The fact, that such a model is not consistent with human stereopsis does not discourage some workers in AI from using this model for machine vision, and an entire book is devoted to it (Grimson, 1981). Let me note that Grimson also emphasizes another maxim of Marr and Poggio in his stereo algorithms—that of striving for uniqueness. This is the more curious, since in my monograph (Julesz, 1971) I devote an entire chapter ("Mental Holography") to *ambiguous* RDS that display two or more distinct surfaces using the same RDS. The human stereopsis system is capable of finding one-by-one these multiple solutions to the matching problem, so striving for uniqueness is not necessary, and what is more it is a requirement that is not used by the human visual system.

The fact that the Marr–Poggio non-cooperative algorithm based on vergence movements is not used by the visual system does not mean that the same hierarchical system could not be used, based on neurological couplings such that low SF channels would introduce ever-decreasing shifts in the higher SF channels. Of course, such a neuronal shifter hierarchy (though much more complex than cooperative neural nets) could still exist, and Anderson & Van Essen (1987) conjecture ways such shifter nets could work.

LUMINANCE VERSUS CYCLOPEAN CHANNELS OF MOTION

In this chapter I restrict myself to RDS and omit a quarter-century-long research with RDC (cinematograms, called by some kinematograms). On the other hand, I devote this section to dynamic RDS and their relationship to movement perception.

As I did point out in my monograph (Julesz, 1971), one of the striking phenomena with dynamic RDS is the fact that the dynamic noise streaming in different depth planes never appears to cross the depth boundaries. The perceived noise appears as a random walk with *reflecting* depth barriers. Each individual dot can be perceived as if moving in a "Brownian motion", say, in the hovering center square, but no dot would be perceived as jumping over to the background. This means that first global stereopsis localizes the individual dots' positions in 3D, and only after this process does apparent motion perception establish correspondence between nearest neighbors in 3D.

One would assume from this insight that stereopsis dominates motion perception. This, however, is only so if the monocular views do not contain conflicting motion information. Indeed, I was lucky that in my research I mainly used RDS that were either static or dynamic (of the Brownian-motion kind) and therefore did not contain some monocularly perceivable oriented motion due to coherence. Some very interesting recent experiments by Jih-Jie Chang show some fundamental rules of how luminance motion affects cyclopean perception. Chang would first create, say, a horizontal cyclopean grating (a corrugated depth grating) moving always vertically down. Of course, a cyclopean grating by itself is infinitely transparent and thus cannot be seen. In order to make such a transparent moving surface visible, one has to project on its surface some texture of luminance patterns. In the case of dynamic noise (of black and white "snowstorm"-like dots) the well-known dynamic RDS is obtained and the dynamic RDS portrays the corrugated depth grating drifting from top to bottom.

However, when a *static* texture of random black and white dots is projected on to the moving cyclopean grating, the grating seems to be at standstill, and instead it appears to move towards and away from the observer in the frontial-parallel plane. If the projected texture contains some coherent direction of apparent movement either in the same, opposite or perpendicular direction to the direction of the moving cyclopean grating, the resulting percept is *always* in the direction of the coherently moving luminance texture. So, the motion of the cyclopean grating is totally dominated by the luminance motion. Of course, in real life we do not see tigers jumping in one direction while the texture of their fur might be detached from the trajectory of the jump and perform some motion of its own.

That luminance channels (contrast) and binocular disparity channels can interact is not a novel finding. We found (Julesz and Oswald, 1978) that a moving depth bar with a disparity gradient under threshold or a contrast gradient under threshold, respectively, would not elicit pursuit eye movements. However, if both parameters (under detection threshold) were presented simultaneously, strong pursuit eye movements were elicited. A model assuming probability summation of luminance (contrast) and cyclopean (disparity) information could account for the observed phenomena.

In contrast, the experiments by Chang demonstrate that in the case of luminance and cyclopean (disparity) motion, the former clearly dominate the perception of the latter. Thus in early vision there seem to be modules for stereopsis, contrast, luminance motion, cyclopean motion, etc., and there are some predetermined interactions between these modules. Whether this interaction is predetermined, or is behaviorally set at an early age, or can be modified at some later age by learning, remains to be seen.

REMARKS

This concludes the article. When I agreed to give an Invited Address at ECVP at the request of the editors, I had already accepted another invitation at SPIE in Los Angeles, to be delivered a few months later. Since I do not want to clutter the literature with similar material on my researches, I decided to have two articles with almost identical abstracts. The abstracts indicate the scope of my present work; however, Part I (this article) is devoted to cyclopean perception, while Part II, just published in the SPIE Proceedings (1989, Vol. 1077, pp. 247–268), is devoted to preattentive texture discrimination. The two, if read in succession (in any order) give a brief account of the present status of the two areas of research in which my coworkers and I are engaged.

REFERENCES

Anderson, C. H. & Van Essen, D. C. (1987). Shifter circuits: A computational strategy for dynamic aspects of visual processing. *Proceedings of the National Academy of Sciences, USA*, **84**, 6297–6301.

Bergen, J. R. & Adelson, E. H. (1988). Early vision and texture perception. *Nature (London)*, **333**, 363–364.

Grimson, W. E. L. (1981). *From Images to Surfaces*. MIT Press, Cambridge, MA.

Hubel, D. H. & Wiesel, T. N. (1962). Receptive fields, binocular interaction and functional architecture in the cat's visual cortex. *J. Physiol., London*, **160**, 106–154.

Julesz, B. (1959). Method of coding television signals based on edge detection. *Bell System Technical Journal*, **38**, 1001–1020.

Julesz, B. (1960). Binocular depth perception of computer-generated patterns. *Bell System Technical Journal*, **39**, 1125–1162.

Julesz, B. (1962). Visual pattern discrimination. *IRE Transactions on Information Theory*, **IT-8**, 84–92.

Julesz, B. (1971). *Foundations of Cyclopean Perception*. University of Chicago Press, Chicago.

Julesz, B. (1981). Textons, the elements of texture perception and their interactions. *Nature*, **290**, 91–97.

Julesz, B. (1984). Toward an axiomatic theory of preattentive vision. In *Dynamic Aspects of Neocortical Function*, G. M. Edelman, W. E. Gall & W. M. Cowan (Eds.), 585–612. Wiley, New York.

Julesz, B. (1986a). Stereoscopic vision, *Vision Research*, **26**(9), 1601–1612. Twenty-fifth Anniversary Issue.

Julesz, B. (1986b). Texton gradients: The texton theory revisited. *Biological Cybernetics*, **54**, 245–251.

Julesz, B., Gilbert, E. N., Shepp, L. A., & Frisch, H. L. (1973). Inability of humans to discriminate between visual textures that agree in second-order statistics—revisited. *Perception*, **2**, 391–405.

Julesz, B. & Kröse, B. (1988). Features and spatial filters. *Nature*, **33**, 302–303.

Julesz, B. & Miller, J. E. (1975). Independent spatial frequency tuned channels in binocular fusion and rivalry. *Perception*, **4**, 125–143.

Julesz, B. & Oswald, H. (1978). Binocular utilization of monocular cues that are undetectable monocularly. *Perception* **7**(3), 315–322.

Marr, D. (1982). *Vision*. Freeman, San Francisco, California.

Marr, D. & Poggio, T. (1976). A theory of human stereopsis. *Proc. R. Soc. B*, **204**, 301–328.

Mayhew, J. E. W. & Frisby, J. P. (1979). Convergent disparity discriminations in narrow-band-filtered random-dot stereograms. *Vision Research*, **19**(1), 63–71.

Mowforth, P., Mayhew, J. E. W. & Frisby, J. P. (1981). Vergence eye movements made in response to spatial-frequency-filtered random-dot stereograms. *Perception*, **10**(3), 299–304.

Ogle, K. N. (1964). *Researches in Binocular Vision*. Hafner, New York.

Ogle, K. N. & Wakefield, J. M. (1967). Stereoscopic depth and binocular rivalry. *Vision Research*, **7**, 89–98.

Poggio, G. F. (1984). Processing of stereoscopic information in primate visual cortex. In *Dynamic Aspects of Neocortical Function*, G. M. Edelman, W. E. Gall & W. M. Cowan (Eds.), 613–635. Wiley, New York.

Poggio, G. F. & Fischer, B. (1977). Binocular interaction and depth sensitivity of striate and prestriate cortical neurons rhesus monkeys. *J. Neurophysiol.*, **40**, 1392–1405.

Saarinen, J. (1987). Perception of positional relationships between line segments in eccentric vision. *Perception*, **16**(5), 583–591.

Sperling, G. (1970). Binocular vision: A physical and neural theory. *J. Am. Psychol.* **83**, 461–534.

Voorhees, H. & Poggio, T. (1988). Computing texture boundaries from images. *Nature (London)*, **333**, 364–367.

3 Visual Perception in People and Machines

V. S. Ramachandran

Psychology Department, C-009, University of California, San Diego, La Jolla, CA 92093, USA

INTRODUCTION: THEORIES OF PERCEPTION

Visual perception may be defined as a biological process whose goal is to rapidly compute a three-dimensional representation of the world that the organism can use for navigation and for object manipulation. How is this achieved?

In the nineteenth century the German physicist Hermann Von Helmholtz pointed out that the visual image is inherently ambiguous and that perception is essentially a matter of resolving ambiguities by using knowledge of the external world. I can think of no better illustration of this principle than the so-called "Ames room"—an example of which may be seen at San Francisco's Exploratorium. The Ames Room is a life-size distorted room, one corner of which is made much bigger than all the others. But if you stand outside the room and look inside through a small peephole using one eye the room looks completely normal! The standard textbook explanation of this illusion is that from this vantage point the retinal image produced by the distorted room is identical with (and therefore indistinguishable from) that of a normal room. But surely this explanation begs the question of how the visual system "knows" which of the two interpretations is normal. Or to put it differently, how does it know the room is *not* distorted? If you shut one eye and look at the room that you are in right now, the image that exists on your retina is in fact compatible with an infinity of distorted Ames rooms. How does the visual system discard this infinity of Ames rooms and home in on a single interpretation? This is the central problem of perception.

If you examine the history of ideas on perception during the last century or so you will notice that there have been three major trends in thinking:*

---

* For some recent discussions on the problem of perception, see Shepard (1981), Hochberg (1981), Cutting (1987), Epstein (1988) and Kanizsa (1979).

AI and the Eye   Edited by A. Blake and T. Troscianko
© 1990 John Wiley & Sons Ltd.

1. *Perception as unconscious inference.* This view emphasizes that the visual image is inherently ambiguous and that the perceptual apparatus resolves ambiguities by using "intelligent" processes that *resemble* conscious reasoning. The idea was originally put forward by Helmholtz (1867) and has more recently been revived by Gregory (1970) and Rock (1983).
2. *Direct perception.* This emphasizes the richness of the visual input and argues that ambiguity exists only in contrived laboratory situations but not in the "real world". A vast amount of information is implicit in the visual image and perception is achieved not by making this information explicit but by direct "resonance". Unfortunately, it is never clearly specified how or where in the brain this resonance is supposed to occur.* I will not elaborate this argument of Gibson (1966) further except to say that it is not quite as silly as it sounds.
3. *Natural computation.* This is the AI approach and attempts to bridge (1) and (2) through formal modelling. One begins by rigorously specifying the computational problem that the organism is confronted with and then develops a computational theory and a set of algorithms to tackle the problem. Information that is only *implicit* in the retinal image is transformed (through computation) into *representations* that make certain aspects of the information more explicit and accessible for further computation. This view is similar to (1) in that it argues that a knowledge of the statistics of the natural world is indispensable for computing representations and it is also similar to (2) in emphasizing the richness of the visual input. However, it is different from (1) in that it takes advantage of constraints that incorporate general properties of the world rather than top-down influences that depend on high-level semantic knowledge of specific objects. Thus the visual system may have built-in knowledge about surfaces, depth, movement, etc., but not about umbrellas, chairs and dalmatian dogs.

Differences Between Human Vision and Machine Vision

The first step toward understanding any complex information-processing system is to clearly identify the *problems* it was designed to solve. The computational approach to vision has been extremely useful in this regard because it allows a much more rigorous formulation of perceptual problems (Ullman, 1979; Marr, 1982; Poggio *et al.*, 1985) than what would be possible with psychophysics or pysiology alone.

Unfortunately, simulation of a biological system does not necessarily tell us how the system actually works.† We must bear in mind, especially, that biological vision differs from machine vision in several important respects:

1. Considerations of optimality have obvious importance in engineering but they have only a limited role in biology. The goal of biological visual systems is to

---

* As Peter Medawar might have phrased it, words such as resonance are "mere analgesics; they dull the ache of incomprehension without removing the cause."
† For a more detailed argument along these lines see Searle (1989) and Penrose (1989).

rapidly compute approximate solutions to perceptual problems. The solutions are always adequate for the job on hand, but rarely optimal.

2. The constraints imposed by the environment (natural constraints) reduce the computational burden on the visual system but they do not impose a *unique* solution to perceptual problems. There are often far too many ways of solving a problem theoretically and the only way to distinguish between them is to do old-fashioned psychophysics and neuroanatomy.

3. The central dogma of computational vision has been that the strategies used by any complex information-processing system can be understood independent of hardware implementation. Contrary to this we would argue that biological vision is strongly constrained by the actual neural machinery that mediates it. There may be certain things that neurons simply cannot do and this automatically eliminates a wide range of theoretically plausible solutions.

4. In science one typically wants to understand the whole pedigree of causes that governs a given phenomenon—not merely the remote ancestral cause. In this sense, specifying natural constraints, although useful, is an incomplete account of visual processes since it doesn't tell us exactly *how* a given constraint is actually exploited. For example, even a child knows that sunlight is a natural constraint for plant growth but this tells us very little about the mechanisms of photosynthesis!

5. Biological systems were not designed from scratch—they often had to be built from preexisting hardware. For example, the bones of the middle ear, which were originally used for chewing food (in our reptilian ancestors) are now used for amplifying sound, i.e. for hearing. This example suggests that nature is inherently opportunistic and will often adopt *ad hoc* solutions that may actually seem very *inelegant* to an engineer.

6. For any given perceptual problem biological systems often seem to use *multiple parallel mechanisms*. The perception of three-dimensional shapes, for example, is made possible by stereopsis, occlusion, shading, relative motion, etc. Why use multiple mechanisms when a single one will suffice on computational grounds? There are at least two reasons. First, by using multiple strategies for any one problem, the system can get away with each of them being relatively crude and, therefore, easy to implement in real neural hardware. As an analogy, consider two drunks, neither of whom can walk unsupported but, by leaning on each other, they manage to stagger along towards their goal! Second, the simultaneous use of multiple parallel short-cuts allows more rapid processing of images and a greater tolerance for noise than what would be possible with a single sophisticated algorithm. It is this remarkable tolerance for noisy (sometimes camouflaged) images that characterizes biological vision and sets it apart from machine vision.

Perception as a "Bag of Tricks". The Utilitarian Theory of Perception

Based on these considerations I would like to replace the three theories of perception I outlined earlier with a fourth "theory" of perception which I call the "utilitarian theory" (Ramachandran, 1985a). According to this view perception does not involve intelligent reasoning as implied by some psychologists; does not involve resonance with the world as suggested by Gibsonians; and does not require creating elaborate internal representations or solving equations as implied by AI researchers. One could argue, instead, that perception is essentially a "bag of tricks"; that through millions of years of trial and error the visual system has evolved numerous short-cuts, rules-of-thumb and heuristics which were adopted not for their aesthetic appeal or mathematical elegance but simply because they *worked* (hence the "utilitarian" theory). This is a familiar idea in biology but for some reason it seems to have escaped the notice of psychologists, who seem to forget that the brain is a biological organ just like the pancreas, the liver, or any other specialized organ. The digestion of food, for example, is not brought about by computation, by intelligent deduction, nor even by resonance. The system uses an arbitrary set of special-purpose tricks (i.e. mastication, peristalsis, sequential cleavage by enzymes, specific satiety signals, etc.) that are tailor-made for achieving a step-by-step denudation of food into easily absorbed constituents. Further, the strategies used are different for different kinds of food and at different points along the gastrointestinal tract (and in different animals). It may not be too far-fetched to suggest that the visual system also uses an equally bewildering array of special-purpose tricks and adaptive heuristics to solve its problems. If this pessimistic view of perception is correct, then the task of vision researchers ought to be to uncover these rules rather than to attribute to the system a degree of sophistication that it simply doesn't possess.*

Does the utilitarian approach to perception imply that the mechanisms of perception are completely chaotic and unlawful in character? Of course not. Clearly, the mechanisms that mediate vision must be locally lawful in a manner that reflects natural constraints. Each of the dozen or so mechanisms that mediate depth perception, for example, has an internal logic that can be profitably studied, but it would be difficult to maintain that processes as different as stereopsis (which uses disparities) and shape-from-shading (which relies on the effects of surface slant on reflected light) are united by a common principle.

CONSTRAINTS IMPOSED BY NEURAL HARDWARE

I doubt if we can ever guess what Natural Selection has achieved, without some help from the way function has been embodied in actual structures. The reason is simple. Natural Selection is more ingenious than we are.

(F. H. C. Crick, 1985)

---

* My criticisms apply mainly to classical Von Neumann-style computation of the kind implied in the theories of Marr (1982). The idea proposed in this chapter—that for any perception problem the visual system uses a set of heuristics or short-cuts—is not inconsistent with modern connectionist or "PDP" approaches to vision (e.g. Ballard, 1986; Feldman, 1986) including those which employ learning algorithms (Sejnowsky & Churchland, 1989). Indeed, what I call short-cuts or "tricks" are precisely what one would expect such algorithms to learn as they interact with the world. In this sense the utilitarian theory of perception provides an effective bridge between Gibsonian and Helmholtzian accounts of perception.

Figure 1 illustrates the flow of information in the primate visual system. It is a summary of the anatomical and electrophysiological work of Hubel & Livingstone (1985), De Yoe & Van Essen (1985) and Shipp & Zeki (1985). To simplify the diagram we have deliberately left out some of the relays in layer 4. Notice that there are three parallel pathways or "streams" which are segregated all the way from the LGN to the visual areas beyond area 18. Physiological recordings from cells at various points along these pathways reveal that they have very different stimulus requirements. The magnocellular stream, which relays through layer 4B in area 17 and terminates in the broad stripes of area 18 (as well as area MT) is dominated by cells tuned to stereoscopic disparity as well as direction of movement. These cells will respond only to contours defined by luminance contrast and are insensitive to chromatic borders at equiluminance. Cells in the thin stripes of area 18, on the other hand, respond well to chromatic borders. Unlike the broad stripe cells, however, they have circular receptive fields and are insensitive to direction, disparity and orientation. And, lastly, cells in the "pale stripes" or interstrips of area 18 are found to be indifferent to disparity and direction of movement but are sharply tuned to *line length*, i.e. they will respond only to line segments of finite length. Their exact role in vision is unclear but it has been suggested that they may be involved in the early stages of shape, curvature or form recognition (Hubel & Livingstone, 1985) or in the perception of visual *texture* (Ramachandran, 1987a).

The anatomical segregation of motion and color pathways in the brain leads to some interesting and counterintuitive predictions. Consider a red object moving

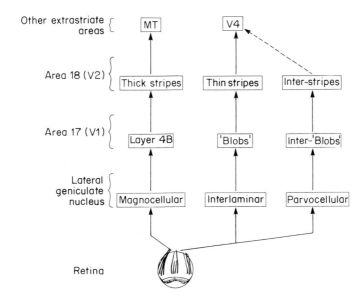

Figure 1.   Three parallel channels in the primate geniculo-cortical pathway (after Rama-chandran, 1987a). This diagram summarizes information from many sources including Van Essen (1979) and Hubel & Livingstone (1985) and Zeki (1978). For clarity we have left out the relay through layer 4C. Also, the interlaminar projection to the "blobs" is still somewhat controversial.

against a green background. If one were to carefully match the luminance of red and green areas, the moving red–green border would no longer be able to excite the direction-selective cells in the broad stripes and consequently one should no longer be able to see the object moving! We had originally intended to use "real" movement of a red object on a green background to test this prediction directly but decided that this would not work because even if the sensation of movement disappeared one might still be able to "infer" movement at some higher level. Since the object was changing position from moment to moment one might be able to *deduce* that it had moved even if one did not actually experience movement directly. To circumvent this problem we used random-dot kinematograms which eliminate positional cues. We began with two random-dot patterns which were identical (point-to-point) except for a central square-shaped matrix which was shifted in the second pattern in relation to the first. We then superimposed the two patterns so that the background dots were in exact registration and then presented them in rapid alternation. The central square was seen to oscillate horizontally as a result of apparent motion. Next, we repeated the experiment using red dots on a green background (instead of black on white) and found that at equiluminance the impression of an oscillating square disappeared completely (Ramachandran & Gregory, 1978). We concluded from this that human motion perception is at least partially "color blind" as predicted by the neuroanatomy.

Oddly enough, we found that although motion was lost at equiluminance in random-dot kinematograms, motion could still be seen quite vividly if simple line targets were used. Why is there such a striking difference between the two kinds of displays? There are at least three possibilities (Ramachandran & Gregory, 1978). First, it is possible that chromatic borders provide a *weak* input to motion perception (rather than no input at all) and this weak input is perhaps more easily revealed when line targets are used rather than random-dot kinematograms. Second, when looking at random-dot kinematograms we had the impression that what was specifically lost at equiluminance was the process of *segregation* from motion rather than motion *per se* (although there was also an obvious reduction in motion as well). This interpretation is consistent with the recent findings of Cavanagh, Boeglin & Favreau (1985). Third, it is possible that the *early* motion system is color blind whereas the "long-range" motion system can use any type of contour including equiluminous chromatic contours. In fact, as we shall see in a later section, the long-range motion system is remarkably versatile in the kinds of inputs it can use.

Similarity of Color can Influence Long-range Motion Correspondence

In the previous section we noted that even though equiluminous chromatic borders provide only a weak input to motion perception, motion can be seen quite readily if a single isolated target is used instead of a random-dot pattern. We will now consider another experiment which suggests that color can be used as a cue for long-range motion correspondence.

Two dots were flashed on diagonally opposite corners of a 1° wide square and then replaced with two dots flashed on the remaining two corners. The display was

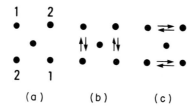

Figure 2. An ambiguous apparent motion display. Two dots are flashed on diagonally opposite corners of a square and replaced by dots appearing on the two remaining corners (a). If the procedure is repeated in continuous cycle one can see either vertical (b) or horizontal (c) oscillation of the spots (Ramachandran & Anstis, 1983).

bistable in the sense that one could see either vertical or horizontal apparent motion and the two percepts were mutually exclusive (Figure 2b and c; Ramachandran & Anstis, 1983, 1986).

As reported by Livingstone & Hubel (1987), if the two top elements were red and the bottom elements were green there was no obvious increase in the tendency to see horizontal motion (between similar elements). Notice that in this display the red and green dots are equiluminous with each other but not equiluminous with the surround. When nine bistable displays were viewed simultaneously, however, we found that all of them became synchronized and horizontal motion was seen in all of these. Surprisingly, the particular bistable display one was looking at could be seen to oscillate either vertically or horizontally but all other displays *always* moved horizontally in accordance with similarity of the tokens (Ramachandran *et al.*, 1987). We conclude that one's attention can override perceptual affinities only in a narrow region corresponding to the "spotlight". Conversely, even small perceptual affinities become amplified when multiple displays are used since the system is forced into a preattentive mode.

Perceptual Coupling of Motion and Stereoscopic Disparity

In the previous section we noted that motion-detecting cells in the visual pathways of primates are clearly segregated from cells which respond to chromatic borders. The separation of movement-sensitive cells from cells tuned to stereoscopic disparity, on the other hand, is not quite as clear-cut; in fact, MT contains cells which are tuned to both these dimensions. One perceptual consequence of this might be the close coupling between stereopsis and motion observed by Ramachandran & Anstis (1986a). They presented two vertically aligned spots in frame 1 of an apparent motion sequence followed by two spots shifted horizontally (Figure 3).

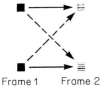

Frame 1   Frame 2

Figure 3. Two vertically aligned spots are flashed in frame 1 (solid black dots) and followed by 2 spots shifted horizontally in frame 2 (grey cross-hatched dots). Horizontal distance between spots was 0.6°. The spots never cross each other's paths (dotted lines) but always move horizontally (solid arrows).

The spots were always seen to jump horizontally and were never seen to cross paths (Kolers, 1972; Ullman, 1979) even if diagonally opposite pairs were made similar in color or form. However, we found that if two diagonally opposite corner dots were in a separate stereoscopic plane from the other two the dots did cross paths (Ramachandran & Anstis, 1986a). This was especially true if several such displays were viewed simultaneously (Figure 4). We may conclude from this result that there is a much stronger link in the brain between motion and stereoscopic disparity than between motion and other stimulus features such as color and form—a conclusion that is consistent with the anatomical results of Livingstone & Hubel (1987).

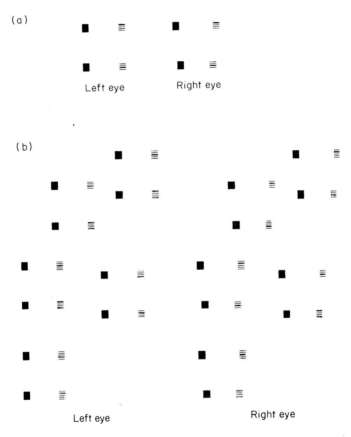

Figure 4. (a) A stereogram constructed using two displays similar to Figure 2. Diagonally opposite pairs of dots now occupy different depth planes and this permits the dots to cross each other's trajectories. Grey (cross-hatched) dots appear in frame 2.   (b) The tendency to cross can be greatly enhanced by simply viewing multiple displays such as (a) simultaneously. The use of multiple displays seems to amplify small preattentive affinities in apparent motion (Ramachandran *et al.*, 1987). Subjects now report seeing two lacy planes crossing each other.

MOTION CORRESPONDENCE

How does the visual system match successive "snapshots" of a moving object to generate an impression of smooth, continuous motion? Does it first extract 3D shapes and outlines from the image and then proceed to match these or is motion correspondence based on a primitive point-to-point matching of luminance distribution? Our experiments suggest that the former strategy is used. Even relatively abstract stimulus features such as equiluminous *texture borders* (Ramachandran *et al.*, 1973), illusory contours (Ramachandran, 1985b) and shape-from-shading (Ramachandran, 1988) can provide an input to the long-range motion system. Of course, moving objects usually differ from the background in terms of their surface reflectance, so under ordinary circumstances the visual system could rely entirely on luminance edges to achieve correspondence. But by using a variety of inputs (such as texture edges, cyclopean edges and chromatic edges), the system is able to tolerate noisy images of the kind it would encounter in the natural world (e.g. a leopard moving against a screen of fluttering foliage). As alluded to earlier, this is one of the major advantages of using multiple strategies for the same visual process.

But if correspondence is established mainly between coarse or salient features —what about the finer features in the image? Consider a leopard leaping from branch to branch while chasing one of our arboreal ancestors. How does the visual system know which spot in any given view or "snapshot" of the leopard corresponds to which spot in the immediately succeeding view?

There have been several approaches to this problem in the past and a particularly ingenious one was introduced by Ullman (1979). He suggests that the visual system tries all possible combinations of matches between the dots and through successive iterations, arrives at the match which yields the *minimum* total distance. This match is chosen as the solution to the correspondence problem.

Contrary to this view, I would like to suggest that in solving the correspondence problem the visual system actually throws away all the information about the individual dots and resorts to the use of a short-cut or "trick" which I call "motion capture". Figure 5 illustrates this effect. Two sparse, uncorrelated random-dot patterns were alternated to generate random incoherent noise or "snowfall" (as in a untuned TV set). A sine wave grating of low frequency and low contrast was then optically superimposed on this display. Notice that the grating is displaced horizontally in frame 2 in relation to frame 1. When the two frames were alternated the grating appeared to jump left and right as one would expect. But to our surprise we found that all the dots in the display also appeared to jump horizontally along with the grating—as though they were "captured" by it. Motion capture was not seen if (a) the spatial frequency of the grating was too high (Ramachandran & Inada, 1985) or (b) if the excursion of the grating was small in relation to dot density (Ramachandran & Cavanagh, 1987).

We attempted to measure these effects by using two displays similar to Figure 5 presented simultaneously, one below the other. The top panel was identical to Figure 5 but in the bottom panel the dots in the two frames were *correlated* in successive frames and they were made to jump horizontally along with the grating.

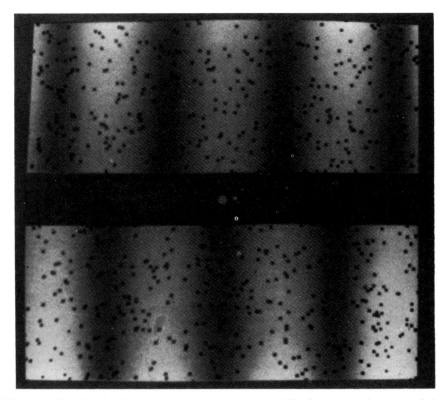

Figure 5. Two frames of an apparent motion sequence. The frames are shown one below the other for clarity but in the original experiment they were optically superimposed and alternated. Even though the dots are uncorrelated in successive frames, they are seen to adhere to the grating and to move with it as a single sheet. In the absence of the grating the dots are simply seen to swirl around incoherently.

Figure 6 (*opposite*). Results of two experiments on motion capture (Ramachandran & Cavanagh, 1985). In Experiment 1, dots in one field were uncorrelated in successive frames and in the other field they were correlated and displaced horizontally (solid line) or vertically (dotted line). A vertical sine-wave grating of 1 cycle/deg and 40% contrast was superimposed on both fields. The subject's task was to gradually reduce the displacement of the grating until the dots were released from capture so that the two fields became discriminable. Above and to the right of the graph the dots were captured and the two fields were indiscriminable. (Each datum point is the mean of four readings.) Note that vertical dot motion is more difficult to capture. Horizontal motion of the correlated dot field in the same direction as the grating (with) does not appear to be either easier or harder to capture than motion in the opposite direction (against). In Experiment 2 the dots were always correlated in successive frames both above and below the central divider. The grating moved in the same direction in both fields but the dots moved in opposite directions. For instance, for vertical dot motion (evenly interrupted line) the dots in the two fields moved either simultaneously towards or away from the central dividing strip. As in Experiment 1, subjects reduced the grating displacement until they could just discriminate the two fields.

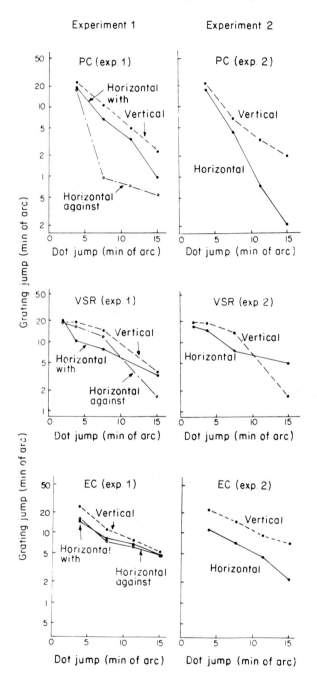

The subject's task was to gradually reduce the excursion of both gratings until he could just discriminate the two panels (Figure 6). We found that over a surprisingly wide range of displacement, subjects could not see the difference between the two panels, i.e. they could not discriminate dots which were *captured* by the grating from dots which actually moved physically along with the grating.

These results suggest that unambiguous motion signals derived from certain coarse image features mask or *inhibit* the signals from the finer image features—a process that serves to eliminate spurious motion signals. However, the inhibition of motion signals from the finer features does not cause them to appear stationary; they are in fact seen to jump along with the coarse features. This suggests that when there are no motion signals from some frequency bands and strong signals from another (lower-frequency) band, the signal from the latter is spontaneously attributed to the former.

Motion Capture with Illusory Contours

Our next experiment shows that other types of features can also generate motion capture. We begin with two illusory squares presented in an appropriately timed sequence to generate apparent motion of an illusory surface (Figure 7; note that the

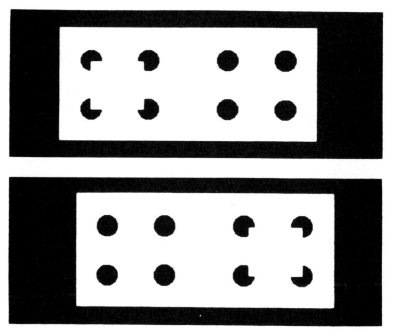

Figure 7. The apparent motion of an illusory square (Ramachandran, 1985a). The two frames of the movie are shown one below the other for clarity, but in the original experiment they were optically superimposed so that the disks were in perfect registration. One has the vivid impression of an opaque illusory surface that jumps left and right while covering (and uncovering) the black disks in the background. Note that all eight disks are present in each frame so that the disks themselves do not move.

disks themselves do not move). In this motion sequence most subjects perceive an opaque oscillating square that occludes and disoccludes the disks in the background; they never report seeing "pac-men" opening and closing their mouths or two illusory squares flashing on and off. When a template of this movie was then projected on a regular grid of dots, the dots appeared to move with the illusory surface even though they were physically stationary (Figure 8). Since there is no evidence that the dots have not moved, the brain assumes, by default, that they have jumped with the illusory square (Ramachandran, 1985a, 1986).

These results suggest a solution to the correspondence problem. The question posed by AI researchers is: How does the visual system "know" which spot in any given snapshot of the leopard belongs to which spot in the succeeding snapshot? Our answer is that the visual system simply does not care. It extracts motion signals from certain conspicuous features (e.g. the leopard's outline) and these signals are blindly attributed to the spots themselves so that they appear to move with the leopard. In doing this the visual system discards enormous amounts of information about the positions of the individual spots. The advantage with this strategy is that it reduces the computational burden on the visual system by eliminating the need to keep track of individual spots on the leopard. The

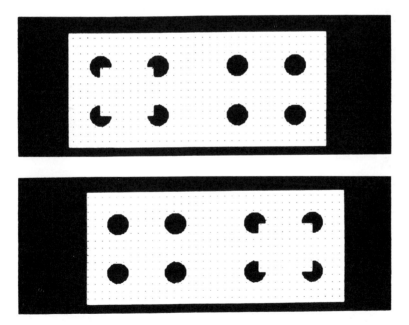

Figure 8. A template of the movie described in the caption to Figure 7 is superimposed on a matrix of dots. The dots are present in both frames and are exactly superimposed on each other so that they can generate no movement signals of their own. However, when the illusory square jumps, all the dots corresponding to its surface also appear to move in the same direction. The reader can view this illusion by using the computer software (Apple floppy disk) provided with a special issue of the journal *Perception* (1985, Vol. 14) on human motion perception. The disk is included inside the back cover of that journal.

disadvantage is that the system would be "blind" to small local excursions of the dots. For instance, if the leopard were to smile as he jumped, you probably wouldn't notice this, but this is a small price to pay if you are trying to run away from him!

Notice that the visual system can afford to use this trick or short-cut only because in the real world spots don't usually fly off leopards. But my point is that although the visual system takes advantage of this constraint it doesn't make very specific or sophisticated use of it. In general, it looks as though the human visual system will do as little processing as it can get away with for the job on hand. There may, of course, be other visual functions which do require the use of individual dot motions—e.g. motion hyperacuity or image segmentation from motion—but those systems, in their turn, would be insensitive to the overall direction of motion of the whole object; a function mediated by the long-range motion system. Which system is dominant at any given instant is dictated by the velocity of the moving object and by the immediate behavioral demands on the organism. When the leopard is standing still the visual system can afford a leisurely inspection of the local movements that define his smile, but if he decides to leap at you, the long-range system takes over to signal the overall direction of movement (and velocity) of the animal as he approaches you.

Interaction Between Color and Motion

When a red object is moved against a green background, the chromatic border associated with the object generates only weak motion signals (Ramachandran & Gregory, 1978; Cavanagh et al., 1983). Yet in the real world when a red object moves across a green background we do see it moving, not standing still. Presumably motion signals are extracted only from the incidental luminance differences that usually accompany the chromatic border, but if this is true why does one also see the *chromatic* border moving? Or, to put it differently, when a colored object moves, how is such perfect perceptual registration maintained between the chromatic and luminance borders if it is indeed true that they are being extracted separately? Our next experiment addresses this issue.

A red square subtending $1°$ was displayed against an equiluminous homogeneous green background. When a sparse pattern of small black dots was superimposed on the square and moved up and down, the square appeared to move in the same direction even though it was physically stationary. The illusion was especially pronounced on eccentric fixation; when we fixated $2°$ away the effect could be seen even for excursions up to $2°$ (Ramachandran, 1987a,b). Similar effects were observed when yellow/grey borders were used instead of red/green ones.

This result suggests that chromatic borders can be captured by moving luminance contours in a manner analogous to the capture of texture elements. We may conclude that whenever a colored object is displaced in the visual field, motion signals are extracted primarily from the luminance borders (by the magnocellular pathway) and then spontaneously applied to chromatic borders that happen to excite the adjacent thin stripes.

Conflict Between Position and Motion-sensing Mechanisms

In the previous experiment we noted that is a sparse random-dot pattern was superimposed on an equiluminous yellow square and moved horizontally the square appeared to move in the same direction as the dots. A curious effect was observed when the dots were moved *continuously* as on a conveyor belt. The square would initially be pulled along for a bit and then it would quite suddenly jump back to its original location. This process of being captured then jumping back occurred repeatedly so long as the random-dot array was made to move continuously in one direction.

It seems likely that this effect occurs because of a conflict between position and motion signals. The motion system is presumably informing the brain that the yellow square has moved but the color system (thin stripes?) is simultaneously signalling the actual location of the yellow square which remains unchanged. When the discrepancy becomes too large the square "returns" to its original location. Perhaps one could use this illusion to measure the magnitude of displacement induced by motion capture (and, indirectly, the position sensitivity of the "blob"/ thin-stripe system). We tried to do this by using the stimulus configuration shown in Figure 9. Notice that instead of a single yellow square we now have a long

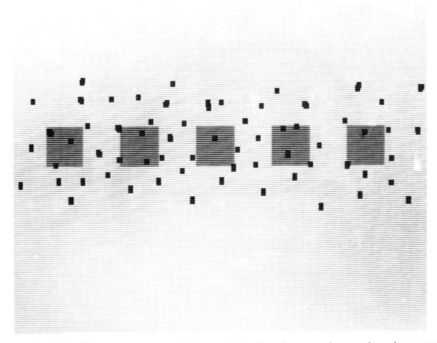

Figure 9. This illustrates capture of chromatic borders by a moving random-dot pattern (Ramachandran, 1987b). A row of yellow squares (depicted dark grey in this illustration) was displayed against an equiluminous grey surround. When a continuously moving "conveyor belt" of random dots was superimposed on the display the yellow squares also appeared to move continuously.

horizontal row of them. The squares subtended 1° each and were separated by 2° intervals. We then found that if the dot pattern was moved continuously the squares also appeared to move along with them *continuously*, and no jumping back occurred. (We had to fixate about 2–3° above the center of the display to generate this effect.) Presumably at this setting the positional displacement induced by motion capture was exactly equal to the spatial separation between the squares.

Loss of Image Segmentation at Equiluminance

As mentioned earlier, Ramachandran & Gregory (1978) reported a loss of motion-based image segmentation at equiluminance. They began with two correlated random-dot patterns (A and B) which were identical except for a square-shaped matrix in the middle that was shifted horizontally in B in relation to A. The two patterns were optically superimposed so that the backgrounds were in perfect registration. When the patterns were presented in rapid alternation one could see the central square oscillating horizontally. However, when the black–white dots in the display were replaced by red–green dots at equiluminance the impression of an oscillating square was destroyed completely, even though the dots themselves were clearly resolvable. Ramachandran and Gregory suggested that there were probably at least two reasons for this disappearance of the oscillating square. First, motion-sensing mechanisms may be partially "color blind"—i.e. they receive only a weak input from chromatic borders. (There is some physiological evidence to support this view, e.g. see Livingstone & Hubel, 1987.) Second, the process that leads to *image segmentation* (or segregation') from motion may be especially dependent on luminance contrast. This would explain why even when some motion was occasionally seen, the square always remained invisible.

Image segmentation based on other types of cues such as occlusion may also be incapable of accepting a chromatic input. Gregory (1977) found that illusory contours (Figure 7) are reduced considerably when the inducing elements are red disks on an equiluminous green background (rather than black on white). The observation suggests that the "blob"/thin-stripes system, which extracts chromatic borders, is probably incapable of signalling the presence of illusory contours (Ramachandran, 1986; Livingstone & Hubel, 1987).

Some very striking visual effects can be produced by superimposing illusory contours on visual textures (Ramachandran, 1986). In Figure 10(a) and (b), for example, the visual texture corresponding to the illusory square is seen to "belong" to the square and is seen in a different depth plane from the surround, even though in some sense it is continuous with the surround. This effect is especially pronounced when some of the texture elements actually coincide with the illusory contours (Figure 11). On the other hand, if the texture elements are made equiluminous with the background color (e.g. yellow dots on a grey background), this effect goes away completely, even though the sectored disks themselves are black—i.e. *non*-equiluminous with the background. The texture elements are now seen as being continuous with the background instead of belonging to the square.

Why are equiluminous textures seen as belonging to the background rather than to the figure defined by the illusory surface? One possibility is that the equilumi-

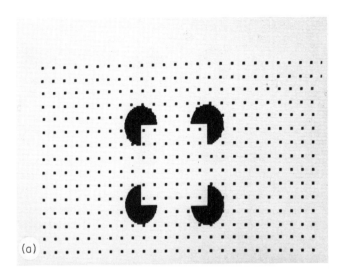

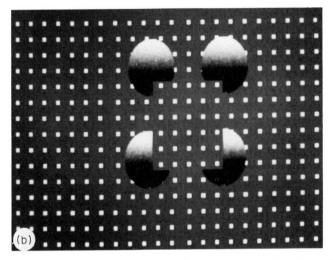

Figure 10.   (a) An illusory square is superimposed on a regular matrix of dots. The dots that fall inside the illusory square are seen as belonging to the illusory surface instead of being seen as part of the background. If the dots are made equiluminous with the background (e.g. yellow dots on a grey background), however, they are seen as being continuous with the dots in the surround. (b) This is identical to Figure 10a except that the pie-shaped wedges have been cut out of four shaded spheres rather than disks. Try blurring the image slightly and view it with one eye shut.

nous elements are "seen" only by the thin stripes and pale stripes, whereas the illusory surface is extracted by the broad stripes and pale stripes (Ramachandran, 1986). To allow the texture to be seen as part of the illusory surface, there has to be adequate communication between the two systems and the connections needed for this simply may not exist at this early stage of processing.

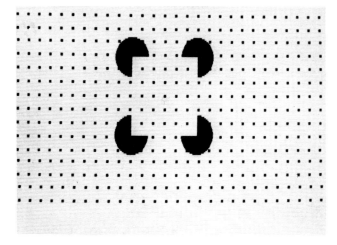

Figure 11. This is similar to Figure 10 except that the locations of some of the dots actually coincide with the illusory edges of the square. This considerably enhances the effect described above, i.e. the impression of a square piece of paper with dots on it. Again, if the dots are made equiluminous with the homogeneous background they are no longer seen as belonging to the square. Similar effects were observed when we used a random-dot matrix in the background instead of a regular array of dots.

Constraints Imposed by Occlusion

The visual world consists largely of opaque objects which often partially occlude each other. It would be surprising, therefore, if the visual system did not take advantage of occlusion as a "natural constraint" to resolve ambiguities in motion perception (Ramachandran *et al.*, 1985; Ramachandran & Anstis, 1986a). As an example, consider, once again, a leopard moving in front of a textured background. As the leopard moves, it successively covers and uncovers leaves in the background and therefore these elements are seen in reverse sequence by, say, retinal motion detectors. The resulting spurious motion signals might be eliminated if the motion signal from the occluder (i.e. the leopard) were to veto the signals from the background texture elements. An ingenious experiment by Sigman & Rock (1974) supports this idea. They found that if an opaque occluder was moved back and forth in front of two stationary light spots so as to occlude them alternately, then no apparent motion of the light spots was seen since the brain could "intelligently" interpret the motion signals as arising from the occluder rather than from the spots themselves.

Here we have stripped this illusion down to its bare essentials and show that even apparent motion of an apparent occluder will eliminate the motion signal from the light spot. We began with the stimulus sequence shown in Figure 7. In the first frame (Figure 7a) eight black disks were displayed simultaneously—four disks on the left and four on the right (see figure legend for details). No sectors were removed from the four disks on the right and hence no illusory contours were seen in this part of the display. The entire display was then switched off and replaced by the second frame (Figure 7b). This frame is identical to Figure 7(a) except that the sectors have now been removed from the four disks on the right rather than the four disks on the left.

The two frames were cycled continuously at a stimulus onset asynchrony (SOA) of 400–500 ms. All eight subjects who viewed this display reported seeing an opaque "subjective" square moving left and right to occlude and disocclude the disks in the background (Ramachandran, 1985b).

Our second display was identical to Figure 7 except that we now added an extra dot in the center that appeared on the right side alone in frame 1 and on the left side alone in frame 2 (Figure 12). Interestingly, these dots simply appeared to blink on and off; one had the distinct impression of an opaque white square moving horizontally so that the two central dots were occluded in rapid succession. It was impossible to see apparent motion between the two spots even though the time intervals were quite appropriate. For instance, one might have expected to see simultaneously the black central dot and the white square moving in opposite directions but this percept could not be obtained. We interpret this finding to mean that the motion signal from the illusory occluder somehow vetoes or inhibits the signal generated by the central spot. We satisfied ourselves that this was indeed the case by simply deleting the outer disks from the display—a procedure which immediately caused apparent motion to be perceived between the central spots.

Does this vetoing depend on the apparent depth of the illusory occluder relative to the central spot? To find out, we presented two patterns similar to Figure 12 separately to the two eyes and introduced horizontal disparities between the cut

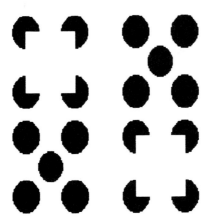

Figure 12.   This is identical to Figure 7 except for the presence of a single additional central disk that appears on the right in frame 1 (top) and on the left in frame 2 (bottom). The two frames were optically superimposed and flashed alternately. Subjects usually see an opaque white illusory square occluding and disoccluding all the other disks. The central disk is *not* seen to move. If the disks in the surround are eliminated the central disk does appear to oscillate quite vividly. This suggests that apparent motion of the illusory square somehow inhibits the motion signal from the central disk. This inhibition can be removed, however, by simply introducing retinal disparities so that the central dot appears stereoscopically nearer than the four black disks.

sectors on the disks. When crossed disparities were used one had the distinct impression of an illusory square standing out clearly from the background (Gregory & Harris, 1974; Ramachandran, 1986). No disparities were introduced between the central spots or between the disks themselves so that they appeared flush with the background at zero disparity. We then switched off the entire stereogram and replaced it with a stereogram in which the illusory square and central spot had simply exchanged places horizontally. The stereoscopic illusory square then appeared to jump left and right horizontally as it occluded and disoccluded a stationary spot in the background, i.e. the percept was identical to what we observed in Figure 12.

Next we altered the disparities in the display so that the illusory square was at zero disparity but the central spot alone was shifted horizontally in one eye. This caused the central spot to float out of the background and we now found that it jumped horizontally quite vividly. The square and the spot were *both* seen to jump but in opposite directions. On the other hand, if the polaroid goggles were switched around to reverse disparity relationships the spot appeared further away than the illusory square and no longer appeared to move horizontally. These effects demonstrate a powerful interaction between occlusion, stereopsis and apparent motion.

These displays have the advantage that they lend themselves quite readily to simple physiological experiments. For instance, many cells in MT are known to respond to apparent motion (Newsome *et al.*, 1986) and one wonders whether these cells would also "see" the illusion described here. Consider a cell confronted with the display shown in Figure 12. If the surrounding sectored disks are eliminated from the sequence the cell should, of course, respond quite vigorously to the apparent motion of the central spot. But what would happen if the sectored disks are now included in the sequence? (They should, of course, be presented outside the classical receptive field.) Would this silence the firing of the cell?

STEREOPSIS

AI researchers often use stereopsis as an example to illustrate that visual mechanisms are highly *modular* (Marr, 1982). A Julesz random-dot stereogram, for example, evokes a powerful sensation of depth even though it is completely devoid of other depth cues and contains no monocularly visible shapes or contours (Julesz, 1971). One may be tempted to conclude, therefore, that stereopsis is a simple point-to-point matching process that does not interact significantly with other visual mechanisms. Our next few experiments suggest, however, that this is not the case.

Stereopsis from Illusory Contours

We created a stereogram using two illusory squares similar to Figure 7(a) by introducing small horizontal disparities between the vertical edges of the cut sectors (Gregory & Harris, 1974). The disks themselves were at zero disparity in relation to the surrounding frame. When the two patterns (Figure 13) are fused by

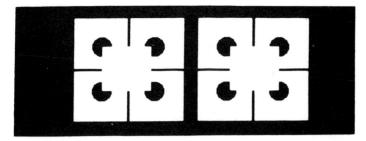

Figure 13. A stereogram produced by using two illusory squares. Small horizontal disparities are introduced between the vertical edges of the cut sectors. When the patterns of the two eyes are fused, a subjective square stands out in stereoscopic depth. All stereograms described in this chapter are printed in reverse to enable easy fusion; the pattern of the right eye is printed on the left and that of the left eye is printed on the right. To experience the illusions described, the reader should cross his eyes while fusing the stereograms. If the reader prefers to diverge his eyes, he should xerox and interchange the positions of the pictures.

crossing one's eyes, the four black disks are seen in the same depth plane as the frame, but the white illusory square stands out quite clearly in front of the background, an observation that suggests a high degree of interaction between illusory contours and stereoscopic depth perception.

Figure 14 depicts the "wallpaper effect". A pattern of repeating stripes is inherently ambiguous when viewed binocularly for it can convey any one of a number of different depth planes (Helmholtz, 1867). At any given instant, however, the entire pattern is seen to occupy only one single plane; the exact plane seen seems to depend mainly on the angle of convergence.

Next, we superimposed a template of the stereogram depicted in Figure 13 on several kinds of wallpaper to generate "wallpaper stereograms" (Figures 15 and 16). In Figure 15 we simply used repeating vertical rows of dots (see figure legends for additional details). When the patterns of the two eyes were fused, the square defined by the subjective contours could be seen standing out clearly in front of the

Figure 14. A well-known stereoscopic illusion called the wallpaper effect. If the reader brings the pattern very close to his nose and changes his angle of vergence while viewing this display, he will perceive corresponding changes in the plane of perceived stereoscopic depth.

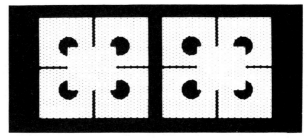

Figure 15. An example of stereoscopic capture. A template of the stereogram shown in Figure 13 was superimposed on Figure 14 to create this display. When the illusory square floats out in front it carries all the corresponding dots with it even though the dots are at zero disparity. Readers should cross their eyes to view the stereogram.

background. Interestingly, the corresponding dot rows on the wallpaper were also carried forward with the plane—an effect we call *stereoscopic capture* (Ramachandran, 1986). Since the disparity of the squares was several multiples of the periodicity of the dot rows, this finding implies that the subjective surface in depth created by the subjective contours was somehow pulling the dots with it even though the dots themselves were at zero disparity in relation to the background. Eight naive subjects who viewed these patterns reported this effect spontaneously. Interestingly, stereo capture can be obtained only with two-dimensional textures. If all the dots in Figure 15 are removed except for a single horizontal row in the middle the effect disappears completely and the dots remain flush with the background.

In Figure 16 we used continuous vertical lines instead of rows of dots in the background. Subjects reported that the illusion was just as compelling here as in Figure 15. In fact, the capture effect was strong enough to overcome the physical continuity of the vertical lines, and caused apparent breaks to appear on the lines at

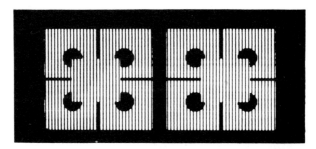

Figure 16. A template of Figure 13 is superimposed on a pattern of repeating vertical stripes. (The spatial frequency of the stripes is 9 cycles/degree.) A subjective square stands out clearly from the background, carrying the lines with it. Also, the capture effect is strong enough to overcome the physical continuity of the lines and causes apparent breaks to appear in the lines. The effect is especially compelling if the disparity between the cut sectors is arranged to be an exact multiple of the grating periodicity.

the upper and lower borders of the illusory square, even though all the lines were at zero disparity.

One explanation for the stereo-capture illusion would be that the unambiguous signals derived from the cut sectors are blindly attributed to finer image features in the vicinity. This explanation is readily disproved by using horizontal lines in the background instead of vertical lines. When we superimposed Figure 13 on horizontal lines (Figure 17) we found that only the horizontal lines actually joining the sectors themselves were pulled forward. All the other lines on the square remained flush with the background, and it was very difficult to break the continuity of these lines in order to partition them into two surfaces. Although horizontal lines are perceptually just as salient as vertical lines, the brain is reluctant to attribute depth signals to them.

The Influence of Occlusion Cues in the Perception of Stereopsis

The stereograms described so far convey *crossed* disparities, i.e. the impression of a square standing out in front of the paper (Figures 15-17). When the disparities were reversed a new percept emerged (see Figure 18). Subjects reported that instead of an illusory square they now saw four "portholes" cut out of an opaque sheet of wallpaper. The black disks which were originally opaque now acquired the subjective quality of being hollow. Through these holes they could now see the four corners of a smaller square piece of wallpaper, as shown schematically in Figure 19. The effect took a long time to crystallize but once it was seen it became quite stable, and was perceptually very compelling (Ramachandran, 1986). The illusory contours were now associated with completion of the holes (disks) rather than the square, and thus the corners which were seen through the holes pulled the corresponding lines of wallpaper with them. This unusual percept of seeing four deeper corners is of considerable theoretical interest, for in this case the illusory contours must be constructed *after* stereoscopic fusion. Further, once they have been constructed, these stereoscopic illusory contours must in their turn influence the subsequent processing of finer image features. This suggests that factors such as occlusion can directly influence the stereoscopic matching process, and it is

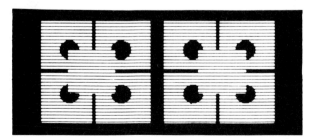

Figure 17.   Capture is considerably weaker if horizontal lines are used. The lines adjoining the sectors themselves are pushed forward but not the lines in between (they remain flush with the background and it is impossible to see subjective breaks).

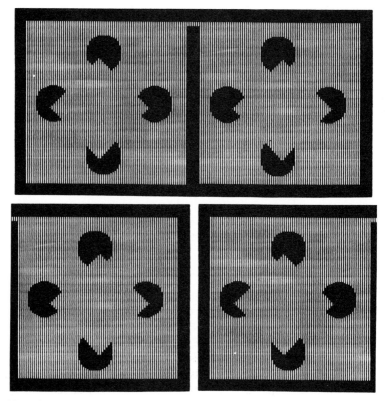

Figure 18. The porthole illusion produced by using uncrossed disparities (bottom panel). Subjects reported seeing four portholes cut out of an opaque sheet of wallpaper. Through these portholes they could see the four corners of a smaller square piece of wallpaper which pulled the corresponding lines with them (see Figure 19).

noteworthy that such a striking change in processing disparity signals can be induced by simply interchanging the pictures of the two eyes.

Unambiguous disparity signals can propagate and influence the matching of ambiguous elements in the vicinity (Julesz & Chang, 1976; Mitchison & McKee, 1985). Is stereo capture caused by a similar propagation of disparity signals from the cut sectors? To find out we tried using a control stereogram (Figure 20) in

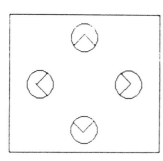

Figure 19. Schematic view of the percept obtained from Figure 18.

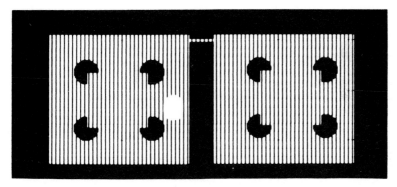

Figure 20. Disparity is introduced between the disks themselves (including cut sectors). Illusory contours are visible in the monocular image, but are actually reduced during stereoscopic viewing. Stereocapture is impossible to obtain. Hence, spread of disparity signals from the sectors alone is not sufficient to explain capture; construction of an illusory 3D surface may be a prerequisite.

which disparity is introduced between the discs themselves (including the cut sectors) and not just between the cut sectors alone. Stereoscopic capture could not be perceived in this stereogram even though the disparities conveyed by the cut sectors (and monocular illusory contours) are identical to those used in our previous experiments. This result suggests that the construction of an illusory stereoscopic *surface* is an important prerequisite for producing stereo capture; the mere propagation of disparity signals will not suffice.

Phase Sensitivity of Stereoscopic Capture

We found that stereoscopic capture was also very sensitive to the spatial phase relationship between the wallpaper and the sectored disks; the subjective square's disparity had to be an exact multiple of the periodicity of the lines. Thus, when the disks themselves were flush with the background, the subjective square occupied exactly the same plane as the enclosed wallpaper that was captured, and this seemed to amplify the illusion. This observation implies that the signal derived from the disparate subjective contours is not merely *attributed* to the elements of wallpaper; there must be some degree of mutual synergy between the two. In this respect stereo-capture may turn out to be different from motion capture (Ramachandran & Inada, 1985, Ramachandran & Cavanagh, 1987).

When a phase shift was deliberately introduced so that the disparity of the cut sectors was, say, 2.5 or 3.5 times the periodicity of the lines, a curious new effect was observed. The lines of wallpaper now occupied a stereoscopic plane that was equivalent to the nearest integer value to that conveyed by the illusory square (e.g. 3 instead of 3.5 or 2 instead of 2.5). Most observers reported seeing a transparent glass sheet through which they could see a square sheet of "captured" wallpaper.

PERCEPTION OF TRANSPARENCY

Transparency in Stereopsis

When resolving ambiguities in perception the human visual system often seems to use rules which reflect a built-in knowledge of the physical world. How far does this knowledge extend? In this section we present a new class of stereograms which convey a striking impression of transparent surfaces. The effects seem to depend strongly on the luminance ratios of different regions within the stereogram; if the ratios are incompatible with a real physical transparent object, then the *perception* of transparency also disappears. Incompatible colors, on the other hand, are readily tolerated by the system, suggesting that the stereoscopic mechanism incorporates tacit knowledge about the physics of transparency in the luminance domain, but not in the color domain. One reason for this may be that the neural pathways that mediate color vision appeared relatively late in primate evolution and may not have become adequately integrated with the phylogenetically older structures that mediate stereopsis.

To explore transparency effects in stereopsis we created displays of the kind shown in Figure 21. This display is very similar to Figure 13 except that the cut sectors of the "pac-men" have been filled in with pie-shaped wedges which have a different luminance. A strong impression of transparency can be obtained from the

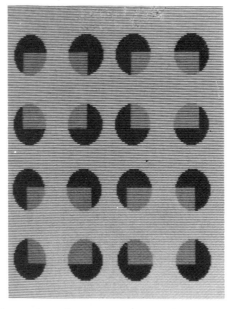

Figure 21.   A vivid impression of transparency (translucency) can be obtained in this stereogram which was created by simply filling in the pie-shaped cut sectors in Figure 11 with wedges of intermediate luminance. Transparency is seen only with crossed disparities (above) and not with uncrossed disparities (below).

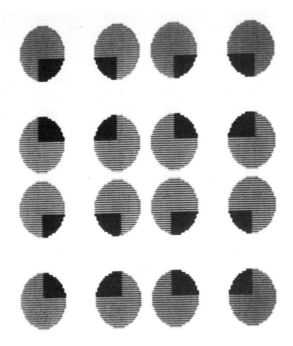

Figure 22.   Transparency can also be obtained if the wedges are made darker than both the pac-men and the background. The effect may take some time to evolve and many subjects report seeing a neutral density filter suspended in front of the four grey disks.

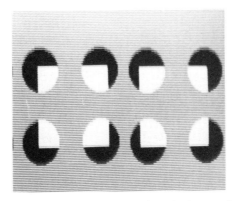

Figure 23.   The wedges are made brighter than both the background and the sectored disks. No transparency is seen in this display. The edges of the cut sectors are often seen in stereo depth but the *surface* corresponding to the square is seen to occupy the same depth as the surround. The implication is that stereoscopic transparency is sensitive to luminance ratios. The reader should diverge his eyes to "fuse" this stereogram.

crossed version of the stereogram (a) but not in the uncrossed version (b). In the uncrossed version one usually perceives four holes cut out of an opaque sheet of grey paper through which one can see the four corners of a partially occluded square. This is similar to the porthole effect described earlier (shown schematically in Figure 19) and it suggests that occlusion cues can strongly influence stereoscopic processing (Ramachandran, 1986; Nakayama et al., 1989).

Monocular transparency effects are known to be strongly influenced by luminance ratios (Metelli, 1974: Beck, 1986) and we wondered whether this was also true for stereoscopic transparency. To find out we kept the luminance of the pac-men (and background) constant and varied the luminance of the pie-wedges gradually over a wide range (Figures 21, 22 and 23). Three distinct percepts could be obtained depending on the luminance setting.* When the pie-wedges were darker than both the background and the sectored disks themselves the stereogram conveyed the impression of a square piece of neutral-density (ND) filter suspended in front of the four disks (Figure 22). The percept often took a long time to develop. When the luminance of the pie-wedges was made *intermediate* to that of the disks and the background (Figure 21) there was a striking change in perception. The illusory square now looked translucent like a "milky" glass plate or square piece of tissue paper suspended in front of the four disks. The effect was much more compelling than in Figure 22 and the illusory square now looked distinctly whiter than the background. None of our subjects had any difficulty in obtaining this percept. Finally, when we made the pie-wedges slightly brighter than both the background and the disks there was a complete loss of translucency (Figure 23). Surprisingly, even the impression of an illusory surface in depth disappeared; what was lost was not merely transparency but stereopsis as well. The vertical edges of the cut sectors themselves were seen tilted forward in depth but there was no impression of an occluding *surface*. This observation has the curious implication that the stereoscopic mechanism has "knowledge" about the physics of transparency. Notice that Figure 23 is a logically impossible object in the real world; there is no ND film or translucent plate that can make the wedge region appear *brighter* than the other two regions, and consequently the visual system rejects this percept.

What would happen if the pie-shaped wedges are made red instead of grey (Figure 24a)? We found that so long as the luminance was appropriate the visual system did not seem to mind this. We could obtain a strong impression of a transparent surface in this display and the surface was sometimes tinged with the same color as the wedges—an example of "assimilation" or "neon spreading" (Van Tuijl, 1975; Grossberg & Mingolla, 1985; Livingstone & Hubel, 1987). Interestingly, as one might expect from the theoretical speculations of Grossberg & Mingolla (1985), the neon spreading stopped exactly at the borders of the illusory contours. If the luminance was made inappropriate, on the other hand, there was a complete disappearance of depth, transparency and assimilation (Nakayama et al., 1989). The cut edges of the pac-men were tilted forward but the square itself remained flush with the background.

---

* Similar effects have also been observed by Nakayama et al. (1989) using a somewhat different stimulus configuration.

(a)

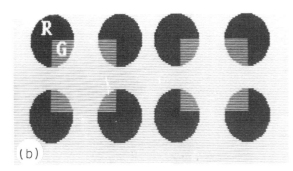

(b)

Figure 24. (a) This stereogram is similar to Figure 23 except that the wedges are red rather than grey. Transparency is seen only when the luminance of the red wedges is intermediate to that of the disks and the background. The entire square then acquires a reddish tinge—an example of "neon spreading" (Van Tuijl, 1975). Transparency disappears if the disparity is uncrossed rather than crossed. (b) In this stereogram the wedges are green and the disks are red. When the luminance of the green wedges is made intermediate to that of the red disks and the grey background one usually sees a transparent greenish tinged square. Again, transparency disappears if (i) the luminance of the wedges is greater than both the disks and the surround and (ii) if disparities are uncrossed rather than crossed. This experiment shows that the visual system will readily accept discordant colors (red and green) but not inappropriate luminance ratios.

Several conclusions emerge from these results. First, striking impressions of transparency can be obtained in stereopsis which are analogous to similar effects that have been previously described for non-stereoscopic (monocular) stimuli (Metelli, 1974; Beck, 1986). Second, the rules that govern the perception of stereoscopic transparency seem to mimic the physics of transparency to a surprising extent. Specifically, the system will not accept luminance ratios that would be incompatible with real transparent (or translucent) objects, which implies that the stereoscopic mechanism must incorporate "knowledge" about the physics of transparency. Inappropriate colors, on the other hand, do not seem to affect the perception of transparency as strongly as inappropriate luminances. (Small effects may exist but we did not encounter any in our experiments.) For instance, in one of our displays (Figure 24b) we could readily observe a green transparent plate hovering in front of red disks in the background even though the overlapping region was green rather than black. It seems remarkable that the system should display such a high degree of tolerance for incorrect colors while at the same time displaying such exquisite sensitivity to luminance ratios. One reason for this might be that our ancestors were nocturnal insectivores that had to rely largely on their luminance-based magnocellular pathways to perceive stereoscopic depth (Livingstone & Hubel, 1987; Snyder & Barlow, 1988). When color vision appeared later as an evolutionary novelty in diurnal frugivorous primates (Allman, 1987, it may not have become adequately integrated with other aspects of visual processing such as stereopsis (Ramachandran, 1986). This may explain why the stereoscopic mechanism is indifferent to discordant colors.

Relationship to Stereoscopic Capture

How does transparency interact with stereoscopic capture? To find out we superimposed Figure 21 on a grid of spots to create the stereogram shown in Figure 25. An illusory transparent square stands out clearly in front, but this time the dots corresponding to the square are not pulled forward, they remain flush with the background. There is, of course, nothing physically impossible about a transparent sheet with dots on its surface but the visual system rejects this percept and prefers to see the dots as lying in the same depth plane as the black disks in the background (Ramachandran & Rogers-Ramachandran, 1989b).

Consider the curious implications of this observation. First of all, seeing the square as transparent or opaque seems to depend critically on luminance ratios as well as the sign of disparity. Yet once a decision has been made that the square is transparent this decision, in its turn, seems to influence the matching of finer elements in the display. Thus, the luminance of the wedges and the disparity between them determines the perception of transparency, and transparency, in turn, affects the processing of retinal disparities conveyed by the texture elements. It seems unlikely that the visual system is actually going through all these iterations but our observations imply that the stereoscopic "module" must interact significantly with many other aspects of image segmentation, such as those conveyed by transparency and occlusion.

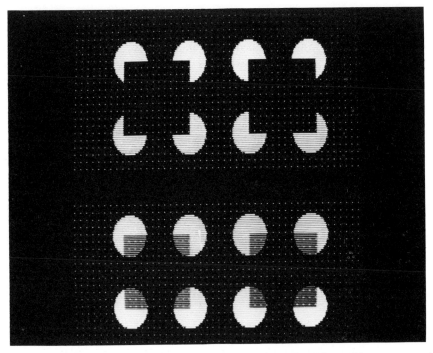

Figure 25. The bottom panel was created by superimposing Figure 21 on a repeating pattern of dots. Notice that the display is identical to Figure 15 except for the fact that the wedges have been filled in with an intermediate grey. Stereoscopic capture is reduced considerably compared with Figure 15 (reproduced here in the top panel); observers usually report seeing the dots through a milky glass plate (compare top and bottom panels).

Effect of Transparency on Perceptual Grouping

Can transparency influence perceptual grouping? To investigate this we created the display shown in Figure 26 in which the regions of overlap between the Bs and the irregular "ink-blot" have a different luminance from the exposed parts of the Bs. Notice that in this display the Bs look very camouflaged and it is not easy to segregate them from the "ink blot". Within each B the luminance fluctuations somehow prevent the fragments from being grouped into a whole B. We then varied the luminance of the overlapping region until each B looked transparent, and in this display (Figure 27) the Bs are once again perceptually salient. The different fragments of each B are grouped together quite readily in spite of the luminance differences since the differences are now compatible with transparency. One is tempted to conclude that transparency must be signalled fairly early in visual processing since it has such a striking influence on image segmentation and perceptual grouping.

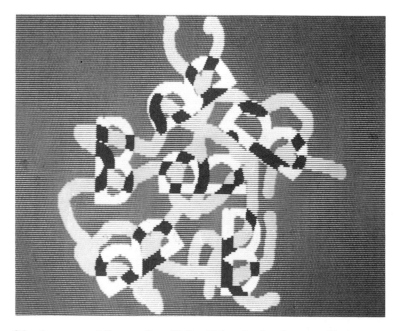

Figure 26. A swarm of "camouflaged" Bs. This stimulus is a modified version of an experiment carried out by Bregman (1981). Notice that unlike Bregman's display, each B in this pattern is composed of a mosaic of segments of different luminances. The fluctuations in luminance within each B are mistaken for object boundaries by the visual system and this tends to camouflage them. Animals such as giraffes and reef fishes have evolved similar tricks to break up their outlines.

Transparency and the Aperture Problem

A question of considerable theoretical interest is the so-called aperture problem that was originally posed by Wallach & O'Connell (1953). When a grating or even a single straight line is moved behind an aperture (so that its ends are not visible) its direction of motion is ambiguous; the retinal image motion generated by the line is in fact compatible with a whole family of velocities and directions (Adelson & Movshon, 1982; Hildreth, 1984). In the absence of other cues one usually sees motion at right angles to the orientation of the grating (Figure 28a).

On the other hand, if two such gratings are superimposed on each other to create a plaid pattern (Figure 28b), the ambiguity is reduced considerably. Instead of seeing the two gratings moving independently (component motion) one usually sees them moving unambiguously in a single direction (pattern motion). If the two gratings are made very dissimilar in spatial frequency and/or contrast they tend to move independently, whereas if they are made identical (or similar) they tend to generate coherent motion (Adelson & Movshon, 1982).

Adelsen and Movshon (1982) and Hildreth (1984) have provided an elegant theoretical analysis of this problem. There are two possible explanations of why coherent motion is seen when a plaid is used. First, the visual system may compute

Figure 27. The luminances of the different components of the mosaic have been altered to convey a vivid impression of transparency. This restores perceptual grouping so that the different fragments of each B are now seen to belong together to constitute individual objects.

the locus of direction and velocity vectors for each grating separately and then use the point of intersection of the two loci to uniquely specify the direction of the coherently moving plaid. Second, the higher-order features produced by the intersections between the two gratings move unambiguously in a single direction and it is possible that this unambiguous motion signal is used to resolve ambiguities in the rest of the display (as in motion capture).

We noted in a previous section that transparency influences the perception of stereoscopic depth. Would the perception of transparency also influence the probability of seeing component vs pattern motion? Some preliminary observations suggested that if the luminance of the intersections was made appropriate, the gratings could be made to look transparent (i.e. as though one grating were being seen through the other). This was especially true if an asymmetrical square-wave grating was used (Figure 28c). On the other hand, if the intersections were either too dark or too light (Figure 28d) the impression of transparency was destroyed and replaced by the appearance of a genuine plaid pattern. Again, these observations are quite consistent with the well known "laws" of perceptual transparency (Metelli, 1974; Beck, 1986), according to which luminance ratios between different regions of the display critically determine the impression of transparency.

Our next step was to move one of these square-wave plaid patterns while at the same time varying the luminance of the intersections. Would the perception of component vs pattern motion be gated by the presence or absence of transparency?

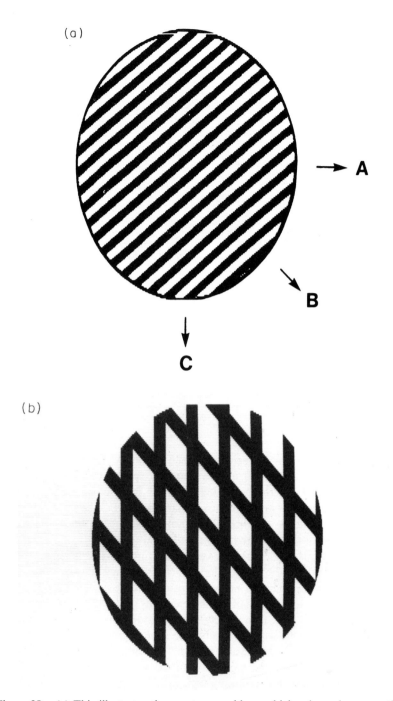

Figure 28. (a) This illustrates the aperture problem, which arises when a grating moves behind a circular aperture. The retinal image motion, produced by this stimulus, is compatible with a whole family of different directions and velocities (e.g. arrows A, B and C). Observers usually see motion at right angles to the grating; i.e. the percept corresponding to arrow B. (b) This was produced by superimposing two gratings. When this pattern was moved the two gratings were seen to move coherently in a single direction (pattern motion) instead of moving independently.

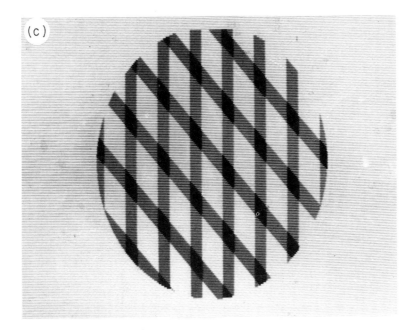

(c)

(d)

Figure 28. (c) If the luminance of the intersections was chosen appropriately, the display conveyed a striking impression of transparency as in this example. When the display was moved horizontally component motion was seen instead of pattern motion. (d) If the luminance of the intersections was inappropriate the impression of transparency was destroyed. When this display was moved horizontally subjects always saw pattern motion rather than component motion.

The results were striking. When the luminance of the intersections was adjusted so that the gratings looked transparent, one almost always perceived component motion rather than pattern motion. If the luminance of the intersection was varied to generate a plaid, however, both transparency and component motion disappeared and were replaced by the appearance of unambiguous coherent motion of the plaid in one direction. The luminance of the intersections thus critically determines both the perception of transparency and the perception of component vs pattern motion. We have recently measured this effect in naive subjects and find that the probability of seeing component motion was highest when the luminance ratios were optimal for seeing transparency (Stoner *et al.*, 1989).

The Role of "Terminators" in Solving the Aperture Problem

In Figure 28(a) the circular patch of grating is usually seen to move obliquely, i.e. at right angles to the orientation of the grating. If the grating is viewed through a narrow rectangular window, however, one always sees it moving horizontally instead of obliquely (Figure 29a). The terminators of the lines now move unambiguously in the horizontal direction and perhaps the motion signals derived from these are used to resolve ambiguities in the rest of the image. (This would be analogous to motion capture.) This is the usual explanation given for the so-called "barber-pole" illusion—the tendency to see the stripes of a barber pole moving vertically instead of horizontally.

What would happen if the occluder looked *transparent* instead of opaque (Figure 29b)? The entire circular patch of grating was now visible through the occluder

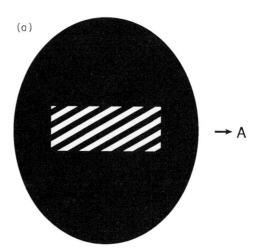

Figure 29.   (a) When the grating is viewed through a horizontal rectangular aperture it is seen to move horizontally (arrow A) independent of its true direction of motion. The motion of the tips of the lines is now unambiguously horizontal and perhaps this captures the motion of the rest of the grating.

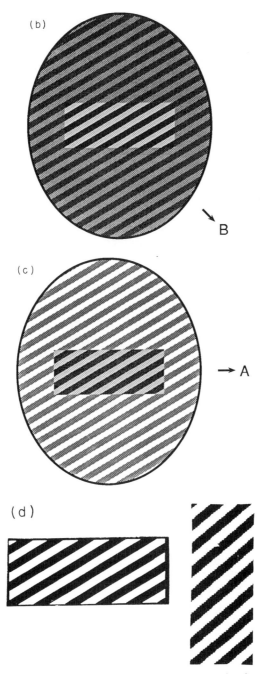

Figure 29. (b) If the occluder is made transparent, oblique motion is seen (arrow **B**) as in Figure 28a. (c) If the luminance ratios are adjusted so that transparency is destroyed, the impression of horizontal motion (arrow **A**) is restored once again. (d) In this display we have a grating moving behind two apertures viewed simultaneously—a vertical one and a horizontal one. Two different percepts could be obtained (see text).

which was made to look transparent by adjusting luminance ratios within different regions of the display. The display conveyed the distinct impression of a circular translucent glass plate from which a horizontal window has been removed. The grating now appeared to move obliquely again and horizontal motion was no longer visible (Ramachandran, 1989a, b; Ramachandran & Rogers-Ramachandran, 1989a). Perhaps the visual system no longer regards the ends of the lines inside the window as terminators since they appear perceptually continuous with the lines behind the transparent occluder.

To test this hypothesis we varied the luminance contrast of the grating outside the aperture so that the occluder no longer looked transparent (Figure 29c). Remarkably, this procedure once again restored the impression of unambiguous horizontal motion. The observation suggests that the motion mechanism must have access to a great deal of tacit "knowledge" about the physics of transparency. It strains the imagination to think of why (or how) such a sophisticated mechanism could have evolved given that transparent objects are not a very common occurrence in nature.

Another interesting display is shown in Figure 29(d). Here we have two apertures viewed simultaneously—a vertical one and a horizontal one. Notice that the grating has the same orientation for both apertures. When both gratings were then moved diagonally in the same direction (i.e. orthogonal to the grating's orientation) the resulting percept was ambiguous and bistable. One could either see two independent "barber poles" that were at right angles to each other so that the gratings moved in orthogonal directions or, alternately, one could voluntarily switch to seeing two windows or holes behind which there was a single grating moving rigidly in one direction. This effect, strongly reminiscent of the stereoscopic porthole effect described earlier (Figure 18), suggests once again that image segmentation and occlusion can strongly constrain the solution to the aperture problem.

Our findings also suggest an obvious physiological experiment. Certain cells in the middle temporal area (MT) of primates are known to show strong direction selective responses to moving gratings. Would these cells also display a sensitivity to transparency? If the cells' "classical" receptive field were to fall entirely within the central rectangular aperture, would it respond differently to Figure 29(b) and (c)? Indeed, the same question could even be asked of an end-stopped hyper-complex-type cell in V1 or V2. Would such a cell be inhibited by the long lines in Figure 29(b) but respond vigorously to the short lines in Figure 29(c)?

Like the correspondence problem, the aperture problem has attracted a great deal of attention from the computer-vision community and several ingenious algorithms have recently been proposed that might account for—or at least mimic—some aspects of motion capture and motion coherence (Yuille & Grzywacz, 1988; Bülthoff *et al.*, 1989). If these models are to provide more than "mere caricatures" (Crick, 1989) of human vision, however, they would have to take into account the role of multiple sources of information and multiple interacting constraints such as those implied by the transparency and occlusion effects reported in this article.

Multiple apertures

Consider the display shown in Figure 30. Here, instead of superimposing two gratings we created a mosaic of orthogonal grating patches moving in two different directions. The circular windows themselves did not move but each grating was made to move in a direction that was orthogonal to its orientation. Notice that unlike the more standard plaid pattern, this display does not contain any higher-order features such as intersections. Since the component directions of motion are identical for both displays, however, an algorithm that relied on spatial integration of velocity measurements alone (Hildreth, 1984; Bülthoff *et al.*, 1989) would signal the same direction of motion for both.

What would subjects actually see when confronted with such a display? The results were clear-cut. When four naive subjects viewed the display they clearly saw the equivalent of component motion rather than pattern motion; the grating patches appeared clearly segregated from each other perceptually and simply moved in orthogonal directions. The equivalent of pattern motion—in this case horizontal motion—was never seen.

If seeing pattern motion were based on an algorithm that spatially integrates motion measurements over an area (Hildreth, 1984; Bülthoff *et al.*, 1989) then one would have expected to see coherent horizontal motion (i.e. the equivalent of pattern motion) in this display; there should have been no difference between the perceived direction of motion of the plaid vs the mosaic. The fact that component motion was seen suggests that for solving the aperture problem either the visual

Figure 30. Multiple circular apertures with orthogonal grating patches moving in two different directions. In this display subjects almost always perceive component motion rather than pattern motion. (In extreme peripheral vision they could occasionally see pattern motion.)

system relies mainly on the unambiguous motion of certain salient image features (e.g. intersections) or that the spatial integration is carried out separately on different "objects" in the visual field. The problem with the latter interpretation, of course, is that the algorithm would have to know in advance what boundaries of the objects were and it is not clear how this could be achieved.

How "Real" is the Motion of an Afterimage?

Our last and most intriguing observation on the aperture problem involved using an afterimage of a vertical grating. First we produced an afterimage by steadily fixating the center of a very large grating that covered almost the whole visual field. Because the afterimage was so large, its outer borders (and terminators) were almost invisible. Whenever the eyes moved horizontally, the afterimage also appeared to move horizontally even though it was stationary on the retina and could not possibly have stimulated motion detectors in the visual pathways. This illusory movement is observed because the visual system assumes (erroneously) that the eyes are "tracking" the afterimage. In other words, the motion seen is entirely due to *reafference* signals from eye movements rather than retinal image motion.

Our next step was to transfer our gaze to an oblique black bar that was tilted 45° and displayed against a bright white background. We then adjusted the luminances of the bar and background so that the afterimage was visible only on the oblique bar—thereby creating the impression of a tilted barber pole. Remarkably, when we now moved our eyes horizontally the lines moved *diagonally*, as they would have on an actual barber pole. Only rarely were they seen to move horizontally. This is a surprising observation since there is no actual motion of the grating on the retina. If confirmed, it would imply that the integration of reafference signals into motion processing must precede the stage at which the aperture problem is solved by the visual system.

DERIVATION OF SHAPE-FROM-SHADING

Consider a ping-pong ball (or any other spherical Lambertian surface) illuminated on one side by parallel rays arising from a single light source. The luminance of this object's surface falls off as a cosine function as one moves away from the illuminated pole toward the "equator". If the illumination and reflectance are held constant, it is possible to calculate surface slant by using the variations in luminance alone and various computer algorithms have been proposed for doing this (Horn, 1975).

Does the human visual system also make use of variations in image intensity in this manner? We created the display shown in Figure 31(a) to answer this question (Ramachandran, 1988). It was produced by superimposing an illusory circle on a simple one-dimensional luminance ramp. The region corresponding to the circle initially looks flat but on prolonged inspection it takes on the appearance of a

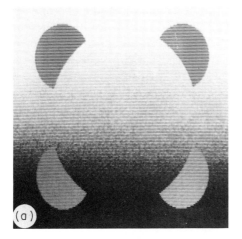

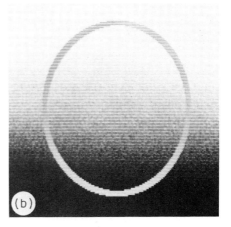

Figure 31. (a) An illusory circle was superimposed on a simple one-dimensional luminance ramp. This creates the impression of an illusory sphere even though there is no change in shading across the border of the sphere (Ramachandran, 1988). (b) If the illusory circle is replaced by a "real" circle, the sphere is no longer seen. This is because illusory contours are more reliable indicators of true object boundaries than "real" luminance-based edges. (c) This photograph illustrates that for extracting object boundaries the visual system relies on multiple mechanisms (e.g. in this case, illusory contours created by occlusion) rather than just luminance edges. If it relied exclusively on zero crossings you would see a hundred zebras here instead of one!

distinct bulge and may even pinch itself off from the background to become an illusory sphere, even though the shading in this region is physically continuous with the background! Also, notice that the curvature is seen along all axes even though the luminance gradient exists along the vertical axis alone. The implication is that the *segmentation boundary* that delineates an object from its background can powerfully influence the processing of shading information. If the visual system were making detailed measurements of shading to recover surface orientation there would be no basis for seeing a sphere in this image since the shading does not change abruptly across the border of the sphere. What the system seems to arrive at is merely a *qualitative* description of a sphere and this is quite different from saying that it computes surface orientation by using variations in luminance. In the next section we shall see how these principles may also apply to the problem of recovering the 3D structure-from-motion.

Oddly enough, illusory contours seem to work even better than real outlines (compare Figures 31a and b). This has the paradoxical implication that as far as the visual system is concerned, illusory contours are more "real" than "real" luminance-based contours! Why? One possibility is that in the natural world luminance edges can arise for a variety of reasons that are unrelated to object boundaries, e.g. edges of cast shadows, changes in reflectance, etc. An illusory contour, on the other hand, is always produced by occlusion which, in turn, can only be produced by a true object boundary. Figures 31(a) and (b) imply that the visual system is aware of this distinction and takes advantage of it. Indeed, if the visual system did not know the difference between reflectance edges and true object boundaries then every time you looked at a zebra (Figure 31c) you would see a hundred zebras instead of one!

Chromatic Edges do not Support Shape-from-Shading

We have seen that edges—even illusory ones—can strongly influence the perception of shape-from-shading. What would happen if the outline were defined by a change of color rather than a change of luminance? We took a typical shaded "sphere" and replaced the homogeneous grey background with a colored background in which the luminance gradient matched that of the sphere (Figure 32b). The result was dramatic; the illusion of depth dissolved and the sphere appeared flattened, even though its outline was distinctly visible because of the constrast in hue. We concluded that the shape-from-shading system cannot make use of edges defined by color differences. One reason may be that our primitive primate ancestors, which resembled tarsiers, were nocturnal and color blind; in their twilight world they may have relied on luminance contrast alone to perceive depth.

Shape-from-Shading as an Input to Perceptual Grouping and Apparent Motion

These demonstrations imply that the brain recovers information about the shape of objects by combining outlines and shading cues. What does the brain do with the shapes once it has recovered them?

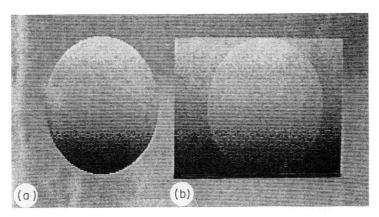

Figure 32. Chromatic borders are ineffective at producing the segmentation that is required for shape-from-shading (compare a and b). The yellow surround is depicted by a darker grey.

An important capacity of perception is the ability to segregate figure from ground. Even in a cluttered scene the visual system can easily decide which features in the image belong together to form objects. The laws of perceptual grouping have been studied systematically by Treisman (1986), Julesz (1981) and Beck (1966). These investigators discovered several important principles. First, they found that an important early stage of visual perception involves extracting certain elementary features, which Julesz calls textons. Examples include oriented edges, color and direction of movement. Once the visual system has extracted the elementary features, similar features are grouped together to form objects. Indeed, Julesz suggests that only elementary features, by definition, can be grouped in this way.

What about three-dimensional objects, though? Our next few demonstrations show that even shapes defined exclusively by shading can serve as elementary features of visual perception. In an array of cavities interspersed with convex shapes, for example, the convex shapes can mentally be grouped together to form a separate depth plane that is clearly segregated from the concave shapes in the background (Figure 33a). The effect is especially striking when the background luminance is exactly equal to the mean luminance of the shaded circular shapes.

We wondered whether the perceptual grouping observed in that display might be the result of some other, more elementary, feature than the three-dimensional shape. For example, because the convex shapes differ from the concave ones in the polarity of their bright-to-dark luminance, one might suppose the grouping is achieved by latching on to luminance polarity. To rule out this possibility, we created a display of objects that have the same luminance polarities as those in the preceding display but that do not carry any depth information (Figure 33b). It is virtually impossible to achieve perceptual grouping in this display. Even after you have spotted all the targets individually, you will not be able to segregate them from the rest of the objects. Clearly the grouping observed in the preceding display must be based on three-dimensional shape rather than on luminance polarity.

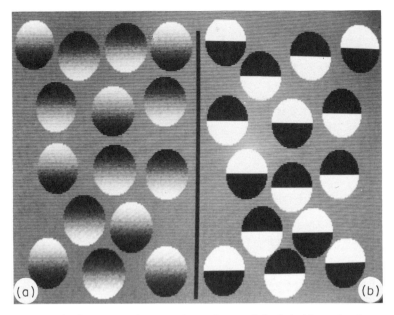

Figure 33. (a) The figure contains a random mixture of shaded objects that have opposite luminance polarities. The ones which are light on top are usually perceived as spheres and they can be mentally grouped together and segregated from the background of concave objects. Hence we may conclude that 3D shapes defined by shading can provide tokens for perceptual grouping and segregation. (b) This is a control for Figure 33(a). No 3D shapes are seen and it is also impossible to perceptually segregate the objects on the basis of luminance polarity. Hence the grouping observed in Figure 33(a) must have been due to 3D shapes.

The illusion of depth is much more powerful when the illumination is from above than when it seems to come from the side. Similarly, lighting from above greatly enhances one's ability to group and segregate images. You can verify this by simply rotating Figure 33 by 90°: the impression of depth will diminish and there will be a considerable reduction in perceptual segregation. This further supports the idea that perceptual grouping must be based on three-dimensional shape. Moreover, these groupings can themselves represent higher-level shapes, such as a triangle (Figure 34). It might be interesting to employ stimuli of this kind to find out whether infants and brain-damaged patients can perceive shape from shading; for example, would an infant respond to spheres arranged to suggest a face?

When one views this display, it appears as though the visual system passes through several stages of processing. In the earliest stage the system performs computations for defining the three-dimensional shapes, taking several seconds. Once the convex shapes have emerged, one has the distinct impression of being able to hold on to them indefinitely in order to group them with similar items in the display. Finally, after the objects are grouped, they are clearly segregated from irrelevant items in the background. The extraction and grouping of textons, then,

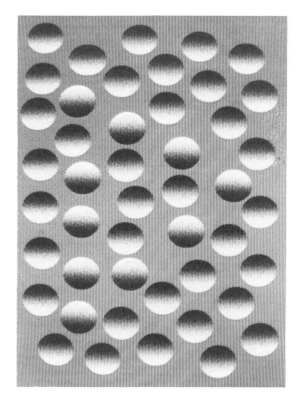

Figure 34.   The large hollow triangle seen in this display is based on shape-from-shading. If the page is rotated by exactly 90° the triangle fades away. Would a shape-detecting cell in visual areas IT or DL respond to shapes such as these that are defined exclusively by shape-from-shading?

although usually described as a one-step operation, may in fact involve several distinct perceptual capacities that act together to delineate figure from ground.

There is, unfortunately, no simple way to disentangle and measure these effects. One promising approach involves the use of apparent motion to determine the extent of perceptual segregation (Ramachandran *et al.*, 1973). An example of this is shown in Figure 35 which depicts two frames (a and b) of an apparent motion sequence. The central texture is shifted *en bloc* in frame (b) in relation to frame (a) but the individual elements comprising the two textures are completely uncorrelated in the two frames. When the frames are alternated one observes vivid apparent motion between the two inner "squares" even though the elements defining them are not correlated. This result suggests that the long-range apparent motion system can accept texture borders as an input.

Perhaps one can use apparent motion as a probe to determine the extent to which one can extract and hold on to a cluster of textons. This is shown in Figure 36. The top frame (a) has a cluster of convex objects on the left whereas in the bottom frame (b) the cluster as a whole is shifted to the right. (The two frames are

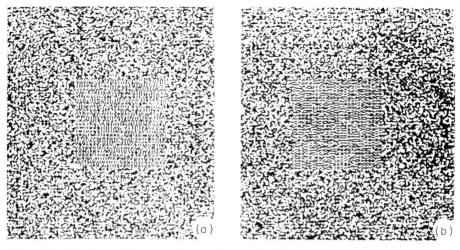

Figure 35. The figure shows two frames of a movie side by side for clarity. The square in frame (b) is shifted horizontally in relation to frame (a), but the elements constituting the squares are completely uncorrelated in successive frames. When (a) and (b) are optically superimposed and alternated, the square is seen to oscillate horizontally suggesting that the motion system can accept texture borders as an input even in the absence of point-to-point luminance correlation (Ramachandran *et al.*, 1973).

shown one below the other for clarity but in the original experiment they were optically superimposed and alternated.) As in Figure 35, the positions of the elements themselves were random and uncorrelated in successive frames. The results were quite striking. As long as there was no depth the elements in the display simply appeared to flicker. Once depth emerged, however, the triangular cluster of convex objects jumped vividly between the two locations as the frames were alternated. Optimum apparent motion was seen when the SOA was about 200 ms. These results suggest that even shapes defined exclusively by shading can provide tokens for long-range motion correspondence. It looks as though the motion system is remarkably versatile in the kinds of inputs it can accept.

The result suggests that the brain must first compute three-dimensional shape before it can perceive apparent motion. Indeed, subjects often take tens of seconds to develop a depth impression, during which time they see no apparent motion. It therefore seems unlikely that the apparent motion could be based on some other, more primitive feature of the image. To demonstrate the point more directly we rotated the entire display by 90°. This reduced the impression of depth considerably and led to an almost complete loss of the apparent-motion effect.

The visual system, then, appears to extract a three-dimensional object from shading cues and to perceive movement based on the three-dimensional image, rather than using the primitive two-dimensional image directly. Certain cells in the visual cortex of the monkey respond to the apparent motion of simple stimuli (Newsome *et al.*, 1986). It might be interesting to see whether these cells would respond to motion based on objects whose shape is defined exclusively by shading.

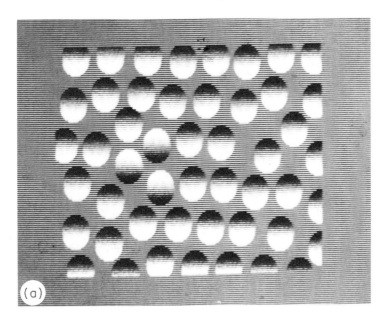

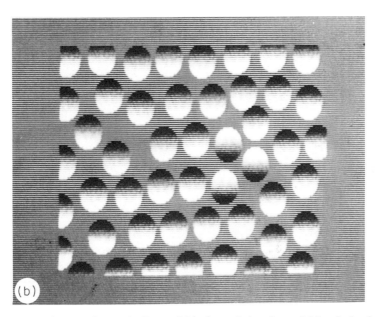

Figure 36. Two frames of a movie. Frame (b) is shown below frame (a) for clarity, but in the original experiment they were optically superimposed and flashed in succession. The positions of the objects are uncorrelated in the two frames but the central cluster as a whole is displaced horizontally. Vivid apparent motion of the central cluster could be seen when the two frames were alternated.

The interpretation of shape from shading also interacts strongly with the visual system's "knowledge" of objects, as is strikingly demonstrated by Figure 37. In these photographs the hollow insides of face masks are illuminated from above; one would therefore expect them to look hollowed out. But the visual system strongly rejects the possibility of hollow shapes and interprets the images as normal faces lit from below. Thus the visual system overrides the assumption of lighting from above in order to be able to interpret the shapes as convex objects.

Now notice the two small shaded disks between the chins of the two faces. Even though the light on the faces is assumed to come from below, the disk on the right generally is seen as convex and the one on the left as concave—as though they were both illuminated from above. Perhaps the brain treats these objects as being quite distinct from the faces and therefore, in interpreting their shading, adheres to the more primitive rule that they are illuminated from above. When the disks are pasted on to the cheek of one of the faces, however, the depth becomes ambiguous: the right-hand disk can appear concave and the left-hand one convex. Finally, when the outlines of the disks are blended into the cheek, they are always seen as being illuminated from below, like the rest of the face. Consequently the disk on the right suggests a dimple and the one on the left looks like a tumor on the zygomatic

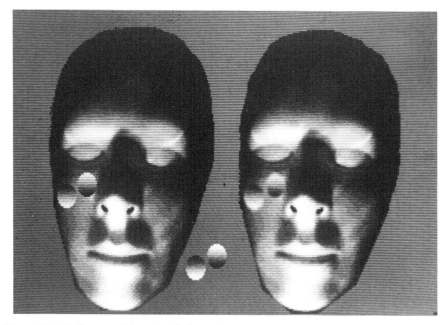

Figure 37. Hollow-mask interiors lit from above produce an eerie impression of protruding faces lit from below. In interpreting shaded images the brain usually assumes light shining from above, but here it rejects the assumption in order to interpret the images as normal, convex objects. Notice the two disks near the chin still appear as though lit from above: the right disk seems convex and the left one concave. When the disks are pasted on to the cheek (left), their depth becomes ambiguous. When blended into the cheek (right), the disks are seen as being illuminated from below, like the rest of the face.

arch. This example once again illustrates the profound influence of image segmentation on shape-from-shading. In the next section we will see how this principle also applies for the perception of three-dimensional structure from motion.

STRUCTURE-FROM-MOTION

A topic that has received a great deal of attention recently is the problem of how we recover the three-dimensional (3D) structure of moving objects. Consider the 2D parallel projection of a rotating transparent 3D cylinder with dots on its surface. The dots describe parallel horizontal paths, and the velocity of each dot varies sinusoidally as it moves from one side of the cylinder to the other and reverses direction. Although this changing pattern of dots is compatible with an infinite set of *non-rigid* interpretations (including that of a single plane of sinusoidally moving dots), observers always report seeing a rigid rotating 3D cylinder, an effect that is often called the *kinetic depth effect* (Wallach & O'Connell, 1953; Braunstein, 1962, 1976) or structure from motion, SFM (Ullman, 1979; Schwartz & Sperling, 1983; Inada *et al.*, 1987).

One approach to this problem originated with Helmholtz (1867) and is based on the assumption that motion parallax and stereopsis are analogous, that is, that 3D structure-from-motion is recovered from velocity gradients in much the same way that stereopsis is recovered from disparity gradients. It has been pointed out by Ullman (1979), however, that velocity gradients by themselves do not convey enough information for extracting 3D structure in the absence of other constraints. He suggested that the derivation of 3D structure from motion may be based, instead, on a special-purpose algorithm that seeks rigid interpretations. First, he showed mathematically that there is enough information in three views of four non-coplanar points to derive a unique 3D structure if the assumption is made that the object is rigid. Second, he suggested that whenever the visual system is confronted with an ensemble of moving points, it tries to home in on this rigid interpretation and discards the infinite set of nonrigid interpretations that are theoretically compatible with the same changing pattern.

What kind of algorithm does the human visual system actually use for recovering 3D structure from motion? Does it simply translate velocity gradients into a sensation of relative depth as originally suggested by Helmholtz? Or does it incorporate the rigidity assumption and proceed to compute the 3D coordinates of the dots by matching three successive views of the cylinder?

We devised a new set of stimuli to try and answer some of these questions (Ramachandran *et al.*, 1988).

Motion Parallax: Multiple Coaxial Cylinders

In this demonstration we displayed two coaxial cylinders of identical diameter superimposed on each other and spinning at two different speeds, 5 rpm and 10 rpm. We found that in this display it was extremely difficult to perceive two cylinders spinning at different velocities (Ramachandran, 1985c; Ramachandran *et al.* 1988). Instead of seeing the dots occupy only the external surface of the cylinder, what was usually perceived was dots occupying two different depth planes and rotating with identical *angular* velocities, as though there were a small cylinder inside a larger outer cylinder. The percept was a curious one since, on careful inspection, it was obvious that all the dots were in fact making identical horizontal excursions.

We believe that this illusion occurs because the brain has a strong propensity to translate velocity gradients into gradients of depth, as originally suggested by Helmholtz (1867). In fact, there may be a built-in assumption that if neighboring points have different velocities, then the slower ones must be nearer to the axis of rotation, even though the ensemble of points has no rigid solution.* This interpretation is somewhat at odds with Ullman's (1979) contention that velocity gradients cannot directly specify gradients of depth or structure from motion. In this example, even though the visual system is given the opportunity for recovering a rigid solution, it actually rejects this interpretation and prefers to respond directly to velocity gradients.

"Cylinder" of Dots Moving at Linear Instead of Sinusoidal Velocity

In this display we had two transparent planes of dots superimposed on each other and moving in opposite directions at a constant linear velocity. As each dot reached one of the vertical borders, it simply reversed direction and retraced its path. Although this display is physically compatible with two flat coplanar sheets of dots moving in opposite directions, what we actually observed was a rotating 3D cylinder. It was as though the mere reversal of direction at the border was sufficient basis for the brain to perceive a depth separation (and a curved motion path), even though the dots were actually moving at a constant linear velocity. The illusion was especially pronounced at high speeds of rotation (> 30 rpm). Notice that no rigid interpretation is theoretically possible in this stimulus, yet the visual system recovers a 3D shape that looks approximately rigid.

Why does this display look three dimensional? In the natural world if there are overlapping sets of points moving in opposite directions they cannot possibly occupy a single depth plane. Conversely, if spatially adjacent elements move with similar velocities (and directions) they probably belong to the same surface and will consequently be assigned the same depth value (or be considered as belonging to the same surface) by the visual system. Notice these constraints follow from the impenetrability and continuity of physical surfaces and, as such, have more in common with the Marr–Poggio stereo algorithm (1979) than with Ullman's rigidity-constraint.

The Role of Segmentation Boundaries: Cylinder Viewed Through a Triangular Aperture

We began with a transparent 3D cylinder and viewed it through a triangular window or aperture, so that only a triangular patch of moving dots was visible (the

---

* This implies, of course, that on the back of the cylinder the faster dots were actually *further* away from the observer than the slower ones.

horizontal base of the triangle was exactly equal in width to the diameter of the cylinder). The display was viewed in complete darkness so that the occluder was not visible. To our astonishment, this display looked very much like a solid 3D cone rather than part of a cylinder. Even though there was no velocity gradient along the vertical axis, the dots near the base of the cone were perceived as being further from the axis of rotation than the dots near the apex at the top. This observation implies that although velocity gradients are often sufficient to specify 3D structure from motion, they are not necessary. Furthermore, the *segmentation boundaries* that delineate the object in motion (i.e. the edges of the triangular window) seem to have a strong influence on the magnitude of perceived depth. We have previously demonstrated the important role played by segmentation boundaries for a variety of other perceptual capacities, such as the perception of apparent motion (Ramachandran, 1985b; Ramachandran & Anstis, (1986b), stereopsis (Ramachandran, 1986), and shape-from-shading (Ramachandran, 1988). It may turn out that the recovery of 3D structure from motion is analogous to seeing shape-from-shading, in that it relies on the combined use of velocity gradients and segmentation boundaries.

In addition to velocity gradients and segmentation boundaries, other factors are also undoubtedly involved in the recovery of 3D SFM. For example, in the displays we have considered so far, the axis of the cylinder was always vertical so that the dots described strictly horizontal excursions. What would happen if the axis were tilted toward the observer in the parasagittal plane? We found that this simple procedure produced a considerable increase in perceived depth. The motion paths were now elliptical rather than horizontal and this seemed to enhance the magnitude of perceived depth even though obviously the 3D structure signalled by the rigidity algorithm remains unchanged.

Cylinder Embedded in a Conveyor Belt

Our next experiment also demonstrates the important role of image segmentation. We began with an opaque 3D cylinder and simply "embedded" it in a conveyor belt of spots moving horizontally. Each spot began its excursion at the left end of the conveyor belt and moved with a constant linear velocity until it reached the cylinder. It then hopped on board the cylinder and its velocity varied sinusoidally until it reached the right-hand border of the cylinder, after which its velocity became linear again as it hopped back on to the conveyor belt (Figure 38).

When the cylinder was viewed in isolation its 3D structure could, of course, be recovered without any difficulty; it looked like an opaque spinning cylinder. When the conveyor belt was added, however, there was a complete loss of depth and 3D structure even though nothing was done to change the velocity gradients on the cylinder itself! Remarkably, this was true even if the dots were allowed to make only short left–right excursions so that no single dot ever crossed the border of the cylinder. The mere presence of flanking dots on either side of the cylinder caused a complete disappearance of 3D structure.

One interpretation of this observation would be that the visual system fails to segment the cylinder from the side flanks and therefore tries to recover a rigid 3D solution for the whole ensemble of points in the visual field (i.e. cylinder and

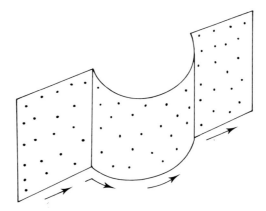

Figure 38.   An opaque 3D cylinder "embedded" in a horizontally moving conveyor belt of spots. When the conveyor belt is switched off the 3D shape of the cylinder is clearly visible, but when the conveyor belt is added to the display the cylinder looks completely flat. This is even true if the excursions of the dot are kept short so that no single dot actually crosses the border of the cylinder.

conveyor belt) rather than the cylinder alone. Since no rigid solution is possible no depth is seen.

If this interpretation is correct it has two implications. First, it suggests that in some situations rigidity may indeed play a role, albeit a limited one, in the recovery of 3D SFM (Ullman, 1979). Second, the deployment of this algorithm must come *after* image segmentation has already occurred, i.e. the algorithm has to be told what points to use as an input. Thus in our scheme, contrary to Ullman's, image segmentation must *precede* the extraction of 3D SFM rather than follow it.

Using Multiple Strategies for Recovering Structure from Motion

I began this chapter by pointing out that the goal of computational vision is to provide a clear description of the problems that the visual system has to solve. A good example of this approach, as we have seen, is Ullman's (1979) elegant formulation of the problem of recovering 3D SFM. He showed that 3D structure from motion can, in principle, be recovered from the changing shadow if the assumption is made that the object producing the shadow is rigid. Given the rigidity assumption, Ullman's SFM theorem proves that there is enough information available in three views of four noncoplanar points to uniquely specify their 3D structure. Furthermore, his argument also has two important implications: (1) without rigidity the problem may be insoluble; and (2) if you assume rigidity then 3D structure can *in principle* be recovered without making any other assumptions.

Yet, paradoxically, our results suggest that instead of a single rigidity-seeking algorithm of the kind described by Ullman, the visual system uses a wide variety of mechanisms to recover 3D SFM. These include (a) velocity gradients, (b) segmentation boundaries, (c) segregation of dots moving in opposite directions into different depth planes, (d) elliptical motion trajectories. Why does the system resort to using so many "hacks" if a rigidity-based algorithm alone will suffice, theoretically, to recover 3D structure? There are at least three answers. First, since evolution has no foresight it may be much easier to evolve multiple crude gimmicks than a single sophisticated mechanism. Second, by using multiple parallel strategies the system can get away with each of them being relatively crude and, therefore, easy to implement in real neural hardware. And lastly, the use of multiple parallel mechanisms allows the visual system to achieve a remarkable tolerance for "noisy" images of the kind it would encounter in the natural world.

I am sometimes asked "Is there a general theory of vision? Does the utilitarian approach negate the possibility of such a general theory?" To a biologist studying vision this question can have no more meaning than, say, the question "Is there a general theory of the liver?" The only general remark that can be made about the liver is that it is concerned with optimal energy utilization, but to a biologist there is a sense in which this is the least interesting aspect of the liver. To him what is interesting about the liver is precisely all the messy details of the two dozen or so diverse metabolic functions it performs (e.g. secreting bile to emulsify fats, glycogen storage and release, gluconeogenesis, fatty acid metabolism, mechanisms for detoxifying portal blood, etc.).

And so it is with vision.* For example, the intricate mechanisms that mediate color vision (i.e. trichromacy at the retinal level followed by opponent processes further upstream and the use of "double opponent" cells in color constancy) were discovered by a combination of painstaking psychophysics and physiology. The particular mechanisms used are in part the result of an interplay between the organism's adaptive needs and certain natural constraints, but also in part due to the organism's evolutionary history. Although it is possible to provide *post hoc* rationalizations for these mechanisms, it seems highly unlikely that any of them could have been deduced from first principles. The lesson to be learned is that in understanding vision, a bottom-up research strategy is just as important as a strictly top-down approach of the kind advocated by Marr.

One general remark that can be made about perception, however, concerns its biological goal—that it has to be extremely rapid and highly tolerant to noisy inputs. Through millions of years of trial and error the organism has "learned" that the best way to achieve this is to simultaneously deploy multiple parallel short-cuts or heuristics for each perceptual problem. Our task as biologists, then, is to unravel the internal logic of each of these mechanisms (preferably at all three levels prescribed by Marr) and to discover how they interact with each other to generate our perceptual experience of the world.

The idea that the visual system may use short-cuts to solve perceptual problems is not entirely new and in fact similar ideas have been previously proposed by Gibson (1966) and Runeson (1977). There are, however, several important

---

* Of course, underlying all these diverse mechanisms, there may be just one or a small number of learning algorithms (Sejnowsky & Churchland, 1989). Even so, a complete understanding of vision will have to include not just a specification of these learning algorithms but also a description of the actual mechanisms that have been (presumably) acquired as a result of the learning.

differences between these earlier approaches and ours. First, Gibson spoke of perception as being direct "pick up" of information and denied the need for intermediate stages of processing, whereas the utilitarian theory explicitly acknowledges the need for such stages. For instance, the specific mechanism we propose for solving the correspondence problem—the inhibition of short-range by long-range motion signals—is very different from the resonance that Gibson would have envisaged. Second, contrary to many psychological theories which emphasize the flexibility and intelligence of perception, we would argue that the mechanisms of perception are often relatively crude, although always *adequate* for the job on hand. What makes vision so efficient and reliable in our scheme is the use of multiple parallel mechanisms for each perceptual task. And lastly, although the idea of using heuristics and short-cuts in vision is a plausible one, there have been very few attempts to devise critical empirical tests that would serve to distinguish this view from Gibsonian, Helmholtzian and computational approaches to vision. Our purpose in this chapter has been to provide examples of such experiments.

Taken collectively, these results support Francis Crick's conjecture that "God is a hacker." They suggest that our final perception of a three-dimensional visual world depends on a rich interaction of information from a variety of sources. The numerous reciprocal cross-connections that are known to exist between different extrastriate visual areas (Van Essen, 1979; Finkel and Edelman, 1989) provide a suitable substrate for mediating these interactions.

ACKNOWLEDGEMENTS

This chapter is based on a talk I gave in September 1988 at the international conference on "How the Brain Works" organized by *Nature*. I thank N. Bourbaki, C. G. H. Tompkins, F. H. C. Crick, K. Nakayama, S. Anstis, P. Cavanagh, D. Rogers-Ramachandran, D. Kleffner and D. Plummer for stimulating discussions. The analogy between the visual system's use of parallel mechanisms and the plight of two drunks staggering towards their goal emerged from a discussion I had with J. A. Deutsch. I also thank the Academic Senate of the University of California and the Airforce Office of Scientific Research for funding this research.

REFERENCES

Adelson, E. H. & Movshon, J. A. (1982). The phenomenal coherence of moving patterns. *Nature*, **300**, 523–525.

Allman, J. (1987). Evolution of the brain in primates. In R. L. Gregory (Ed.) *Oxford Companion to the Mind*. Oxford University Press, Oxford.

Ballard (1986). Cortical connections and parallel processing: structure and function. *Behavioural and Brain Sciences*, **9**, 67–120.

Braunstein, M. (1962). Depth perception in rotation dot patterns: effects of numerosity and perspective. *Journal of Experimental Psychology*, **64**, 415–420.

Braunstein, M. L. (1976). *Depth Perception Through Motion*. Academic Press, New York.

Beck, J. (1966). Effect of orientation and of shape similarity on perceptual grouping. *Perception and Psychophysics*, **1**, 300–302.

Beck, J. (1986). Perception of transparency in man and machine. In A. Rosenfeld (Ed.) *Human and Machine Vision*, Vol. 2. Academic Press, New York.

Bregman, A. (1981). Asking the "what for" question in auditory perception. In M. Kubovy & J. R. Pomerantz (Eds) *Perceptual Organization*, pp. 99–119. Lawrence Erlbaum, Hillsdale, NJ.

Bülthoff, H., Little, J. & Poggio, T. (1989). A parallel algorithm for real-time computation of optical flow. *Nature*, **337**, 549–553.

Cavanagh, P., Boeglin, J. & Favreau, O. E. (1985). Perception of equiluminous kinematograms. *Perception*, **14**, 151–162.

Cavanagh, P., Tyler, C. W. & Favreau, O. (1985). Perceived velocity of moving chromatic gratings. *Journal of the Optical Society of America*, **A1**, 893–899.

Crick, F. H. C. (1989). The recent excitement about neural networks. *Nature*, **337**, 129–132.

Cutting, J. (1988). *Perception with an Eye for Motion*. Bradford Books, MIT Press, Cambridge, MA.

DeYoe, E. A. & Van Essen, D. C. (1985). Segregation of efferent connections and receptive fields in visual area V2 of the macaque. *Nature*, **317**, 58–61.

Epstein, W. (1988). Has the time come to revive Gestalt theory? *Psychological Research*, **50**, 2–6.

Feldman, J. A. (1986). *Behavioral and Brain Sciences*, **8**, 265–289.

Finkel, L. H. & Edelman, G. M. (1989). Integration of distributed cortical reentry: a computer simulation of interactive functionally segregated visual areas. *Journal of Neuroscience*, **9**(9), 3188–3208.

Gibson, J. J. (1966). *The Sense Considered as Perceptual Systems*. Houghton Mifflin, Boston.

Gregory, R. L. (1970). *The Intelligent Eye*. McGraw-Hill, New York.

Gregory, R. L. (1977). Vision with isoluminant color contrast—I. A projection technique and observations. *Perception*, **6**, 113–119.

Gregory, R. L. & Harris, J. P. (1974). Illusory contours and stereo depth. *Perception and Psychophysics*, **15**, 411–416.

Grossberg, S. & Mingolla, E. (1985). Neural dynamics of form perception: boundary completion, illusory figures, and neon color spreading. *Psychological Review*, **92**, 173–211.

Helmholtz, H. L. F. von (1867). *Handbuch der Physiologischen Optik*. Leipzig.

Hildreth, E. (1984). *The Measurement of Visual Motion*. MIT Press, Cambridge, MA.

Hochberg, J. (1981). Levels of perceptual organization. In M. Kubovy and J. R. Pomerantz (Eds) *Perceptual Organization*. Lawrence Erlbaum, Hillsdale, NJ.

Horn, B. K. P. (1975). Obtaining shape from shading information. In P. H. Winston (Ed) *The Psychology of Computer Vision*. McGraw-Hill, New York.

Hubel, D. H. & Livingstone, M. S. (1985). Complex unoriented cells in a subregion of primate area 18. *Nature (London)*, **315**, 325–327.

Inada, V., Hildreth, E., Grzywacz, N. & Adelson, E. H. (1987). The perceptual build-up of 3-D structure from motion. *Investigative Ophthalmology and Visual Sciences*, **28** (Suppl.), 142.

Julesz, B. (1971). *Foundations of Cyclopean Perception*. University of Chicago Press, Chicago.

Julesz, B. (1981). Textons, the elements of texture perception and their interactions. *Nature*, **290**, 91–97.

Julesz, B. & Chang, J. J. (1976). Interaction between pools of disparity detectors tuned to different disparities. *Biological Cybernetics*, **22**, 107–119.

Kanizsa, G. (1979). *Organization in Vision. Essays on Gestalt Perception*. Praeger, New York.

Kolers, P. (1972). *Aspects of Motion Perception*. Pergamon Press, New York.

Livingstone, M. S. & Hubel, D. H. (1987). Psychophysical evidence for separate channels for the perception of form, colour, movement and depth. *Journal of Neuroscience*, **7**, 3416–3468.

Marr, D. (1982). *Vision*. Freeman, San Francisco.

Marr, D. & Poggio, T. (1979). A computational theory of human stereo vision. *Proceedings of the Royal Society (London), Series B,* **204**, 301–328.

Mitchison, G. & McKee, S. (1985). Interpolation in stereoscopic matching. *Nature (London),* **315**, 402–404.

Metelli, F. (1974). The perception of transparency. *Scientific American,* **230**, 90–98.

Nakayama, K., Shimojo, S. & Ramachandran, V. S. (1989). *Perception,* in press.

Newsome, W. T., Mikami, A. & Wurtz, R. H. (1986). Motion selectivity in macaque visual cortex—III. Psychophysics and physiology of apparent motion. *Journal of Neurophysiology,* **55**, 1340–1351.

Penrose, R. (1989). *The Emperor's New Mind.* Oxford University Press, Oxford.

Poggio, T., Torre, V. & Koch, C. (1985). Visual perception and regularization theory. *Nature,* **138**, 645–647.

Ramachandran, V. S. (1985a). Apparent motion of subjective surfaces. *Perception,* **14**, 127–134.

Ramachandran, V. S. (1985b). Guest editorial: the neurobiology of perception. *Perception,* **14**, 97–105.

Ramachandran, V. S. (1985c). Inertia of moving visual textures. *Investigative Ophthalmology and Vision Research* (Suppl.).

Ramachandran, V. S. (1986). Illusory contours capture stereopsis and apparent motion. *Perception and Psychophysics,* **39**, 361–373.

Ramachandran, V. S. (1987a). Visual perception of surfaces: a biological theory. In S. Petry & G. Myer (Eds) *The Perception of Illusory Contours.* Springer, New York.

Ramachandran, V. S. (1987b). Interaction between color and motion in human vision. *Nature,* **328**, 645–647.

Ramachandran, V. S. (1988). Perception of depth from shading. *Scientific American,* **269**, 76–83.

Ramachandran, V. S. (1989a). Interactions between motion, depth, color and form: the utilitarian theory of perception. In C. Blakemore (Ed.) *Vision: Coding and Efficiency.* Cambridge University Press, Cambridge.

Ramachandran, V. S. (1989b). Visual perception in people and machines. Presidential special lecture given at the annual meeting of the Society for Neuroscience.

Ramachandran, V. S. & Anstis, S. M. (1983). Perceptual organisation in moving displays. *Nature,* **304**, 529–531.

Ramachandran, V. S. & Anstis, S. M. (1986a). Perception of apparent motion. *Scientific American,* **254**, 102–109.

Ramachandran, V. S. & Anstis, S. M. (1986b). Figure–ground segmentation influences in apparent motion. *Vision Research,* **26**, 1969–1975.

Ramachandran, V. S., Anstis, S. M. & Rogers-Ramachandran, D. (1987). Correspondence strength in apparent motion. *Investigative Ophthalmology and Vision Research* (Suppl.).

Ramachandran, V. S. & Cavanagh, P. (1987). Motion capture anisotropy. *Vision Research,* **27**, 97–106.

Ramachandran, V. S., Cobb, S. & Rogers-Ramachandran, D. (1988). Recovering 3-D structure from motion: some new constraints. *Perception and Psychophysics,* **44**, 390–393.

Ramachandran, V. S. & Gregory, R. L. (1978). Does colour provide an input to human motion perception? *Nature (London),* **275**, 55–56.

Ramachandran, V. S. & Inada, V. (1985). Spatial phase and frequency in motion capture of random-dot patterns. *Spatial Vision,* **1**, 57–67.

Ramachandran, V. S., Inada, V. & Kiama, G. (1985). Perception of illusory occlusion in apparent motion. *Vision Research.*

Ramachandran, V. S., Rao, V. M. & Vidyasagar, T. R. (1973). Apparent motion with subjective contours. *Vision Research,* **13**, 1399–1401.

Ramachandran, V. S. & Rogers-Ramachandran, D. (1989a). Occlusion and transparency in motion perception. *Society for Neuroscience Abstracts.*

Ramachandran, V. S. & Rogers-Ramachandran, D. (1989b). Transparency and stereoscopic capture. In preparation.

Rock, I. (1983). *The Logic of Perception*. MIT Press, Cambridge, MA.

Runeson, S. (1977). On the possibility of "smart" perceptual mechanisms. *Scandinavian Journal of Psychology*, **18**, 172–179.

Schwartz, B. J. & Sperling, G. (1983). Nonrigid 3-D percepts from 2-D representations of rigid objects. *Investigative Ophthalmology and Visual Science*, **24** (Suppl.), 239.

Searle, J. (1989). Is the brain's mind a computer program? *Scientific American*, in press.

Sejnowsky, J. & Churchland, P. (1989). Computational neuroscience. *Science*, in press.

Shepard, R. (1981). Psychophysical complementarity. In M. Kubovy & J. R. Pomerantz (Eds) *Perceptual Organization*. Lawrence Erlbaum, Hillsdale, NJ, pp. 279–343.

Shipp, S. & Zeki, S. M. (1985). Segregation of pathways leading from area V2 to areas V4 and V5 of macaque monkey visual cortex. *Nature (London)*, **315**, 322–324.

Sigman, E. & Rock, I. (1974). Stroboscopic movement based on perceptual intelligence. *Perception*, **3**, 9–28.

Snyder, A. & Barlow, H. (1988). Revealing the artist's touch. *Nature (London)*, **331**, 117–118.

Stoner, E., Albright, T. & Ramachandran, V. S. (1989). Transparency and coherence in human motion perception. Submitted for publication.

Treisman, A. (1986). Features and objects in visual processing. *Scientific American*, **225**, 114–126.

Ullman, S. (1979). *The Interpretation of Visual Motion*. MIT Press, Cambridge, MA.

Van Essen, D. C. (1979). Visual cortical areas. In W. M. Cowan (Ed), *Annual Reviews in Neuroscience*, Vol. 2, pp. 227–263. Palo Alto Annual Reviews, Palo Alto.

Van Tuijl, H. F. J. M. (1975). A new illusion: neonlike color spreading and complementary color indication between subjective contours. *Acta Psychologica*, **39**, 441–445.

Wallach, H. & O'Connell, D. N. (1953). The kinetic depth effect. *Journal of Experimental Psychology*, **45**, 205–217.

Yuille, A. L. & Grzywacz, L. (1988). A computational theory of coherent motion perception. *Nature (London)*, **333**, 71–74.

Zeki, S. M. (1978). Functional specialization in the visual cortex of the rhesus monkey. *Nature (London)*, **274**, 423–428.

4   Deploying Visual Attention: The Guided Search Model

Jeremy M. Wolfe and Kyle R. Cave

Department of Brain and Cognitive Sciences, Massachusetts Institute of Technology, Cambridge, MA 02139, USA

INTRODUCTION

No visual system is able to completely analyze all of the input that it receives. Sophisticated computer vision systems and sophisticated biological visual systems are required to allocate their resources. If nothing about the input is known in advance, the system must have a mechanism, preferably a fast mechanism, that can direct other more thorough processing mechanisms to the most important parts of the input on the basis of a preliminary analysis of that input. Thus a visual system is likely to have two major stages: an early stage that must be able to rapidly process all of the input in order to identify the most important portions (parallel, preattentive processing), and a later stage that is capable of thoroughly processing only a limited portion of the input at any one time (serial attention). The later stage should be guided by the output of the early stage. Moreover, it should be possible to request specific information from the early stage in those situations in which something is known about the input in advance. In this chapter, we will review evidence that the human visual system is constructed along these lines with an early, fairly simple-minded parallel processing stage guiding the subsequent serial deployment of more sophisticated, but spatially limited, processes.

Are Two Stages Necessary?

Regardless of the realities of biological systems, it could be argued that an ideal system would not be required to use serial processes but would execute all of its functions in parallel. However, two classes of argument strongly suggest that it will

© 1990 John Wiley & Sons Ltd.

not be possible to build visual systems without a two-stage, parallel–serial architecture. First, there is a theoretical constraint. Some tasks seem to be inherently "serial". Ullman (1984) has identified a number of such essentially sequential processes. Examples include tracing a curve and identifying the region inside a closed boundary. It is difficult to imagine parallel algorithms that could perform these computational tasks.

Second, there are practical constraints. For instance, assume that visual objects are identified as a collection of basic features such as color, orientation, size, depth and motion. Assume also that there are detectors for each of these kinds of feature covering all locations in the visual field. Identifying a particular object should be a simple matter of finding the right combination of features. However, there are too many possible combinations of features to make it possible to have separate detectors for all combinations of all features at all locations in the visual field. One solution is to have detectors for visual objects respond whenever the required features appear anywhere in the visual field. Feldman (1985) tries this solution in his "four-frames" model. As Feldman points out, though, when two different objects appear in the visual field, the system has no way of knowing which features belong to which object. This problem, which Hinton *et al.* (1986) have called "the binding problem", can be avoided by adding a mechanism that suppresses input from all but one location. By accepting inputs from different locations at different times, the system can determine what feature combinations occur at what locations. Of course, such a mechanism is a mechanism of serial attention.

The preceding example is a single example of a general limitation. Consider virtually any of the algorithms that analyse shapes, combine them into object representations or compare them against representations in memory. In each case a prohibitive amount of hardware would be necessary to perform the operation independently at all locations across the visual field. Higher-level processing tasks of this sort might best be implemented with a limited amount of hardware that can be applied to different parts of the input at different times. Given these theoretical and practical constraints, it seems clear that any complex visual system will need a good selection mechanism to allow it to allocate its spatially limited processing resources appropriately.

The problems that such a selection mechanism must solve are not easy. At a minimum, it must work quickly and with limited information. This problem is something like confronting a box of chocolates. You can only choose one among many, and to make the best choice you have to bite into each one first. Since that is is not possible, you have to make the best choice you can with very limited information. In this chapter we will focus on selection in the human visual system. Perhaps the selection mechanisms used by this successful visual system can be applied in artificial systems.

Previous Approaches to the Selection Problem in Human Vision

The distinction between the early parallel processing stage, and the later limited stage has been around for some time. Neisser (1967) proposed that a set of preattentive processes separated a visual display into its individual elements and directed focal attention from one element to another. The preattentive processes operated in parallel across the visual field, but "they could provide neither fine structure nor emotional content" (p. 103). Focal attention could process stimuli in great detail, but could only operate over a limited region of the visual field at one time, and thus was forced to process each element serially.

These concepts have endured. Currently two of the leading theories of visual selection are built upon this general framework. Treisman's "feature integration theory" (Treisman & Gelade, 1980; Treisman & Schmidt, 1982; Treisman, 1986) and Julesz's "texton theory" (Julesz & Bergen, 1983; Julesz, 1984) both posit a fast but incomplete parallel stage followed by a spatially limited serial stage. These two theories are similar in form. Whereas Neisser was vague about the specific differences in processing between the parallel and serial stages, Treisman and Julesz have an abundance of additional data that allow them to make more specific claims.

A large part of this evidence came from experiments in visual search. In these experiments, subjects search for a particular visual element embedded in a group of randomly positioned elements. The results from a particular search task are determined by the property of the target that distinguishes it from the distractor elements. For instance, if a target is red while all of the distractors are green, subjects will find it very quickly. More importantly, if more distractors are added to the display, the time it takes subjects to respond will increase very little or not at all. The same pattern appears if the target has a different orientation from the distractors. Because the time necessary to find these differences in color or orientation is more or less independent of display size, Treisman concludes that these feature differences are detected by a preattentive stage that can process information in parallel across the visual field. Figure 1 shows data from our laboratory for such a search. (Note: in this and subsequent graphs, where we show our data, we are showing RTs averaged across 10 subjects with 300 or more trials per subject.)

Treisman contrasts these parallel searches with searches for targets that are defined by two features. For instance, if the target is a red vertical line, and the distractors are all either red horizontal lines or green vertical lines, then information about either color or orientation alone is not enough to find the target. In these searches, the target is defined by a conjunction of features, and subjects must consider both the color and orientation of an element before deciding whether or not it is a target. Treisman found that response times for these conjunction searches increased as the number of elements in the display increased. An example, replotted from Treisman & Gelade (1980), is shown in Figure 2. Apparently, their subjects processed one element (or group of elements) at a time until they found the target. Thus Treisman and Gelade concluded that conjunction searches are performed by a serial processing stage.

Additional evidence comes from other experimental paradigms. For instance, if a field of horizontal lines is placed next to a field of vertical lines, a salient texture boundary appears between the two fields. Obvious texture boundaries can also be produced with fields that differ in the color of their elements. However, if one field is made of red vertical and green horizontal elements while the other is made of

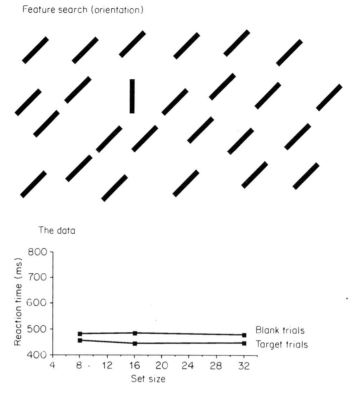

Figure 1. In a "feature" search, the target is distinguished from distractors by a single, unique feature; here, orientation. Reaction time (RT) is independent of set size, suggesting that all items are processed in parallel. In this and other graphs of our data, RTs are averaged over 10 subjects.

green vertical and red horizontal elements, no salient boundary appears (Treisman & Gelade, 1980; Beck *et al.*, 1983; Julesz & Bergen, 1983). According to feature integration theory, within the parallel stage information about different features is represented independently. Only the serial stage can combine information from different feature processes and it can only operate at one location at a time. (Julesz's texton theory is similar, and for the remainder of this discussion we will speak entirely in terms of feature integration theory.) Any task that requires conjoining different features, such as the conjunction search described above, will rely on the serial stage.

Feature integration theory accounts for a large body of data from visual search, texture segregation and a number of other experimental paradigms (Treisman & Gelade, 1980). Moreover, it is appealing for its simplicity. The parallel stage only needs to compare values within a particular feature dimension. The operations it requires are simple and can be quickly carried out in parallel across the visual field. Also, failure of the parallel processes to find conjunctive targets is just the sort of failure to be expected given the binding problem described above.

Conjunction search (color × form)

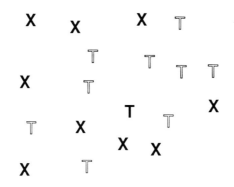

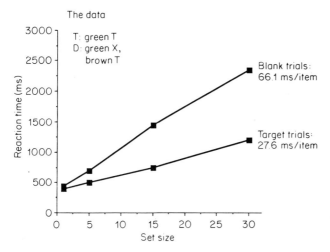

Figure 2. In a "conjunction" search, no single feature distinguishes target from distractors. Here the target is a black T, a conjunction of color and form (or, in this case, orientation). Data are replotted from Treisman & Gelade (1980), where the target was a green T. Treisman & Gelade found that RT increased linearly with set size. Moreover, the slope of the RT × set size function for blank trials was twice that for target present trials, suggesting a serial self-terminating search for this conjunction.

GUIDED SEARCH

Although feature integration theory accounts for Treisman's experimental data quite well, the constraints it imposes seem very severe, given the speed at which everyday visual processing can occur. We can generally recognize complex scenes very quickly, even when we know nothing about them in advance (Biederman, 1981). Usually this recognition will require conjoining many different features at a number of different locations. In order for all these conjunctions to be done rapidly, it is imperative that the serial stage be quickly directed to the most important locations in the scene. However, these locations will usually not be marked by a unique feature (color, orientation, etc.). It is not clear how normal scene perception could occur within the bounds of feature integration theory.

Luckily, the parallel stage in feature integration theory can be enhanced within the constraints imposed by the binding problem, and this enhancement can result in more efficient visual searches. Although it may not be possible to have parallel detectors for every conjunction of features at every location in the visual field, it should be possible for the parallel stage to guide the serial search for conjunctions by combining information from different feature processes. Thus, the intersection of information about the location of "red" items and "vertical" items should be useful in the search for "red vertical" items. Our data suggest that such guidance is possible. The remainder of this chapter will outline our "guided search" model. The model allows for the combination of information from different processes at each location to determine whether or not that location should be processed more fully. Under this scheme, the mechanisms required for the parallel stage are still very simple and could easily be carried out quickly across the visual field. We will present the model as a set of propositions. For each proposition, we will offer supporting data from visual search experiments. More detailed information about these experiments can be found in previously published work (Wolfe & Franzel, 1988; Wolfe *et al.*, 1989; Cave & Wolfe, 1989; Wolfe *et al.*, 1989a).

Proposition 1.   The Visual System Processes a Set of Basic Features in Parallel

The physiology of the visual system suggests that at every location in the visual field there are cells sensitive to simple visual features including color, motion, size (or spatial frequency) and orientation (Bishop, 1984). This is not to say that all parts of the visual field are equally sensitive to each feature. The decline in response to high spatial frequency outside the fovea is an obvious example of variation across the visual field. Still, though the parameters may change, the entire visual field is covered by the receptive fields of cells that respond differentially to variation in spatial frequency.

This hardware should make it possible to simultaneously process information at multiple locations. Put another way, these basic features should be processed in parallel. Evidence from visual search experiments suggests that they are. As noted above, if the amount of time required to find a target is independent of the number of distractor items, then we generally conclude that the target can be found by means of a parallel search of all locations at the same time (though see Townsend, 1972, for important qualifications).

There is not complete agreement about the set of basic features, though there is agreement about many members of the set. Most of the features that have been used to stimulate single cells support parallel visual processing (color, orientation, size, motion, stereoscopic depth). In addition, there are a number of other stimulus properties that appear to support parallel search (e.g. binocular lustre, various pictorial depth cues, curvature, line terminators). Some of these may be based on other, more primitive, features, a matter discussed toward the end of this chapter.

Proposition 2. Information Combined from Two or More Feature Maps can be used to Guide Visual Search for Conjunctions

Individual feature processes (or "maps") can perform only very limited visual tasks. The combination of information from several maps is at the heart of our guided search model. This combination allows for the execution of more sophisticated tasks. The model combines two lines of thought. Hoffman (1978) has proposed that a parallel front end of the visual system guides later serial stages. Treisman (Treisman & Gelade, 1980; Treisman, 1986) and others have demonstrated that this front end processes only a limited set of simple features.

Consider a search for a conjunction of two features: luminance and orientation. In Figure 3, the target is a black vertical item. Distractors are white vertical and black horizontal items. The target cannot be located either by knowing its luminance polarity or its orientation. A model that lacks parallel guidance of serial search would predict that search for the target would be a random, serial, self-terminating search. Figure 4 shows an example of such a search.

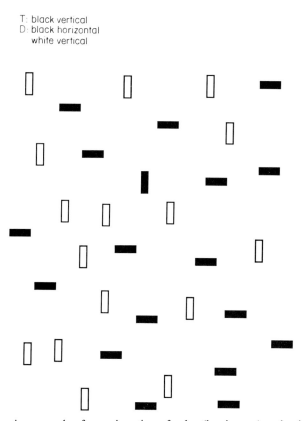

Conjunction of luminance and orientation

T: black vertical
D: black horizontal
   white vertical

Figure 3. An example of a conjunction of color (luminance) and orientation.

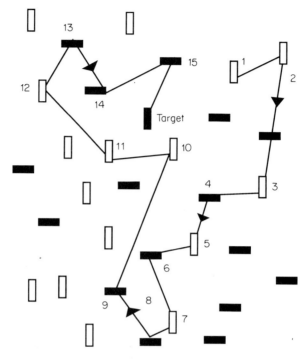

Figure 4.   An example of a random-walk, serial, self-terminating search for a conjunction.

If the parallel processes do guide serial search, that search need not be random. While a parallel process for luminance cannot identify the black vertical item, it can locate the set of all black items (Figure 5a). Similarly, the parallel process for orientation cannot find the black vertical item but can locate the set of all vertical items (Figure 5b). The intersection of these two sources of information locates the black vertical item or items (Figure 5c).

Examples of searches for conjunctions from our laboratory are shown in Figure 6. The slopes from one of Treisman & Gelade's (1980) conjunction searches are replotted from Figure 2 for comparison. Clearly, our slopes are shallower. We believe that subjects are able to combine information from different feature maps in order to guide search toward the target item. If the data shown in Figure 6 were the result of a serial self-terminating search, then the ratio of blank trial and target trial slopes should be 2:1. Though average slopes are in a roughly 2:1 relationship, individual subjects range from as low as 1:1 to as high as 30:1, making it unlikely that subjects are performing regular serial searches (Wolfe *et al.*, 1989a). Moreover, the shallow slopes would imply movement of the spotlight at a rate much faster than previous estimates (e.g. Bergen & Julesz, 1983a; Julesz, 1984).

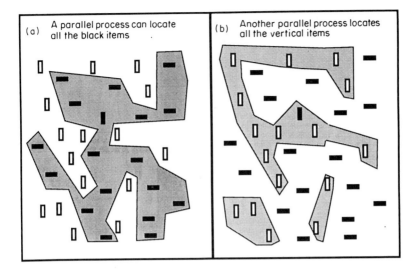

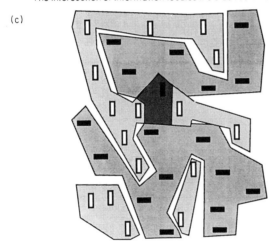

Figure 5. Even if no individual parallel process can locate a conjunction, the parallel processes, taken together, can guide serial attention toward a conjunction. Here a parallel "color" process locates all black items (a) and a parallel "orientation" process locates all vertical items (b). Combining these two sources of information, attention could be guided toward the black vertical target (c).

Proposition 3.   Guidance is Not Perfect but Depends on Stimulus Salience and Internal Noise

If this parallel guidance were perfect, as it is in Figure 5, then the search for conjunctions would be as independent of set size as the search for simple features. As a general rule this is not the case. We conceive of this as a problem of detecting a signal in noise. Consider a red target among green distractors. The large difference

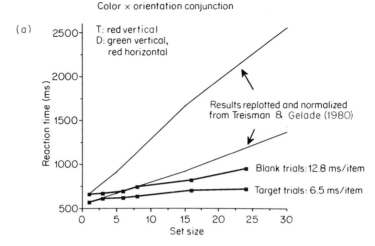

Color × orientation conjunction

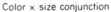

Color × size conjunction

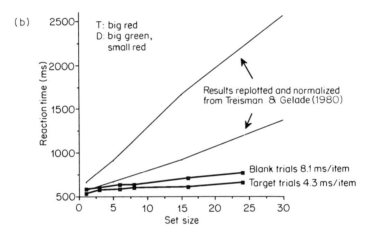

Figure 6. Conjunction searches that suggest parallel guidance of serial attention. For color × orientation (a) and color × size (b) conjunctions, our RT × set size functions are much shallower than those reported by Treisman & Gelade (1980). Their data (from Figure 2) are replotted in this figure. Their RTs are normalized to our data for target trials at set size 1. The slopes for our conjunction searches are similar to those reported elsewhere for feature searches.

in color ensures that the signal about the location of the red item will be larger than virtually any random noise in the system. However, suppose that in a search for a red target the distractors were orange or reddish-orange. At some point, noise will obscure the signal differentiating the target from the distractor. In searches for targets defined by a single feature it has been found that large differences between target and distractors support search independent of set size, while small differences require what appears to be more serial search (Bergen & Julesz, 1983b; Duncan, 1989).

For reasons explained below, parallel guidance in searches for conjunctions is more likely to be obscured by noise than guidance for simple features. Therefore, in most conjunction searches, serial attention will check a few of the distractors before finding the target. An example of this imperfect guidance is shown in Figure 7. As the level of noise increases, the target is less likely to be found quickly, more distractor locations will be checked, and as a result searches will tend to take longer. If the level of noise is extremely high, then information from the feature processors will be totally obscured, and search will be completely random and serial.

Differences in signal-to-noise ratio may explain why some experiments show steep slopes for conjunction searches while others do not. Figure 8 shows data from

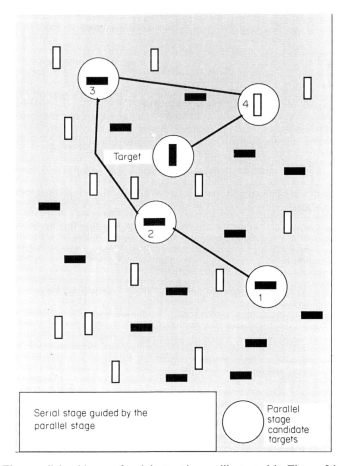

Figure 7. The parallel guidance of serial attention as illustrated in Figure 5 is perfect. In reality, it appears to be limited by noise. In a search for a conjunction, parallel processes identify several candidate locations for the target, effectively reducing the set size. A serial search is done only for these candidate locations. In this illustration, four false target locations are checked before the true target is found.

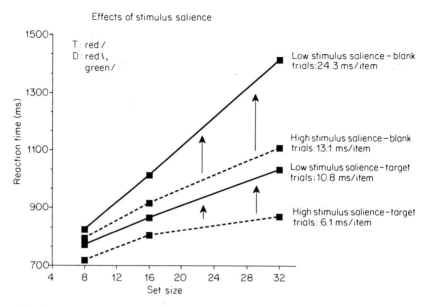

Figure 8. One way to manipulate the amount of noise and, thus, the quality of the parallel guidance, is to manipulate stimulus salience. That is, better guidance is obtained with a greater difference between target and distractors on any dimension. In this example, it can be seen that reducing stimulus salience increases the slope of the RT × set size functions.

two versions of a color × orientation search. In one case, colors are vivid and on a black background; in the second case, the colors are desaturated and on a gray background, further reducing the contrast. Obviously, slopes are steeper in the second case.

Proposition 4.   Additional Sources of Information Improve Parallel Guidance of Attention

In a search for a conjunction, there are two sources of information about target location: the parallel processes for the two relevant features. If guidance is accomplished by combining information across parallel processes, it follows that adding more relevant features would improve guidance. This prediction is borne out experimentally in searches for triple conjunctions (Quinlan and Humphreys, 1987; Wolfe *et al.*, 1989a). In Figure 9, we show data from a search for a triple conjunction of color, size and form. The target is a big red o. The distractors each share one feature with the target. There is a BIG green ×, a small RED ×, and a small green o. Compared to a simple conjunction of color and form, it is clear that the additional size information makes search more efficient.

In Figure 9, the target differs from the distractors on two dimensions. Triple conjunction searches can be designed so that targets differ from distractors on only one dimension (e.g. Target: big red o; Distractors: BIG RED ×, small RED o,

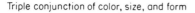

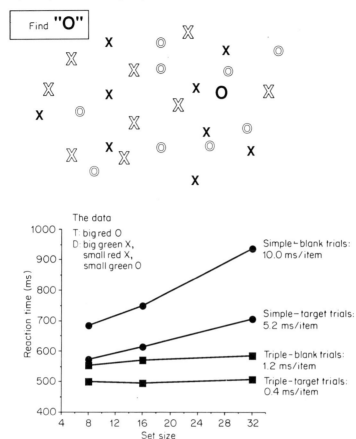

Figure 9. If attention is guided toward conjunctions by combining information from two parallel feature processors, it seems likely that better guidance could be obtained by combining information from three feature processors. Here the target is defined by a triple conjunction of color, size and form. Each distractor shares one attribute with the target. Slopes are very shallow and are significantly shallower than those obtained with simple conjunctions.

BIG green o). In this case, the information is comparable to that available in the simple conjunction and in our experiments slopes are comparable as well (Wolfe *et al.*, 1989a).

Proposition 5.   Parallel Guidance is Based on Two Sources of Information: Bottom-up and Top-down

Thus far, we have said that parallel processes guide attention to likely targets in visual search tasks but we have said little about how the parallel processes act to select those targets. The data suggest that there are two mechanisms. One of these requires knowledge of the nature of the target item. It can be called top-down selection. The other mechanism is strictly stimulus driven and can be labelled bottom-up.

Proposition 5(a).   Bottom-up activation guides attention toward the items that differ from all other items

When a red item is presented in a field of green items, it does not matter if the observer knows that "red" is the designated target. Attention will be automatically attracted to the unique item. In fact, it is hard to ignore a salient unique item even if it is known that it is *not* the target (Pashler, 1988). Contrast this to a display containing a single red item in a field of items, each with its own unique color. Clearly, the red item will not immediately attract attention unless it is known that "red" is the target. The salience of the unique red item in the first instance can be understood as the product of a mechanism that determines the difference, within some featural dimension, between an item and all other items. In the first example, the red item is different from all of the green items while each green item is different from only the single red item. In the second example, each item is different from all other items and, thus, the red item has no special status.

A 'gedanken experiment' should be adequate to show that the bottom-up mechanism can provide adequate information to conduct a visual search task. Imagine that on each target trial all items are identical except for a unique target item. The particular target and distractor colors change from trial to trial. Blank trials consist of a homogeneous set of distractors. This experiment could be done with any of the basic features (orientation, size, motion, etc.). It should be intuitively clear that the search for an "odd-man-out" among homogeneous distractors will be easy even if the identity of the target is not known in advance. As a fanciful control, we may imagine the same task with heterogeneous distractors. Clearly, if the identity of the target is not known and can change from trial to trial and if each item has a unique color, then neither parallel nor serial search will be possible.

When nothing is known about the input, it is important to identify those parts that are likely to be most informative. Bottom-up activation does this by identifying those visual elements that differ the most from their surroundings. In other situations, the viewer will have certain expectations about the upcoming input, and will direct attention accordingly. If something unexpected appears in a different part of the visual field, the bottom-up activation will ensure that attention is redirected to it.

Proposition 5(b).   Top-down activation is based on differences between an item and the designated target

Of course, it is possible to search for a "red" target among heterogeneous distractors if the subject knows in advance that the target will be red. This suggests a second mechanism that determines the similarity of each item to the known target. For each feature, top-down activation guides attention toward those elements that are most similar to the target.

To prove that such a mechanism exists at a preattentive, parallel stage in processing, we need to show that it is possible to search for an item among heterogeneous distractors independent of the number of those distractors. Figure 10 shows data from such an experiment. The red target was located in a set of eight different colored distractors. The RT × set size slopes for target and blank trials are essentially flat. Red is at one extreme of color space. The experiment was repeated with a purple target that was less isolated in color space. The slopes increase a little but remain much shallower than predicted by serial self-terminating search. Duncan (personal communication) has done similar experiments with similar results.

Top-down activation is useful whenever something is known about the target being sought. Even if there are other objects surrounding the target that share some of its features, top-down activation can guide attention. In the presence of noise, this guidance will not always be perfect, but it can still make searches much faster than they would be otherwise.

The existence of these two mechanisms of parallel guidance of attention make it easier to explain the results described above. In a simple feature search, top-down and bottom-up sources of information both help to find the target. The target is known and is displayed on a homogeneous background of distractors. By contrast, a standard conjunction presents a much more difficult problem. In a search for a red vertical item among green vertical and red horizontal distractors, the bottom-up mechanism is of no use. Half of the items are red, half green. Half the items are vertical, half horizontal. Only the top-down activation can provide information to

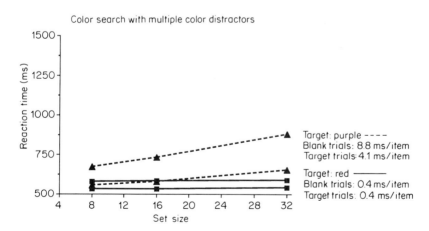

Figure 10. Parallel guidance has two aspects: top-down and bottom-up. Bottom-up guidance is based on the differences between a given item and all other items. A unique item attracts attention. Top-down guidance is based on similarity between an item and a known target attribute. Here the target is of a unique color. The distractors' colors are heterogeneous, so bottom-up guidance is lacking. Top-down guidance is adequate, in this case, to provide for parallel or nearly parallel search.

guide attention. In the triple conjunction case shown in Figure 9, bottom-up information is again useful, although not as useful as in a feature search. If the target item is a big red ○ among BIG green × s, small RED × s, and small green ○s, then the target will be similar to only one-third of the distractors in color, size or orientation. For each feature, the bottom-up activation should guide attention toward the subset of items with the correct target attribute. As noted above, search is further enhanced by the presence of three relevant sources of information. This parallel mechanism with its top-down and bottom-up components is similar to Duncan's (1989) similarity model. However, Duncan believes that similarity is computed across all features rather than separately for each feature (color, orientation, etc.).

Proposition 6.   When No Guidance is Possible, Search is Serial and Self-terminating

It is possible to design search tasks in which neither top-down nor bottom-up information is available. With preattentive, parallel guidance precluded, the resulting search must be either serial or impossible depending on the capabilities of the serial stage of processing. Figure 11(a) gives an example of such a search Ts and Ls each contain one vertical and one horizontal line. There is no orientation information to guide search for a T among Ls. If the letters can be rotated, other dimensions are irrelevant as well. (Note: without rotation, some "form" information remains. Relatively efficient search is possible for an upright T among upright Ls.) As can be seen in Figure 11(b), the resulting search produces the steep slopes and the 2:1 slope ratios characteristic of serial search.

Figure 12 gives an example of a task that foils even the serial stage. The target is presented to one eye while the distractors, otherwise identical, are presented to the other. The serial stage lacks access to eye-of-origin information. The resulting search is neither serial nor parallel: it is impossible (Wolfe & Franzel, 1988). There are a number of other, less interesting, failures of the serial stage. Many of these involve acuity limitations. If a task cannot be done without making a foveating eye movement, it contributes little to our understanding of serial and parallel processes. In the absence of appropriate controls, tasks with slopes of, say, 125 ms/item on target trials and 250 ms/item on negative trials should be regarded with suspicion.

Search can be made more efficient even if only partial guidance is provided. For instance, it is easier to find a red L among red Ts and green Ts than among Ts that are all red. Even though no parallel process can discriminate Ts from Ls, half of the distractors can be eliminated by parallel guidance from the color mechanism (see also Egeth *et al.*, 1984).

Proposition 7. Attention can be Guided Toward Only One Instance of a Feature at a Time

The power of the parallel stage of processing is the ability to simultaneously determine the presence or absence of specific stimulus attributes in several stimulus

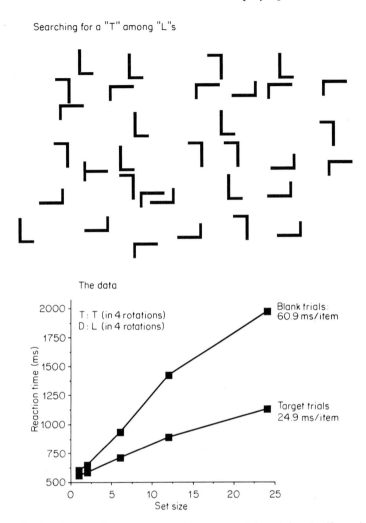

Searching for a "T" among "L"s

The data

Figure 11.   In the absence of any parallel guidance, search is serial and self-terminating. In this case, both the target, T, and the distractors, L, contain one horizontal and one vertical contour. Thus, orientation information is useless. The resulting search has the normal hallmarks of a serial self-terminating search.

dimensions. Thus, a color processor can locate all "red" items at the same time that an orientation processor locates all "vertical" items. A significant limitation on that ability appears if we attempt to simultaneously search for two types within a single dimension. In Figure 13, for example, the target is the item that is vertical and oblique; a conjunction of two orientations. The distractors are vertical and horizontal, and oblique and horizontal. The two line segments are of different luminance polarity because if they were both black or both white, the overall shape/orientation of the item would become a cue. These tasks are difficult. Figure 14(a) shows data from such an orientation × orientation search. Figure 14(b)

Is "eye-of-origin" information a feature?

T: spot presented to the right eye
D: spots presented to the left eye

Figure 12.   Some tasks lack information that can be used by either the serial or the parallel stages of processing. Here the target is a spot presented to the right eye while distractors are presented to the left eye. Though cells early in visual processing are selective for eye of origin, this information is not available to guide either serial or parallel visual search. Subjects reply at random.

Orientation × orientation conjunction

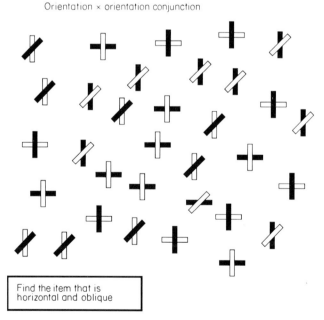

Find the item that is
horizontal and oblique

Figure 13.   Though conjunctions may be found by combining information about two different types of feature (e.g. color × orientation) the same does not appear to be true for conjunctions of two examples of the same feature (e.g. orientation × orientation). In this figure, the search for the item that is horizontal and oblique is quite difficult.

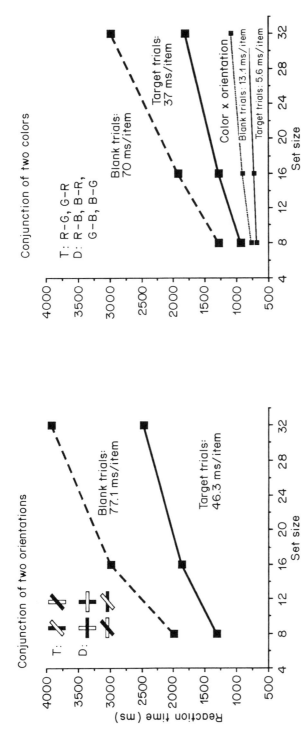

Figure 14. Data from orientation × orientation and color × color searches. In both cases, RT × set size functions are consistent with self-terminating search. Indeed, slopes are steeper than many other apparently serial searches (cf. Figure 11).

shows data from a similar search for color × color conjuntions (target: red and green; distractors: red and blue, green and blue). Variations of the stimulus configuration make little or no difference to the steep serial nature of the results.

Several conclusions follow from these results.

1. Separate representations of "red" and "green" or of "vertical" and "oblique" do not appear to exist, at least not in the sense that color and orientation are represented separately. While it is possible to combine information from color and orientation processes in order to guide search for a red vertical item, it is not possible to combine red and green information in order to guide search for a red-green item.
2. Within a process (color or orientation), it is not possible to activate two types of item. That is, it does not appear to be possible to ask, top-down, for all the red items and all the green items and then to guide search to the item that is activated twice.
3. Finally, search cannot be guided by steering attention away from a set of items. In Figure 13, all distractors contain a horizontal line. In the color example, all distractors contain blue. It is not possible to forbid attention to visit blue or horizontal locations.

Note that the limitations on guidance described here are primarily top-down limitations. If a subject needs to look for a single red and a single green item on a field of blue distractors, bottom-up processing will mark both of these locations as significantly different from all other items.

A different hypothesis could be used to explain the highly serial nature of orientation × orientation or color × color conjunctions. Two colors or two orientations must occupy two spatial locations while a single color can be conjoined with a single orientation at a single location. It is possible to conclude that the difficulty in searches of the sort described here is not with conjunctions within a stimulus dimension but with conjunctions across space. Though two colors cannot occupy the same space and time, this hypothesis can be tested by separating color and orientation and examining the effects on search. Sample stimuli are shown in Figure 15. The color is carried on an unoriented ring while the orientation is carried on an uncolored central bar. For comparison, color and orientation can both be carried on the central bar with an uncolored, unoriented ring remaining in order to keep the overall configuration constant. In this experiment, slopes were actually somewhat steeper in the case where color and orientation information occupied the same spatial location. Certainly there was no evidence that separating color and orientation produced the sort of steeply sloped serial results seen with color × color or orientation × orientation conjunctions.

Proposition 8. Complex Searches can be Performed as an Automatized Series of Simple Searches

The limitations on parallel guidance of attention are quite severe. Consider the following search for two possible targets. The targets are a big red item or a little

Color × orientation conjunctions
Attributes can be on the same or on different stimulus elements

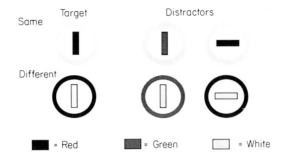

Figure 15. In color × color and orientation × orientation searches, the two relevant attributes are spatially separated. In a color × orientation search, color and orientation are expressed on the same stimulus element. To eliminate spatial configuration as an explanation of the results shown in Figure 14, search experiments were conducted with stimuli shown here. In the "different" case subjects still search for color × orientation conjunctions, but color is expressed on the unoriented circle and orientation on the white bar. The slopes for the "different" case were actually shallower than those for the "same" case in this experiment.

green item. The distractors are big green and little red (cf. Nakayama & Silverman, 1986). The preceding discussion indicates that the parallel processes cannot guide attention toward red and green items simultaneously. Moreover, since information about the location of red and green items does not appear to reside in separate parallel maps, directing attention to all red and green items would merely have the effect of directing attention to all items; hardly a useful strategy. An identical analysis holds for the size dimension.

The system appears to solve this problem by doing two sequential guided searches; first for one target type (e.g. "little red") and then for the other (e.g. "big green"). Broken down in this way, the search can be guided by the parallel processes. There is a cost to be paid, the "overhead" on an extra search. However, that seems to be worthwhile when compared to the cost of serial self-terminating search. From this example we can see the possibility of doing quite elaborate searches by a series of simple steps, much in the manner that a computer program might carry out an elaborate operation with a sequence of more basic operations (Wolfe *et al.*, 1989b).

Proposition 9. An Observer Terminates Guided Search on Blank Trials Using a Criterion Based on the Distribution of Reaction Time on Target Trials and that Observer's Tolerance for Error

The mechanics of guided search or of completely parallel search are easy enough to understand when there is a target to find. Blank trials, however, pose a problem. When should a search be terminated? The safest alternative is to search until every element has been processed. However, because of the guidance from the parallel stage, the target is likely to be found relatively early (as long as the noise is not extremely high). If the target has not been found after a certain amount of time, the search can be abandoned with little risk of missing a target. Once subjects have practiced a particular type of search, they should have the information they need to be able to judge when it is safe to stop searching. Experimental data indicate that subjects do end many searches before serial attention can reach every element. The slopes for trials without targets are usually steeper than for trials with targets, but not as steep as they would be if every element were processed.

Proposition 9 is more speculative than the preceding points because, to be honest, we are still working on the problem. It is possible to offer a hypothesis and some evidence in support of it. A subject might adopt the following strategy for terminating a search without finding a target. Assume that the subject learns the approximate mean, X, and standard deviation, S, for the time it takes to find a target when it is present. During any subsequent trial, the subject can estimate the probability that a target has been missed. That is, if the subject has waited two standard deviations beyond the mean RT, then the probability that a target will be discovered is less than 3%. Put another way, for any RT, there is a corresponding Z-score that indicates the probability that a target has been missed.

$$Z(RT) = (RT - X)/S$$

The larger $Z(RT)$, the less likely it is that a target has been missed. If the subject adopts a criterion, $Z(crit)$, that tolerates $N\%$ errors then the subject could safely terminate any search when $Z(RT) > Z(crit)$. For any subject, we can estimate $Z(crit)$ that was used for each size in an experiment as

$$Z(crit) = \frac{[\text{average RT(blank trials)} - \text{average RT(target trials)}]}{\text{SD (target trials)}}$$

Given $Z(crit)$, several hypotheses may be tested. We will describe two. First, when $Z(crit)$ is compared across subjects, it should correlate negatively with error rate; that is, the more conservative a subject's criterion, the lower the error rate should be for that subject. We have examined three sets of data from each of ten subjects. These data are from color × color, color × orientation and color × size conjunctions. There was a significant negative correlation between $Z(crit)$ and error rate across subjects (for three experiments, correlation coefficients varied from 0.55 to 0.72). Given this relationship, it is not surprising to find that $Z(crit)$ varies across subjects, as some subjects will be more careful (and slower) than others. The pattern of variation is similar for different experiments. A subject who is conservative in one experiment will tend to be conservative in others. Correlations of $Z(crit)$ scores across experiments are high (correlation between pairs of experiments range from 0.67 to 0.79).

Examining the standard deviations for target trial RTs, we find that SD increases with set size. Under these circumstances, if observers adopt a consistent $Z(crit)$ across set size, then larger $Z(crit)$ scores will be accompanied by steeper slopes on blank trials. This means that the more conservative the subject, the more closely the blank trial searches will approximate an exhaustive serial search. We find significant positive correlations between $Z(crit)$ and blank trial slopes.

This model for blank trial searches is not perfect. The $Z(crit)$ scores predict higher error rates than seen in the data. Further, while many subjects seem to have similar $Z(crit)$ values for all set sizes, some show a tendency to be more conservative [higher $Z(crit)$] as set size increases. Nevertheless, we believe that this approach is a promising beginning to an understanding of this problem.

REMAINING PROBLEMS

The preceding set of propositions accounts for a substantial body of visual search data. However, several problems remain unresolved. The list of basic features is not satisfactory. For example, some workers find that intersections behave as features (Bergen & Julesz, 1983a; Julesz & Bergen, 1983) while others find that they do not (Treisman & Gormican, 1988; Bergen & Adelson, 1988; but see Julesz & Krose, 1988). Similar difficulties surround other proposed features (Treisman, 1986; Treisman & Paterson, 1984). What is needed is a clear understanding of the primitives of form perception (Biederman, 1987).

The model outlined above treats all items as equal. It ignores effects of distance. Comparisons between items are influenced by the spacing and layout of those items (Treisman, 1982; Nothdurft, 1985; Julesz, 1986). In our work with color × color conjunctions, we have found that local color contrast can be used as a cue to support parallel search. Thus, a red–green item will pop out of red–red and green–green items (Wolfe *et al.*, 1989b) not because of any ability to combine red and green information but because attention is attracted to the high local color contrast between red and green halves of the same item. Indeed, these local effects may be a source of confusion in our understanding of the primitives of form. Consider curvature: perhaps our ability to detect curves among straight lines is actually an ability to direct attention to areas of high local orientation contrast. This is consistent with Treisman's finding that detection of curvature among straight elements is easy while detection of straight among curved elements is not.

Finally, in all of the experiments discussed here and, indeed, in most visual search experiments, the independent variable is the number of items. The notion of an item seems clear until examined more closely. In discussing color × color conjunctions, we noted that a target that is half red and half green might be considered to be two items. In those experiments, the visual system seems to treat these targets as a single item, but these are islands of color in a sea of black. In the real world, patches of color tend to fill the field. What, then, are the items? Is a black and white cat an item? Is its head an item? Is one of its black spots an item? If we hope to generalize from the realm of laboratory visual search experiments to the realm of real world visual search tasks, we will need to understand how the visual system parses complex scenes into items.

CONCLUSION

The experiments and computer simulations described here suggest that the human visual system uses fast, efficient, parallel algorithms to guide the later serial stages of visual processing. This attentional system can use information about expected stimuli when it is available, but will identify unusual parts of the input whether or not they are expected. These parallel mechanisms are very limited, both in their accuracy and in what they can do, but by guiding the allocation of higher-level, limited-capacity processes, they can speed visual processing considerably. Computer vision systems can probably benefit from employing similar simple and efficient mechanisms to quickly identify those parts of the input that should be processed immediately.

ACKNOWLEDGEMENTS

We thank Karen Yu, Amy Shorter, Alice Yee, Charles Pokorny, Felicitas Treue, Marni Stewart, Robert Siguirra and Susan Franzel for help with these experiments. We thank IBM for the loan of YODA graphics boards. This research was supported by the National Eye Institute of NIH, the Whitaker Health Sciences Fund, the Educational Foundation of America and the MIT Class of 1922.

REFERENCES

Beck, J., Prazdny, K. & Rosenfeld, A. (1983). A theory of textural segmentation. In J. Beck, B. Hope & A. Rosenfeld (Eds) *Human and Machine Vision*, pp. 1–38. Academic Press, New York.

Bergen, J. R. & Adelson, E. H. (1988). Early vision and texture perception. *Science*, **333**, 363–364.

Bergen, J. R. & Julesz, B. (1983a). Parallel versus serial processing in rapid pattern discrimination. *Nature*, **303**, 696–698.

Bergen, J. R. & Julesz, B. (1983b). Rapid discrimination of visual patterns. *IEEE Transactions on Systems, Man and Cybernetics*, **SMC-13**, 857–863.

Biederman, I. (1981). On the semantics of a glance at a scene. In M. Kubovy & J. R. Pomerantz (Eds) *Perceptual Organization*, pp. 213–253. Lawrence Erlbaum, Hillsdale, NJ.

Biederman, I. (1987). Recognition-by-components: a theory of human image understanding. *Psychological Review*, **94**, 115–147.

Bishop, P. O. (1984). Processing of visual information with retinostriate system. In I. Darian-Smith (Ed.) *Handbook of Physiology*. American Physiological Society, Baltimore, MD.

Cave, K. R. & Wolfe, J. M. (1989). Modeling the role of parallel processing in visual search. *Cognitive Psychology*, in press.

Duncan, J. & Humphreys, G. (1989). Visual search and stimulus similarity. *Psychological Review*, **96**, 433–458.

Egeth, H. E., Virzi, R. A. & Garbart, H. (1984). Searching for conjunctively defined targets. *Journal of Experimental Psychology: Human Perception and Performance*, **10**, 32–39.

Feldman, J. A. (1985). Four frames suffice: a provisional model of vision and space. *Behavioral and Brain Sciences*, **8**, 265–289.

Hinton, G. E., McClelland, J. L. & Rumelhart, D. E. (1986). Distributed representations. In D. E. Rumelhart, J. L. McClelland & the PDP Research Group (Eds) *Parallel Distributed Processing*, Vol. 1, pp. 77–109. MIT Press, Cambridge, MA.

Hoffman, J. E. (1978). Search through a sequentially presented visual display. *Perception and Psychophysics*, **23**, 1–11.

Julesz, B. (1984). A brief outline of the texton theory of human vision. *Trends in Neuroscience*, 7, 41–45.

Julesz, B. (1986). Texton gradients: the texton theory revisited. *Biological Cybernetics*, **54**, 245–251.

Julesz, B. & Bergen, J. R. (1983). Textons, the fundamental elements in preattentive vision and perception of textures. *Bell System Technical Journal*, **62**, 1619–1645.

Julesz, B. & Krose, B. (1988). Feature and spatial filters. *Science*, **333**, 302–303.

Nakayama, K. & Silverman, G. H. (1986). Serial and parallel processing of visual feature conjunctions. *Nature*, **320**, 264–265.

Neisser, U. (1967). *Cognitive Psychology*. Appleton-Century-Crofts, New York.

Nothdurft, H. C. (1985). Sensitivity for structure gradient in texture discrimination tasks. *Vision Research*, **25**, 1957–1968.

Pashler, H. (1988). Cross-dimensional interaction and texture segregation. *Perception and Psychophysics*, **43**, 307–318.

Quinlan, P. T. & Humphreys, G. W. (1987). Visual search for targets defined by combinations of color, shape, and size: an examination of the task constraints on feature and conjunction searches. *Perception and Psychophysics*, **41**, 455–472.

Townsend, J. T. (1972). Some results on the identifiability of parallel and serial processes. *British Journal of Mathematical and Statistical Psychology*, **25**, 168–199.

Treisman, A. (1982). Perceptual grouping and attention in visual search for features and for objects. *Journal of Experimental Psychology: Human Perception and Performance*, **8**, 194–214.

Treisman, A. M. (1986). Features and objects in visual processing. *Scientific American*, **255**, 114B–125.

Treisman, A. M. & Gelade, G. (1980). A feature-integration theory of attention. *Cognitive Psychology*, **12**, 97–136.

Treisman, A. M. & Gormican, S. (1988). Feature analysis in early vision: evidence from search asymmetries. *Psychological Review*, **95**, 15–48.

Treisman, A. M. & Paterson, R. (1984). Emergent features, attention, and object perception. *Journal of Experimental Psychology: Human Perception and Performance*, **10**, 12–31.

Treisman, A. M. & Sato, S. (1990). Conjunction search revisited. *Journal of Experimental Psychology: Human Perception & Performance*, in press

Treisman, A. M. & Schmidt, H. (1982). Illusory conjunctions in the perception of objects. *Cognitive Psychology*, **14**, 107–141.

Ullman, S. (1984). Visual routines. *Cognition*, **18**, 97–159.

Wolfe, J. M., Cave, K. R. & Franzel, S. L. (1989a). Guided Search: An alternative to the Feature Integration Model for Visual Search. *Journal of Experimental Psychology: Human Perception and Performance* **15**, 419–433.

Wolfe, J. M. & Franzel S. L. (1988). Binocularity and visuals search. *Perception and Psychophysics*, **43**, 81–93.

Wolfe, J. M., Yu, K. P., Stewart, M. I., Shorter, A. D. & Cave, K. R. (1989b). Limitations on the parallel guidance of visual search. Manuscript submitted for publication.

5 Imperceptible Intersections: The Chopstick Illusion

Stuart Anstis

Department of Psychology, York University, North York, Ontario, Canada

How do we know in which direction a visual object is moving? A single receptor is not enough, since it registers only flicker without direction when a contour moves across it. So to sense direction you need two nearby receptors coupled together into a directionally selective unit. But directional selectivity alone cannot reveal the direction in which an object moves. A single local reading of velocity is not sufficient to recover the true motion in an image, because a moving line viewed through a moving aperture could be moving in any of a wide (180°) range of directions. We shall give a brief review of models of directional selectivity and of solutions to the so-called "aperture problem" and then turn to a new phenomenon which we call the "chopstick illusion". The visual system is unable to sense the motion path of the *intersection* of two moving lines.

DIRECTIONAL SELECTIVITY

Reichardt (1961) proposed a model of directional selectivity based upon his ingenious experiments on motion detection in the insect eye. The output from a receptor A (Figure 1) is delayed and then compared with the undelayed output from a nearby receptor B. When the transit time for the contour to move from A to B is equal to the internal delay dt then the output from the comparator is maximum and the whole unit responds. The unit is silent when a contour moves in the null direction from B to A. Reichardt's comparator was a multiplicative correlator. Barlow & Levick (1965) suggested that the rabbit retina makes comparisons based on subtractive inhibition, and this gives similar results. More recent models of

AI and the Eye   Edited by A. Blake and T. Troscianko
© 1990 John Wiley & Sons Ltd.

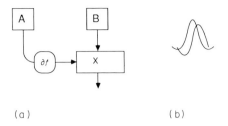

(a)   (b)

Figure 1. Generic direction-selective motion sensor. (a) When a contour passes from A to B (the preferred direction) the output of A is delayed then compared with the output of B. When the two outputs match the unit responds. Comparison could be a multiplicative correlation (Reichardt, 1961) or subtractive inhibition (Barlow & Levick, 1965). (b) Possible receptive fields for receptors A and B.

directional selectivity examine motion separately in different spatial-frequency bands, as proposed by Marr & Ullman (1981), van Santen & Sperling (1984), Adelson & Bergen and Watson & Ahumada (1985). Some of the evidence is discussed by Moulden & Begg (1986) and by Anstit (1988), and van Santen & Sperling (1985) have written a good critical review.

THE APERTURE PROBLEM

As Adelson & Movshon (1982) have pointed out, a single local reading of velocity is not sufficient to recover the true motion in an image; to disambiguate the so-called aperture problem, readings from at least two moving straight lines are needed. When a moving line is viewed through an aperture (Figure 2a), or through the receptive field of a directionally selective unit, only the motion orthogonal to the line is visible because motion parallel to the line causes no change in the stimulus. Because there is a family of physical motions of various directions and speeds that appear identical, the motion of the line is ambiguous. Any of the physical motions indicated by the arrows in Figure 2(b) will appear the same when viewed through the aperture. The situation can be depicted graphically in "velocity space", a space in which each vector represents a velocity: the length of a vector corresponds to speed, and its angle corresponds to direction. The motion of the line is consistent with a family of motions that lie along a line in velocity space; this line is parallel to the moving line and orthogonal to the vector representing its "primary" motion. This effect was originally called the barber-pole illusion (Wallach, 1935) but is now more generally known as the aperture problem (Ullman, 1979). It applies equally well to an observer viewing a line through a hole in a shutter, as to a directionally selective motion-sensitive neuron (reviewed by Berkley, 1982) which views moving contours within the small region bounded by its receptive field. One might think that it would be easy, given such neurons, to compute the velocity at each region in the visual field, but this is not so. If two moving gratings are superimposed (Adelson & Movshon, 1982), the resulting tartan or plaid pattern moves with a speed and direction that can be predicted from

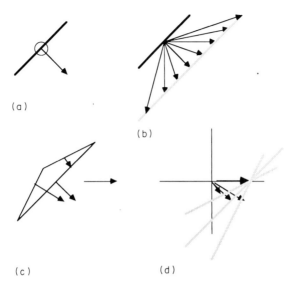

(a)

(b)

(c)   (d)

Figure 2.   (a) A moving line viewed through a stationary aperture is ambiguous. (b) Its true motion could be as shown by any of the arrows. (vectors). The length of each arrow represents speed. Note that all arrowheads lie on the grey line—the "velocity constraint line". (c) Motion of each of three sides of a triangle is ambiguous, as in (a). (d) However, the velocity constraint lines all meet at one point which defines the true motion of the triangle (horizontal arrow) (after Adelson & Movshon, 1982: Movshon *et al.*, 1985). Note that this direction is not the vector sum or average of the motion of the three lines.

the velocity space construction; the two loci of possible motions intersect at a single point, corresponding to the motion of the coherent pattern (Figure 3). Note that this velocity space combination rule is different from a vector sum or vector average (Figure 2c, d; Figure 3). In Figure 3, two gratings move down and to the right. Their vector sum or average also moves down to the right, but the velocity space construction is a motion up and to the right, the motion that observers report when the gratings are seen to cohere. Nothing requires that coherent motion be seen, and instead of a single rigidly moving plaid, observers sometimes reported two transparent gratings sliding over each other in incoherent motion. In general, observers were more likely to report incoherent motion when the angle between the two gratings was made larger, as their speeds increased, and as the spatial frequency increased, although this spatial frequency effect was rather weaker than the others. Under ideal conditions (identical spatial frequencies, low speeds and a modest angle), the two gratings always cohered into a single moving plaid.

Movshon *et al.* (1983) proposed a two-stage model of motion perception. The first stage contained direction- and orientation-selective units with elongated receptive fields, which responded to motion of the component gratings. The second stage contained motion analysers, which combined the signals from several units in the first stage, sensing the intersection of velocity constraints by means of coincidence detectors or "and" gates. These analysers responded to the motion of the plaid. Movshon *et al.* found that 40% of neurons in area MT of the macaque

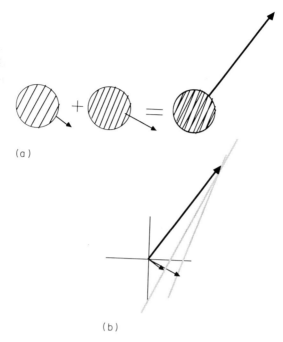

(a)

(b)

Figure 3. (a) Two gratings move down to the right at different velocities. The perceived velocity of the compound grating is not a vector sum, but is up and to the right. (b) Velocity constraint lines of the two moving gratings define the motion of the compound grating, up and to the right (after Adelson & Movshon, 1982).

were component direction selective and 25% were plaid direction selective. They obtained psychophysical evidence for their model with a 2 × 2 adaptation experiment. Adaptation to a grating makes it harder to see a test grating of the same spatial frequency and orientation, so they attempted to adapt the first and second stages of their model differentially. Adaptation to component motion ought to elevate detection thresholds for the component gratings, whereas adaptation to pattern motion ought to affect coherence. Their adapting and test patterns consisted of a horizontally moving grating of vertical bars, and a horizontally moving diagonal plaid pattern composed of two oblique gratings. They found, for instance, that adapting to the vertical grating did not elevate the threshold for the component gratings but did reduce the perceived coherence of the pattern motion.

   Do we really need a two-stage model of motion perception? Perhaps the visual system merely tracks the intersections of the two crossed gratings, that is, the moiré fringes. These fringes are beat frequencies that contain no Fourier energy, but if there were an early non-linearity in the contrast response function this could produce intermodulation distortions in the mixture of two sinusoidal gratings which would supply Fourier energy at the moiré fringe frequency and orientation. This would suffice to provide a motion perception using only very-low-level receptive fields. If this were the case, there might be no need to argue for the synthesis of differently oriented velocity signals. Furthermore, the moiré fringes move in just the direction predicted by the velocity constraint model, and the adaptation experiment described above does not disprove the moiré fringe hypothesis. However, Welch (1988) obtained experimental evidence against a moiré fringe story. She noted that speed discrimination can be much worse at low than at medium speeds. She measured just noticeable differences in velocity for plaids moving at speeds five times the component gratings, and found that speed discrimination followed the speed of the component gratings, not that of the moiré fringes. Speed discrimination for the plaids was not matched by a grating mimicking the speed and spatial separation of the fringes. These results support the velocity constraint model.

Terminators Affect the Perceived Direction of Movement

Wallach (1935) viewed a moving grating through an elongated aperture. The motion appeared to run parallel to the long axis of the aperture. Shimojo *et al.* (1988) added stereoscopic depth, and found that motion parallel to the long edges was stronger if the grating lay in depth in front of the aperture because the grating appeared to be the same size as the aperture and the ends of the bars were perceived as "object terminators". Motion parallel to the long edges was weaker if the grating lay in depth behind the aperture because the grating appeared to extend behind the aperture, and the ends of the bars were perceived as "occlusion intersections".

Nakayama & Silverman (1988a, b) moved a vertically oriented cumulative Gaussian waveform (Figure 4) upward. This figure looked highly non-rigid when it moved. Moving "terminators", defined as the ends of line segments, were then added, lying either "on" the line, appearing as gaps, or "off" the line, appearing as

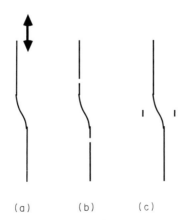

(a)   (b)   (c)

Figure 4. (a) When this cumulative Gaussian curve is translated up and down in the plane of the page (arrow), it appears highly non-rigid. (b) (c) Adding terminators (ends of line segments) dramatically increases the rigidity of the figure, especially if the segments are gaps "on" the line as in (b) rather than short line segments "off" the line as in (c) (after Nakayama & Silverman, 1988b).

short line segments having the same length as the gaps. The figure now looked far more rigid, especially when the terminators lay "on" the line. The authors derived strong support from their results for Hildreth's (1984) model of motion perception, in which local differences in velocity are integrated (smoothed) but only along contours. Hildreth's scheme computes the velocity field which minimizes differences in velocity along contours yet is consistent with constraints dictated by the aperture problem. For our purposes, the powerful influence of terminators upon motion perception should be carefully noted.

In the aperture problem the motion of a stimulus is inherently ambiguous. We shall now describe some new illusions from moving stimuli: first an "Etch-a-Sketch phenomenon", in which the stimulus motion of an intersection is unambiguous but the visual system is unable to sense the motion, and then a new "chopstick illusion", in which motion of an intersection is misperceived because it is perceptually captured by motion of the terminators.

THE ETCH-A-SKETCH PHENOMENON

It is easy to perceive the motion path of a small moving object. When a fly buzzes around in circles we can see the fly and we can also perceive the circles; and without much trouble we can read words written in the air by a moving finger, or written on a screen by a small cross-shaped cursor that leaves no visible trail behind it. Such small moving objects are unambiguous. But suppose that a word is being handwritten on a screen, not by a moving finger or cursor but by Etch-a-Sketch cross-hairs with long horizontal and vertical lines that extend off the edge of the screen, hiding the ends of the lines. As one watches the movement the two lines are not seen as a rigid cross but appear to slide over each other. Surprisingly enough, it is now almost impossible to read the word. Why? The centre of the cross traces out the same path as before, and all that is missing is the information from the terminators—the tips of the cross. Hiding them makes the word hard to read, yet when they were present they added no new information at all because they simply duplicated the movements of the centre of the cross. It seems that we pay more attention to the tips of lines (terminators) than we do to the crossings of lines (intersections). This is the basis of the chopstick illusion.

THE CHOPSTICK ILLUSION

When a single line moves behind an aperture, the stimulus is ambiguous because there is not enough visual information to determine the true motion path. When a pair of crossed lines move orthogonally in the Etch-a-Sketch phenomenon, the path of the intersection is fully determined but we seem to be unable to perceive this unambiguous information. We shall now describe a "chopstick illusion" in which misleading information from the tips of two moving lines or chopsticks alters the perceived path of their intersection.

We put the tips of the lines (the terminators) into competition with their centres. The left hand holds a chopstick and moves it along a clockwise path while keeping it vertical, like a cabin on a Ferris wheel. The right hand moves a second chopstick along a clockwise path while keeping it horizontal (Figure 5). The two clockwise motions are in the same plane but in counterphase so that when the vertical chopstick moves through the highest point of its circular path the horizontal chopstick moves through its lowest point. When the chopsticks do not overlap, each one is seen veridically. However, when they overlap to form a cross so that they slide over each other, an illusion appears. The intersection of the two sticks physically traces out an anticlockwise path, like a Lissajous figure, but perceptually it appears to rotate clockwise, captured by the closkwise motion of the line tips (Figure 6). Thus the perceived motion of the tips propagates back to the intersections, which are incorrectly seen as moving along the same paths as the tips.

The static diagrams shown as figures are no substitute for seeing the motion, and the reader is encouraged to try out the effects by rubbing two pencils together. The skill can be picked up in a few moments. The illusion works just as well when the observer is moving the pencils while viewing them, and in fact the clockwise illusion is so compelling that it is often hard to accept that the intersections are really moving anticlockwise.

To give better stimulus control the chopsticks were replaced by a vertical and a horizontal line on a monitor screen controlled by a Commodore Amiga computer (Anstis, 1986). As before, each line moved along clockwise paths in counterphase, and the intersection, which actually traced out an anticlockwise path, appeared to rotate clockwise. This illusion was very robust; it was impossible to perceive the

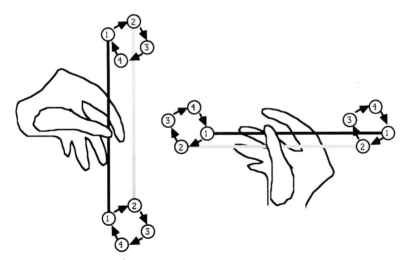

Figure 5. To generate the chopstick illusion, the left hand holds a pencil or chopstick vertical and moves it along a circular clockwise path as shown by the numbers, keeping it always vertical. The right hand moves a horizontal chopstick along a clockwise path which is 180° out of phase with the vertical chopstick—compare the numbers in the small circles, which show the positions of the ends of the two chopsticks at times 1–4. Chopsticks are drawn in black for time 1 and in grey for time 2.

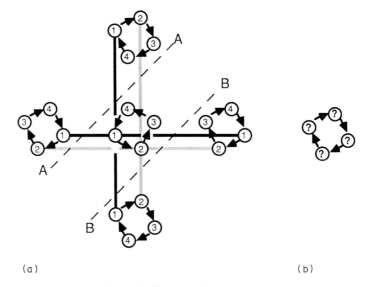

(a)   (b)

Figure 6. (a) Results of the chopstick illusion. The two moving chopsticks shown in Figure 5 now overlap at their centres. The motion path of the intersection is actually anticlockwise, as shown by the numbers at the centre. (b) However, the intersection gives the illusion of moving clockwise, under the influence of the paths of the terminators. Numbers in the circles are replaced by question marks because the order in which the intersection appears to pass clockwise through various points is not clear. Of course it does not actually pass clockwise through any points. The importance of the terminators is confirmed by clipping the ends of the chopsticks along the oblique lines A--A, B--B. Results of this are shown in Figure 7.

true anticlockwise rotation of the intersection. Also, the intersection did not look like a rigid cross (like two rods welded together), but the lines appeared to slide over each other. If the intersection was viewed through a small stationary circular window that hid the terminators, the illusion disappeared and one correctly perceived a rigid cross moving anticlockwise. However, the illusion reappeared at full strength as soon as the screen was removed.

Objectively, whenever the vertical line moved to the right then the intersection also moved right. When the horizontal line moved to the right it merely slid along its own length and the intersection stayed where it was. However, the subjective situation was the opposite of this. When the (tips of) the horizontal line moved to the right this percept propagated along the line and the intersection falsely appeared to move to the right. When the vertical line moved to the right the intersection was barely seen to move. In other words the horizontal component of the intersection's motion was objectively constrained by the horizontal oscillations of the vertical line, but it was subjectively constrained by the moving tips of the horizontal line. To verify this the ends of the lines in Figure 6 were clipped along the oblique lines A--A and B--B, giving the stimulus shown in Figure 7. This kept the central part of the cross untouched, as if viewed through an invisible window with oblique edges. Thus the tips of the vertical line moved obliquely up to the right while the tips of the horizontal line moved down to the left. As a result, the

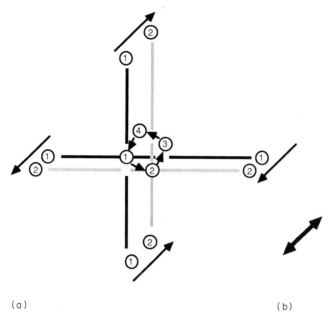

(a)   (b)

Figure 7. (a) Stimulus is the same as in Figure 6 except that the terminators have been clipped along 45° oblique lines. The terminators of the vertical and horizontal chopsticks now move obliquely in antiphase. The central intersection moves along the same circular anticlockwise path as in Figure 5. (b) But now the intersection gives the illusion of moving back and forth obliquely.

intersection now also appeared to move obliquely, up-right and down-left, parallel to the terminators, although it was hard to perceive the phase of its motion. This illusion was moderately robust, and could be overcome by an effort of will. Viewing the intersection through a small stationary round aperture confirmed, as before, that it was still really moving anticlockwise.

Rigidity and Coherence

When a rigid cross translates in its own plane, the distance from each terminator to the intersection remains constant. When two lines slide over each other these distances are continually changing. What kind of "rigidity assumptions", if any, does the visual system make?

There are two possibilities; it might perceive either the intersection or the rods as rigid. In the first case it would perceive a rigid (glued or welded) intersection of two rubber rods as the rods changed in length. In fact this is never reported. Instead the visual system parses each line as being rigid (and unchanging in length, as the terminators assert), but the intersection is parsed as a non-rigid sliding region. We might say that when given a choice the visual system prefers to perceive sliding or occluding objects rather than rubbery objects. This may reflect the statistical properties of the physical world, in which objects constantly occlude and move past each other, but rubbery objects are uncommon.

Necessary conditions

The illusion occurred when the lines intersected at any angle between about 30°
and 90°, and the lines could be solid or dashed, straight or curved. Even
intersecting circles gave the illusion (not shown). Our standard intersections were
X-junctions, but we found that T-junctions and L-corners were also captured by
their terminators, although to a lesser extent. Link & Zucker (1988) discuss
psychophysical sensitivity to static L-corners.

It is not the case that the outermost parts of the display simply capture the
central parts, whatever these might be. If the tips of the lines and the intersection
were each replaced by isolated spots (Figure 8) the illusion broke down and the
motion of the central dot was seen veridically, and now it was seen not as an
intersection but as a separate moving object, circling anticlockwise in the opposite
direction to the terminator dots. Intersections are captured not merely because
they happen to be in the central region of the stimulus, but because they are
intersections.

The chopstick illusion does not result simply from the fact that terminators
outnumber intersections. An array of eight parallel horizontal lines intersected with
an array of eight parallel vertical lines. As before, the vertical and horizontal lines
all moved clockwise but with a phase shift between them. This array had 64
intersections and only 32 terminators, but when the array was set in motion the
terminators moving clockwise around the edges of the array still captured the
intersections. As before, the intersections were really moving anticlockwise but
appeared to move clockwise.

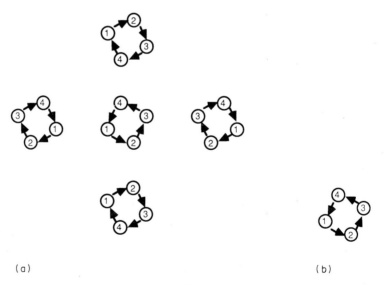

(a)   (b)

Figure 8. (a) Stimulus is the same as in Figure 6 except that the chopsticks have been
removed. Terminators and intersection have been replaced by spots which circled respectively clockwise and anticlockwise. (b) Result: no illusion. The central spot was correctly
seen as circling anticlockwise.

Terminators need not lie around the outer perimeter of the stimulus. "Blobs" and gaps in the interior of the figure are equally effective as terminators. The array of eight vertical and eight horizontal lines was made to fill the whole screen, which now acted like a large rectangular aperture hiding the ends of the lines. Now that the terminators were hidden by the edges of the screen, observers reported seeing a rigid square mesh circling coherently in an anticlockwise direction. This veridical percept showed that the chopstick illusion was absent. Next, gaps were introduced into the vertical and horizontal lines at four points surrounding one intersection. The gaps in the horizontal lines moved clockwise, and so did the gaps in the vertical lines but with the usual phase shift. Result: the single intersection that was surrounded by gaps appeared to move clockwise although all the other intersections still appeared to move anticlockwise. This shows that gaps in lines acted as efficient terminators and constrained the motion of the intersection that they surrounded. However, their influence was local and did not extend to more distant intersections. If gaps were added to surround every intersection then all the intersections showed the chopstick illusion and appeared to move clockwise. A curious phenomenon of direction of gaze was noted: with these gaps, all the intersections appeared to move clockwise when the centre of the screen was viewed, but if the gaze was deflected by some 10° so that the screen was viewed in peripheral vision, the intersections appeared to reverse in direction and move anticlockwise, in the veridical direction. The reason was that peripheral acuity was too low to resolve the gaps, which therefore lost their effectiveness. Blurring the screen with tracing paper in central vision had the same effect as using peripheral vision.

DISCUSSION

Comparison with Earlier Studies

Our results are really complementary to those of Adelson & Movshon (1982) in that they examined the conditions that gave coherent motion of two crossed gratings when they combined into a plaid, whereas we examined the conditions that gave our chopstick illusion, which is an instance of incoherent motion of two crossed lines as they slid over each other. Our percept of a rigid cross corresponds to their coherent motion of a (rigid) plaid, and our percept of rods sliding over each other corresponds to their incoherent motion of two transparent gratings. They showed that coherent plaids always seemed to move in the same direction as the moiré fringes or intersections of the two gratings. (This is a rule of thumb, not a model for their results.) Motion was always coherent except when their two gratings differed markedly in orientation, contrast, speed or spatial frequency. Since they always used a fixed circular aperture, line terminators had little systematic effect on their results. In our studies motion was nearly always incoherent and terminators played a crucial role. We asked (as they did not) what was the perceived direction of the intersections during incoherent motion. Stated differently, when two gratings cohere the two stimulus motions reduce to a single perceived motion. Our question was: when two lines (or gratings) do not cohere, such that two transparent motions are seen, can a *third* motion be seen, namely the motion of the intersections? We find that the answer is generally no.

The Role of Covering and Uncovering

If a man walks along in front of a picket fence, his body successively covers up pickets ahead of him and uncovers pickets behind him. As he walks to the right, pickets disappear on the right and other pickets reappear on the left. These pickets generate spurious signals of apparent motion which the visual system suppresses or ignores (Ramachandran & Anstis, 1986). Also, the edges of his body define a moving shape which is of perceptual interest, but the intersections of his curved or oblique body contours with the vertical edges of the pickets define occlusion intersections that do not correspond to any physical object. These intersections generate spurious signals of vertical movement up and down the pickets, which the visual system ignores. So the visual system's seeming inability to process moving intersections may be not a design fault but a useful and adaptive rejection of spurious motion signals whose uncritical acceptance would hamper, not help, our interpretation of a moving visual world.

ACKNOWLEDGEMENT

This work was supported by Grant A0260 from the Natural Science and Engineering Research Council of Canada (NSERC).

REFERENCES

Adelson, E. H. & Bergen, J. R. (1985). Spatiotemporal energy models for the perception of motion. *Journal of the Optical Society of America*, **A2**, 284–299.
Adelson, E. H. & Movshon, J. A. (1982). Phenomenal coherence of moving visual patterns. *Nature*, **300**, 523–525.
Anstis, S. M. (1986). Visual stimuli on the Commodore Amiga: a tutorial. *Behavioral Research Methods, Instrumentation and Computers*, **18**, 535–541.
Anstis, S. M. (1988). Models and experiments on directional selectivity. In M. Bouma & B. Elsendoorn (Eds) *Working Models of Human Perception*. Academic Press, London.
Barlow, H. B. & Levick, W. R. (1965). The mechanism of direction selective units in rabbit's retina. *Journal of Physiology*, **178**, 477–504.
Berkley, M. (1982). Neural substrates of the visual perception of motion. In A. H. Wertheim, W. A. Wagenaar & H. W. Leibowitz (Eds) *Tutorials on Motion Perception*. Plenum Press, New York.
Hildreth, E. C. (1984). *The Measurement of Visual Motion*. ACM Distinguished Dissertation Series, MIT Press, Cambridge, MA.
Link, N. K. & Zucker, S. W. (1988). Corner detection in curvilinear dot grouping. *Biological Cybernetics*, **59**, 247–256.
Marr, D. & Ullman, S. (1981). Directional selectivity and its use in early visual processing. *Proceedings of the Royal Society (London), Series B*, **211**, 151–180.
Moulden, B. P. & Begg, H. (1986). Some tests of the Marr–Ullman model of movement detection. *Perception*, **15**, 139–155.

Movshon, J. A., Adelson, E. H., Gizzi, M. & Newsome W. T. (1985). The analysis of moving visual patterns. *Experimental Brain Research*, **11** (Suppl.), 117–151.

Nakayama, K. & Silverman, G. (1988a). The aperture problem—I. Perception of nonrigidity and motion direction in translating sinusoidal lines. *Vision Research*, **28**, 739–746.

Nakayama, K. & Silverman, G. (1988b). The aperture problem—II. Spatial integration of velocity information along contours. *Vision Research*, **28**, 747–753.

Ramachandran, V. S. & Anstis, S. M. (1986). Figure–ground segregation modulates apparent motion. *Vision Research*, **26**, 1969–1975.

Reichardt, W. (1961). Autocorrelation, a principle for the evaluation of sensory information by the central nervous system. In W. A. Rosenblith (Ed.) *Sensory Communication*. MIT Press, Cambridge, MA.

Shimojo, J., Silverman, G. H. & Nakayama, K. (1988). Occlusion and the solution to the aperture problem. *Investigative Ophthalmology and Visual Science*, **29** (Suppl.), 264.

Ullman, S. (1979). *The Interpretation of Visual Motion*. MIT Press, Cambridge, MA.

Van Santen, J. P. H. & Sperling, G. (1984). Temporal covariance model of human motion perception. *Journal of the Optical Society of America*, **A1**, 451–473.

Van Santen, J. P. H. & Sperling, G. (1985). Elaborated Reichardt detectors. *Journal of the Optical Society of America*, **A2**, 300–321.

Wallach, H. (1935). Uber visuell wahrgenommene Bewegungsrichtung. *Psychologische Forschungen*, **20**, 325–380.

Watson, A. B. & Ahumada, A. (1985). Models of human visual-motion sensing. *Journal of the Optical Society of America*, **A2**, 322–342.

Welch, L. (1988). Speed discrimination and the aperture problem. *Investigative Ophthalmology and Vision Science*, **29** (Suppl.), 264.

Zucker, S. & Iverson, L. (1986). From orientation selection to optical flow. *Computer Graphics and Image Processing*, **37**, 196–220.

6 Integration of Stereo, Shading and Texture

Heinrich H. Bülthoff[1] and Hanspeter A. Mallot[2]

[1]*Center for Biological Information Processing, Massachusetts Institute of Technology, Cambridge, MA, USA*, and* [2]*Institut für Zoologie III, Johannes Gutenberg-Universität, Mainz, FRG*

INTRODUCTION

Integration of cues is one of the key features of natural vision that underlie its performance and robustness. In this chapter, we investigate the integration of various depth cues into different percepts related to three-dimensional structure.

Most of the depth cues known in psychophysics have been formalized in terms of computational theory and have been implemented as single modules in machine vision systems. Mutually related studies from psychophysics and computational theory exist mainly for stereo (Julesz, 1971; Marr & Poggio, 1979; Mayhew & Frisby, 1981) and shading (Ikeuchi & Horn, 1981; Pentland, 1984; Blake *et al.* 1985; Mingolla & Todd, 1986). There are also a number of studies on depth from texture (Bajcsy & Lieberman, 1976; Kender, 1979; Witkin, 1981; Pentland, 1986), line drawings (Barrow & Tenenbaum, 1981), surface contours (Stevens, 1981; Stevens & Brooks, 1987), and structure-from-motion (Ullman, 1979; Longuet-Higgins & Prazdny, 1981; Grzywacz & Hildreth, 1987). Machine implementations are quite successful for synthetic images but less reliable for natural images. On the contrary, the human visual system deals much better with natural images and multiple depth cues than with single depth cues in synthetic images (e.g. random-dot stereograms). In order to study the superior performance of human vision in the integration of multiple depth cues, we developed methods for quantitative measurement of depth perception with complex yet well-controlled images.

---

*Now at Department of Cognitive and Linguistic Sciences, Brown University, Box 1978, Providence, RI 02912, USA.

AI and the Eye   Edited by A. Blake and T. Troscianko
© 1990 John Wiley & Sons Ltd.

Integration of Multiple Depth Cues

The visual system derives a variety of information about the three-dimensional structure of the environment from different depth cues. This is illustrated in Figure 1 where three pairs of ellipsoids are shown whose axes of elongation are orthogonal to each other. The orthogonal orientation is best seen in Figure 1(c), where texture and specular shading provide sufficient 3D information. If texture is used without shading (Figure 1a), the orientation of the objects can usually be perceived correctly while the objects themselves appear flat. Vice versa, if shading is the only

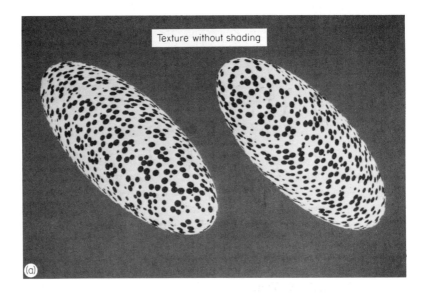

Texture without shading

(a)

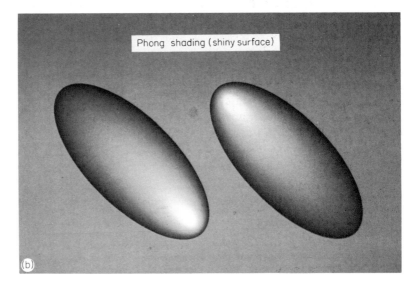

Phong shading (shiny surface)

(b)

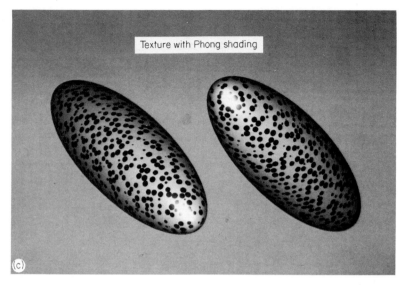

Figure 1. (a–c) Different depth cues provide information about different 3D-descriptors.

cue (Figure 1b), the objects appear nicely curved but it is difficult to see them orthogonal to each other. We therefore argue that at least at a low level of abstraction, multiple representations of three-dimensional structure exist, which will be called *3D-descriptors* in this chapter. These 3D-descriptors are sufficient for simple visual behavior and it is unclear whether a single complete representation of visible surfaces exists at all.

Our approach is schematically described in Figure 2.

Two Aspects of Integration

Raw data from depth cues such as shading, texture or disparity can be thought of as a trivial, or zero-order, representation of the spatial structure of a scene. Based on these data, higher-order descriptors are derived that make interesting spatial properties of the viewed scene explicit. The question of what an interesting 3D-descriptor is, has to be answered in the light of the action that it should subserve. For example, a pointwise depth map is useful for threading a needle, while curvatures might be sufficient for the recognition of complex 3D shapes (such as faces). Eventually, this process may or may not lead to a single complete representation of visible surfaces as was proposed by Marr & Nishihara (1978). In this framework, integration involves two largely independent processes:

1. *Assignment of descriptors to cues.* Which cues are relevant to one particular 3D-descriptor? For example, occlusion contributes more readily to depth ordering than to surface curvature. Shading contributes more qualitatively to curvature than quantitatively to a depth map, or texture more to object orientation than

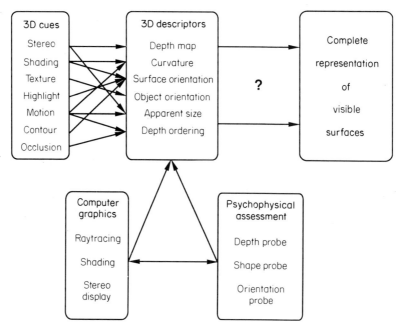

Figure 2. Integration of depth cues. 3D structure perceived from 2D images can be represented at different levels of abstraction. The depth cues themselves constitute multiple *zero-order* representations. Higher-order representations, i.e. the *3D-descriptors*, can be derived from interaction and integration of several of these zero-order representations. Different psychophysical experiments (much as computer vision tasks) involve various combinations of the 3D-descriptors. It is not clear whether a unique 3D representation exists that serves as a common data basis for all types of behavior dealing with the spatial structure of the environment.

to object form. The latter two cases can be qualitatively verified by observing Figure 1.

2. *Cue interaction per descriptor.* From the computational point of view we can ask how are the cues contributing to the computation of a particular descriptor combined? In principle, there are several types of useful interactions which are not mutually exclusive:

(i) *Accumulation.* Information from different cues could be accumulated in different ways such as probability summation or the linear summation model for the integration of stereo and proximity luminance covariance proposed by Dosher *et al.* (1986). A more computational approach to accumulation is joint regularization, where constraints from different cues are accounted for by means of a common cost function (Poggio *et al.*, 1985; Terzopoulos, 1986).

(ii) *Cooperation.* Especially in the case of poor or noisy cues, modules might work synergistically. Here we think of the non-linear interactions of different cues which can be treated, for example, with the coupled Markov random field approach (Marroquin *et al.*, 1987).

(iii) *Disambiguation.* A particular case of a non-linear interaction is the case where information from one cue is used to locally disambiguate a representation derived from another one [e.g. stereo can disambiguate shading (Braunstein *et al.*, 1986)] or specular highlights can disambiguate the convex–concave ambiguity of shading (Blake & Bülthoff, 1989).

(iv) *Veto.* There can be unequivocal information from one cue that should not be challenged by others.

Most computational approaches to integration have focused on the second problem, i.e. the combination of different data types in one representation which is often thought to be unique. In our psychophysical experiments, we addressed both of the above questions by (a) measuring the contribution of individual cues in different matching tasks that correspond to certain 3D-descriptors, and (b) comparing these contributions in each of the matching tasks quantitatively.

Psychophysical 3D Measurements

The perception of three-dimensional scenes relies on many different depth cues and leads to various descriptions of that scene in terms of distance, surface orientation, and curvature, shape or form. We addressed various of these 3D-descriptors (depth map, curvature and object orientation) and depth cues (stereo, shading, highlight, texture).

3D-descriptors and matching tasks

1. *Perceived depth* was mapped with a small probe or cursor that was interactively adjusted to the perceived surface. The depth of this probe was defined by edge-based stereo disparities and all other cue combinations were compared to the percept generated by edge-based stereo. All images were viewed binocularly with the depth cursor superimposed. Each adjustment of the probe gives a graded measurement of distance, or local depth, i.e. this experiment corresponds to the 3D-descriptor *depth map* mentioned in the scheme of Figure 2.
2. *Global shapes* of two objects with different combinations of depth cues were compared directly. Since all images showed end-on views of ellipsoids with different elongation, this measurement corresponds to *curvature* or *form* as a 3D-descriptor.
3. *Object orientation* can be measured in a matching task where long ellipsoids of different orientation have to be compared. While surface orientation is apparently hard to determine for human observers (Todd & Mingolla, 1983; Mingolla & Todd, 1986), the orientation of entire objects (e.g. orientation of *generalized cylinders*) can be measured easily in a matching task.

Depth cues and computer graphics

The relation of shading (with and without highlights), stereo and texture in the 3D perception of smooth and polyhedral surfaces was studied with computer graphics psychophysics. For polyhedral and textured objects, stereo disparities were associated with localized features, i.e. the intensity changes at the facet or texel boundaries, while for the smooth surfaces only shading disparities occurred. In addition, contours such as rings or lines could be drawn on the smooth surfaces to provide sparse edge information. The objects (ellipsoids of revolution viewed end-on) were chosen for the following reasons:

1. As is shown later, in the section on "Images without zero-crossings", images of Lambertian shaded smooth ellipsoids with moderate eccentricities do not contain Laplacian zero-crossings when illuminated centrally with parallel light.
2. The surfaces are closed and are naturally outlined by a planar occluding contour. This contour was placed in the zero disparity plane and did not provide any depth information.
3. Convex objects such as ellipsoids do not cast shadows or generate reflections on their own surface. Therefore, shading (attached shadows) could be studied without interference from cast shadows or mutual illumination.
4. End-on views of ellipsoids can be thought of as a model for the depth interpolation of a surface patch between sparse edge data.

METHODS

Computer Graphic Psychophysics

Images of smooth- and flat-shaded (polyhedral) ellipsoids of revolution were generated by either ray-tracing techniques or with a solid modeling software package (S-Geometry, Symbolics Inc.). The polyhedral objects were derived from quadrangular tesselations of the sphere along meridian and latitude circles. The objects were elongated along an axis in the equatorial plane of the tesselated sphere. Thus, the two types of objects differed mainly in the absence or presence of edges. As compared to spheres, the objects were elongated by the factors 0.5, 1.0, 2.0, 3.0, 4.0 and 5.0. With an original radius of 6.7 cm, this corresponds to depth values between 3.3 and 33.3 cm. In the following, all semi-diameters (elongations) are given as multiples of 6.7 cm. In Experiments 1 and 2, all objects were viewed end-on, i.e. the axis of rotational symmetry was orthogonal to the display screen. In Experiment 3, objects could be rotated around a diagonal axis in the display plane. As an example, the objects displayed in Figure 1 are rotated around that axis by plus and minus 45°, respectively.

The imaging geometry used in the computer graphics is shown in Figure 3. It differs from the usual camera geometry in that the image is constructed on a screen which is not perpendicular to the optical axis of the eyes. Note that the imaging geometry, and therefore the image itself, does not depend on the fixation point as long as the nodal points of the two eyes remain fixed at the positions E_l and E_r, respectively. Images were computed for a viewing distance of 120 cm and an interpupillary separation of 6.5 cm. When a point 10 cm in front of the center of the screen is fixated, Panum's fusional area of $\pm$ 10 min of arc (cf. Ardity, 1986) corresponds to an interval from 4.3 cm to 15.2 cm in front of the screen.

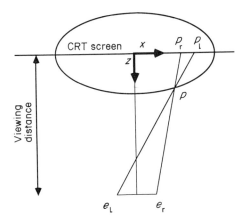

Figure 3. Imaging geometry. Projection onto the x-z-plane. Viewing distance is 120 cm. e_1, e_r: nodal points of the left and right eye, respectively. The distance between e_1 and e_r is 6.5 cm. A point $\mathbf{p} \in \mathbf{R}^3$ is imaged on the screen at $\mathbf{p}_1$ for the view from the left eye and at $\mathbf{p}_r$ for the view from the right eye.

For the computation of the smooth-shaded ellipsoids, a ray-tracing operation was performed.* The illuminant was modeled as an infinite point source (parallel illumination) centrally behind the observer. For some control experiments, oblique directions of illumination (upper-left and lower-right) were used. Surface shading was computed according to the Phong model (Phong, 1975), i.e. consisting of an ambient, a diffuse (Lambertian) and a specular component. For Lambertian shading, the ambient and specular components were zero, while for specular shading (sometimes called highlight in the sequel), a combination of 30% ambient, 10% diffuse and 60% specular reflectance (specular exponent 7.0) was chosen. Since our objects were convex, no cast shadows or repeated reflections had to be considered.

---

* We write the equation of the ellipsoid as

$$\mathbf{x}^T \mathbf{A} \mathbf{x} = 1, \qquad \mathbf{A} = \begin{pmatrix} a^{-2} & 0 & 0 \\ 0 & b^{-2} & 0 \\ 0 & 0 & c^{-2} \end{pmatrix}, \tag{1}$$

where a, b, c denote the semi-diameters. With $a = b = 1$, we have an ellipsoid of revolution. For a ray from e to p',

$$\mathbf{x} = \mathbf{e} + \mu(\mathbf{p}' - \mathbf{e}), \mu \in \mathbf{R}^+, \tag{2}$$

the ray-tracing amounts to the solution for μ of the quadratic equation:

$$(\mathbf{e} + \mu(\mathbf{p}' - \mathbf{e}))^T \mathbf{A}(\mathbf{e} + \mu(\mathbf{p}' - \mathbf{e})) = 1. \tag{3}$$

The image intensity at point p' was computed from this solution for an ideal Lambertian surface illuminated by parallel light from the z-direction. Note that for a point $\mathbf{x}$ on the surface of the ellipsoid $\mathbf{x}^T \mathbf{A} \mathbf{x} = 1$, the surface normal is simply $\mathbf{A}\mathbf{x}/\|\mathbf{A}\mathbf{x}\|$. The viewing direction and the axis of revolution of the ellipsoid were aligned.

Disparity and edge information (Experiment 1)

In a first series of experiments, we crossed disparity and dense edge information in shaded images. Four different image types were tested (Figure 4a, b):
1. Flat-shaded ellipsoid with disparity and edge information (D^+E^+).
2. Smooth-shaded ellipsoid with disparity but without edge information (D^+E^-). Both Lambertian and specular shading were tested.
3. Flat-shaded ellipsoid without disparity but with edge information (D^-E^+).
4. Smooth-shaded ellipsoid with neither disparity nor edge information (D^-E^-). Both Lambertian and specular shading were tested.

Illuminant direction (Experiment 2)

In a second series of experiments, we studied the influence of the illuminant direction in Lambertian shaded images with and without disparities (D^+E^-; D^-E^-). While in the first series illumination was from exactly behind the observer, we chose upper-left and lower-right directions ($\pm 14°$ azimuth and $\mp 13.6°$ elevation from the viewing direction).

Edge vs shading disparity (Experiment 3)

The third series of experiments addressed the interaction of smooth shading and sparse edge information provided by a small dark ring placed at the tip of the ellipsoid (contrast 0.11, radius 7.5 mm, covering less than 1% of the ellipsoid's image). Disparities of shading and ring were varied independently, leading to the following combinations (Figure 4c):

1. Disparate ring and disparate shading.
2. Disparate ring and non-disparate shading.
3. Non-disparate ring and disparate shading.
4. Non-disparate ring and non-disparate shading.
5. Disparate ring in front of uniformly grey non-disparate disk.

All experiments were performed with 4–6 different elongations (0.5–5.0) of the ellipsoids. The elongations were unknown to the observers.

Global shape comparison (Experiment 4)

The local depth probe technique used in the previous three experiments has some disadvantages with depth cues which have to be viewed preferably monocularly. Therefore, we developed a global shape comparison technique which allows the depth cues to be viewed monocularly and compared with a stereoscopically viewed shape reference.

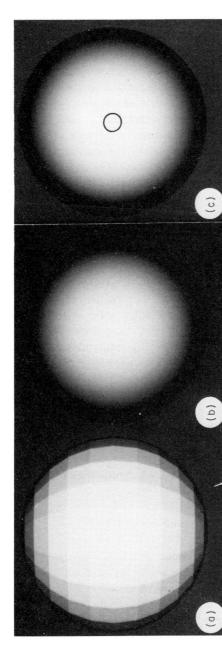

Figure 4. Flat- and smooth-shaded surfaces. (a), (b) Discontinuous and smooth intensity variations in images of polyhedra and ellipsoids provide cues for edge-based stereo, shape-from-disparate-shading and shape-from-shading (Experiment 1). (c) Smooth ellipsoid with sparse edge information has been used in experiments on the interaction of edge-based stereo and shape-from-shading (Experiment 3). All images could be displayed as stereograms or as pairs of identical images. In image (c), the disparities of shading and edge token (ring) could be varied independently.

Experimental Procedure

We displayed either a pair of disparate images (stereo pair) or a non-disparate view of the object as seen from between the two eyes on a CRT Color Monitor (Mitsubishi UC-6912 High-Resolution Color-Display Monitor, Resolution (H × V) 1024 × 874 pixels; bandwidth ± 3 dB between 50 Hz and 50 MHz, short persistence phosphor). The disparate images were interlaced (even lines for the left image and odd lines for the right image) with a frame rate of 30 Hz. This technique allows the left and right views to be displayed at about the same location on the monitor and therefore treats any geometric distortion of the monitor equally to both eyes. Non-voluntary disparities are therefore avoided. Both disparate and non-disparate images were viewed binocularly through shutter glasses (Stereo-Optic Systems Inc.) which were triggered by the interlace signal to present the appropriate images only to the left and right eye. The objects were shown in black and white with a true resolution of 254 grey-levels using a 10-bit D/A-Converter. The background was uniformly colored in half-saturated blue. The screen was viewed in complete darkness.

Local depth probe technique

Perceived depth was measured by adjusting a small red square-shaped (4 by 4 pixel) depth probe to the surface interactively (with the computer mouse). This probe was displayed in interlaced mode together with the disparate images. This is a computer graphics version of a binocular rangefinder developed by Gregory (1966), called "Gregory's Pandora's Box" by some investigators, with the additional advantage that the accommodation cue is eliminated. Measurements were performed at 45 vertices of a Cartesian grid in the image plane in random order. The initial disparity of the depth probe was randomized for each measurement to avoid hysteresis effects. Subjects were asked to move the cursor back and forth in depth until it finally seemed to lie directly on top of the displayed test surface. After some training sessions, subjects felt comfortable with this procedure and achieved reproducible depth measurements. Subjects included the authors (corrected vision) and one naive observer, all with normal stereo vision as tested with natural and random-dot stereograms.

Global shape comparison technique

The global shape comparison technique was used mainly for those cues which required monocular viewing. It is also useful for cues which are processed more globally and would be hindered by a too focused attention to the local probe. Depending on the task this technique was used in two different ways. To measure shape from shading and/or texture with the global probe we displayed a stereoscopically viewed reference object in the same orientation as the probe. The task of the subject was to change the shading or the texture (or both together) in order to match the shape with the reference object. This could be done almost in real time by fast recall from computer memory of precomputed images of different shapes and/or orientations. The reference object did not contain any shading or texture cue beside the disparate rings on its surface to avoid any cross-comparison with the depth cues to be tested.

Data Evaluation

Depth probe technique

The depth probe technique leads to a depth map measured locally at 45 positions in the image plane. In order to derive a global measure of perceived depth we performed a principal component analysis on all data sets, treating each one as a point in 45-space. Variance of the perceived shapes was found mainly (94%) along the first principal axis, whose corresponding loading was very close to an ideal ellipsoid (or sphere). The second component accounted for only 1.4% of the total variance. We therefore chose the overall elongation, i.e. the coefficient associated to the first principal component, as a measure of perceived depth for a given cue combination (Figure 6).

Shape comparison technique

The depth comparison data were averaged over different runs and over 2-4 subjects. The mean number of runs was about 180 and the average correlation between displayed and estimated shape was 0.83. In order to distinguish easily between over- or underestimation of depth we give the mean slope for each depth cue. A slope of 1.0 is naturally the veridical perception and a slope >1 is an underestimation of curvature (see Figure 10).

RESULTS

Disparity and Edge Information (Experiment 1)

In the first series of experiments 165 measurements were performed, each consisting of 45 adjustments of the depth probe to the perceived surface. Results were consistent in all three subjects and were pooled since the differences were noticeable only in the standard deviation. The 16 plots of Figure 5 show the averaged results of all subjects for the four types of experiments and four different elongations of Lambertian shaded ellipsoids.

The perceived elongation in the images with consistent cue combinations depends on the amount of information available. As can be seen from Figure 6, the perceived elongation is almost correct when shading, intensity-based and edge-based disparity information are available (D^+E^+). In the case of smooth-shaded disparate images (D^+E^-), the edges are missing and depth perception is reduced. When shading is the only cue (D^-E^-), perceived elongation is much smaller and almost independent of the displayed elongation. Phong shading (highlights)

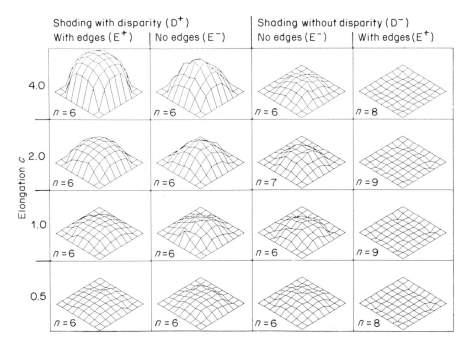

Figure 5. Perceived surfaces (Experiment 1). Each plot shows the average of 6–9 sessions from three subjects. Perceived depth decreases with the following sequence of cue combinations: disparity, edges and shading (D^+E^+); disparity and shading but no edges (D^+E^-); shading only (D^-E^-); contradictory disparity and shading (D^-E^+). The elongation of the displayed objects is denoted by c (depth not drawn to scale).

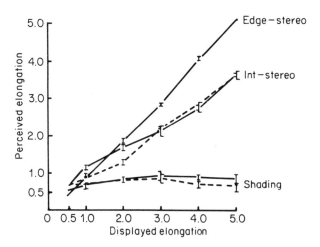

Figure 6. Perceived elongation. Depth perception decreases with fewer cues available. The significant separation between the middle and lower curves (smooth shading with and without disparity) illustrates the influence of disparity information even in the absence of edges. Solid lines: Lambertian shading; dashed lines: Phong shading.

instead of Lambertian shading did not change perceived depth significantly (dashed lines).

In experiment D^-E^+, two identical images (no disparity) of polyhedral ellipsoids (edges) were shown. Although shading alone provided some depth information as shown in experiment D^-E^-, the fact that edges occurred at zero disparity was decisive. The perceived depth did not vary with the elongation suggested by the shading (and perspective) information and took slightly negative values which, however, were not significantly different from zero.

Depth can still be perceived when no disparate edges are present. This is not surprising, since shading information was still available. A comparison of the results (Figure 6) for smooth-shaded images with and without disparity information, however, establishes a significant contribution of shading disparities. The curves for D^+E^- and D^-E^- are significantly separated for all elongations except 0.5.

Illuminant Direction (Experiment 2)

Since the lighting conditions used in the preceding experiments were degenerate (no self-shadows) we measured smooth-shaded ellipsoids (D^+E^-, D^-E^-) with oblique directions of illumination. Light sources were placed in the upper-left and the lower-right in front of the object ($\pm 14°$ azimuth and $\mp 13.6°$ elevation towards the viewer). The results of these experiments (41 measurements, data pooled from all subjects) are depicted in Figure 7. The slight asymmetries present at elongation 4.0 result exclusively from the fact that no depth values were determined in the dark (shadowed) parts of the images. The data are in line with those of Experiment 1: shading disparities produce a significantly stronger depth perception than non-disparate shading (shape-from-shading). Furthermore, when illumination is from

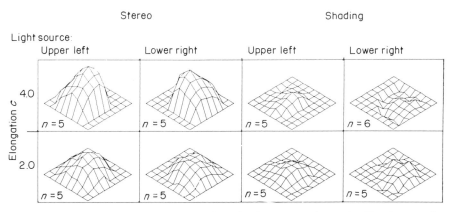

Figure 7.   Perceived surfaces for oblique illuminations (Experiment 2). The data confirm the relevance of disparate shading and show the independence of the findings of Experiment 1 from the lighting conditions. No depth was measured in the self-shadow regions.

the lower-right, stereo prevents depth inversion which occasionally occurred in the non-disparate images (cf. negative depth in Figure 7; shading, lower-right).

Edge vs Shading Disparity (Experiment 3)

In contrast to the original measurements with polyhedral objects where edge information was distributed all over the surface, we now placed a small dark ring at the tip of the ellipsoid. Altogether, 126 measurements were performed with four different elongations. Figure 8 shows the results for the ring at zero disparity combined with non-disparate (a) and disparate shading (b). While the overall results resemble those of Experiment 1 (D^+E^- and D^-E^-, respectively), zero depth is perceived in the vicinity of the ring. The cases with disparate edge information are summarized in Figure 9: in Figure 9(a), edge and shading disparities are consistent and the percept is in between the results of D^+E^+ and D^+E^- from Experiment 1. If the disparate ring appears on a non-disparately shaded ellipsoid, two different perceptions were reported. Especially for large disparities, some observers saw the ring floating in front of a rather flat surface. Others fused the edge-token and the surround into one coherent surface passing through the ring. This surface looked more transparent than those produced by the other cues and was also perceived as a cone-like *subjective surface* when a ring floated in front of a uniformly grey disk (Figure 9b).

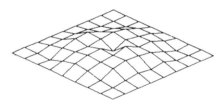

Shape-from-shading and zero-disparity edge
Perceived depth: 16%

Intensity-based stereo and zero-disparity edge
Perceived depth: 66%

Figure 8.   Zero-disparity edge token overrides shading (Experiment 3). (a) Shape-from-shading ($n = 7$). (b) Shape-from-disparate-shading ($n = 6$). Only data for elongation 4.0 are shown.

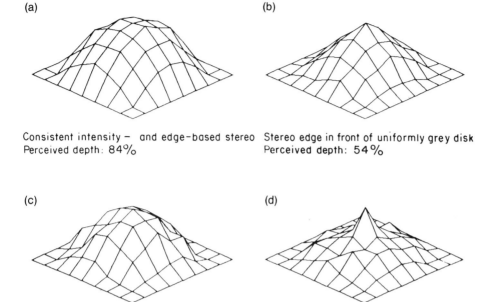

(a)

Consistent intensity − and edge−based stereo
Perceived depth: 84%

(b)

Stereo edge in front of uniformly grey disk
Perceived depth: 54%

(c)

(d)

Stereo edges in front of "shaded" disk (without disparity)
Subjects ISA and HAM: 63%   Subject HHB: 41%

Figure 9. Surface interpolation for sparse edge data (Experiment 3). (a) Shape-from-disparate-shading plus disparate edge information leads to an almost correct percept ($n = 6$). (b) A single edge token in front of a uniformly grey disk yields a cone-like subjective surface ($n = 6$). (c), (d) Shape-from-shading plus disparate edge information leads to an ambiguous perception ($n = 3 + 3$). Only data for elongation 4.0 are shown.

Shape Comparison (Experiment 4)

All images with single cues lead to large errors in perceived shape. With *shading* and *texture* curvature is underestimated (Figure 10a, b), with a highlight it is overestimated (Figure 10c). One remarkable result of the comparison technique is that the shape-from-shading performance is much better with this technique than with the local depth probe technique. The adjusted shading scales with the displayed elongation of the stereoscopically displayed ellipsoid and does not level off as in the case of the depth probe measurements. A highlight on the shaded surface also seems to have a much larger influence with this technique and leads to an overestimation of curvature. But the most interesting result is the strong interaction between shading and texture as shown in Figure 10(d), (e). If shading and texture cues can be used simultaneously the perceived shape is almost veridical with a small bias towards under- or overestimation depending on the shading model [highlight absent (Figure 10d), or present (Figure 10e)].

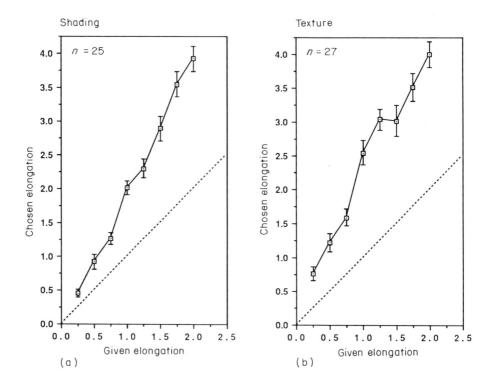

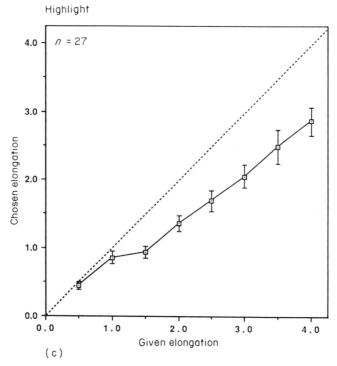

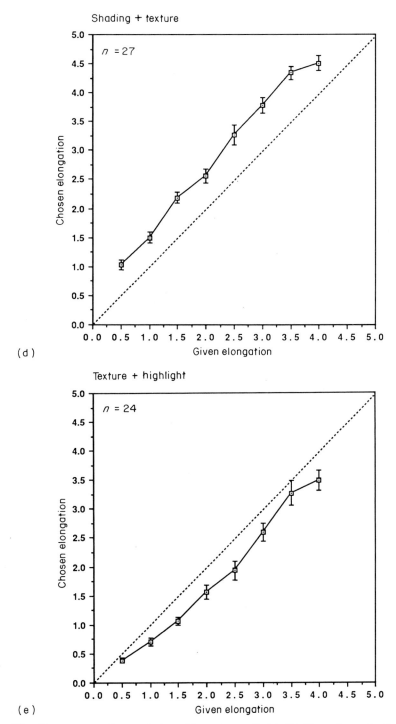

(d)

(e)

Figure 10. Shape comparison technique (Experiment 4). (a), (b) Shape-from-shading and shape-from-texture lead to an underestimation of shape (slope > 1). (c) If a highlight is added to the shading (Phong shading) model the shape is overestimated in the adjustment task. (d) If shading and texture are presented simultaneously the shape is adjusted almost correctly (slope = 1) with a bias to adjust a larger elongation than necessary. (e) If a highlight is added the slope stays the same but the bias changes towards an overestimation of shape.

DISCUSSION

Images without Zero-crossings

One of the most important constraints in early vision for recovering surface properties is that the physical processes underlying image formation are typically smooth. The smoothness property is captured well by standard regularization (Poggio *et al.*, 1985) and exploited in its algorithms. On the other hand, *changes of image intensity* often convey information about physical edges in the scene. The location of sharp changes in image intensity correspond very often to depth discontinuities in the scene. Many stereo algorithms use dominant changes in image intensity as features to compute disparity between corresponding image points. In order to localize these sharp changes in image intensity, zero-crossings in Laplacian filtered images are commonly used (Marr & Hildreth, 1980).

The disadvantage of these feature-based stereo algorithms is that only sparse depth data (along the features) can be computed. This forces an additional stage in which sophisticated algorithms (Grimson, 1982; Blake & Zisserman, 1987) allow the interpolation of the surface between data points. In order to test for the ability of human stereo vision to get denser depth data by using in addition features other than edges or even a completely featureless mechanism we computed images without sharp changes in image intensity. We show that for an orthographically projected image of a sphere with Lambertian reflection function and parallel illumination, zero-crossings in the Laplacian are missing.

Consider a hemisphere given in cylindrical coordinates by the parametric equation

$$z = \sqrt{1 - r^2}. \tag{4}$$

In the special case of a sphere, the surface normal simply equals the radius, i.e.

$$\mathbf{n} = (r \cos \varphi, r \sin \varphi, \sqrt{1 - r^2}). \tag{5}$$

For the illuminant direction $l = (0, 0, 1)$ and the Lambertian reflectance function, we obtain the luminance profile

$$\mathbf{I}(r) = I_0(\mathbf{l} \cdot \mathbf{n}) = I_0\sqrt{1 - r^2}, \tag{6}$$

where I_0 is a suitable constant, i.e. the image luminance is again a hemisphere. For the Laplacian of I, we obtain

$$\nabla^2 I(r) = I''(r) - \frac{1}{r} I'(r) = -I_0 \frac{r^2}{(1 - r^2)^{3/2}}. \tag{7}$$

This is a non-positive function of r, with $\nabla^2 I(0) = 0$; i.e. the Laplacian of I has no zero-crossings.

Unfortunately, this result does not hold for ellipsoids with $c \neq 1$. A similar computation for an ellipsoid with elongation c yields

$$I_c(r) = I_0 \frac{\sqrt{1 - r^2}}{\sqrt{1 - (1 - c^2)r^2}}, \qquad (8)$$

which reduces to equation (6) for $c = 1$. In Figure 11(a), where luminance profiles are plotted for the elongations $c = 0.5, 1.0, 2.0$ and 4.0, it can be seen that for $c \geq 2$ the curves are no longer convex. That is to say that the second derivatives of these profiles in fact have zero-crossings, and a similar result holds for the Laplacians. However, when filtering with the Laplacian of a Gaussian or with the difference of two Gaussians (DOG) is considered, it turns out that these zero-crossings are insignificant for the elongations used here. Pixel-based convolutions failed to show the "edges" unequivocally, and even a Gaussian integration algorithm run on the complete function rather than on the sampled array produced no zero-crossings beyond the single-precision truncation error. We therefore conclude that the slight zero-crossings in the unfiltered Laplacian of our luminance profiles do not correspond to significant edges. For the oblique illuminations used in Experiment 2, we found numerically that the self-shadow boundary corresponds to a level-crossing rather than a zero-crossing in the DOG-filtered image.

Independent from our own work, images of ellipsoids may be useful in the study of the psychophysical relevance of Laplacian zero-crossings. We feel that images of ellipsoids are superior to the gratings or filtered images often used for this purpose (Daugman, 1985).

Receptor Non-linearities in Early Vision

Since the visual system does not work directly on image intensities, but on spatially and temporally filtered and compressed (non-linear) signals, the effects of early visual processing in the retina have to be taken into account. Signal compression alone can significantly change image interpretation. Non-linearity in the photo-receptors, for example, can lead to an illusory motion perception for time-varying signals that do not entail motion information (Bülthoff & Götz, 1979). In analogy, these non-linearities could induce edge information that is not present in smooth-shaded images. An additional source of zero-crossings not present in our image arrays is the non-linearity of the color monitor. If arbitrary non-linearities are considered, zero-crossings can be induced in every non-constant image, however smooth (e.g. by discretization).

Retinal non-linearities in both vertebrates (Naka & Rushton, 1966; Hemilä, 1987) and invertebrates (Kramer, 1975) have been modeled by saturation-type characteristics of the form

$$f(I) = \frac{I}{I + I_{0.5}}, \qquad (9)$$

where $I_{0.5}$ is a constant, given by the luminance which produces 50% of the maximal excitation. We repeated experiments D^+E^- and D^-E^-, i.e. those involving smooth-shaded images, compensating for the compression non-linearity with the inverse of equation (9). Since $I_{0.5}$ depends on the adaptation of the eye, four different choices of the constant $I_{0.5}$ were used. Monitor non-linearities were compensated as well. Depth perception from disparate shading was not affected significantly by this procedure.

Figure 11(b) shows the luminance profile for an ellipsoid with elongation 4.0, and the effect of the non-linearity of equation (9) for the tested values of $I_{0.5}$. It turns out that in our experiments, the presumed receptor non-linearities tend to cancel the shallow zero-crossings rather than to create new ones. This is further support for our assumption that edges cannot be extracted from the smooth-shaded images. Mechanisms relying on zero-crossings in the original image cannot account for the shape-from-disparate-shading performance found in our experiments. Under the assumption of compression-type non-linearities, this holds also for the first neural representation of the zero-crossing free images.

Shape-from-Disparate-Shading

The major finding of this study, as far as single depth cues are concerned, is the strength of depth perception (70%) obtained from disparate shading under various illuminant conditions and reflectance functions. In computational theory, most studies have focused on edge-based stereo algorithms (for review, see Poggio & Poggio, 1984). This is due to the overall superiority of edge-based stereo which is confirmed by our finding that edge-based stereo gives a better depth estimate than disparate shading (Blake *et al.*, 1985). However, in the absence of edges and for surface interpolation, grey-level disparities appear to be more important than is usually appreciated.

Grimson (1984) makes explicit use of binocular shading differences for the interpolation of surfaces between good matches (i.e. between edges). Unfortunately, his model is not directly comparable to our study for the following reasons. First, the information that Grimson's algorithm recovers from shading is the surface orientation along zero-crossings. In our experiments with smooth ellipsoids, the only zero-crossing contour is the occluding contour of the object where the surface orientation does not depend on the total elongation of the object; it is always perpendicular to the image plane. Second, Grimson's model requires a specular component in the reflectance function of the object. Quite to the contrary, we did not find significant differences between Lambertian or Phong shading. From this we may conclude that a mechanism different from the one proposed by Grimson is involved.

Shape-from-Disparate-Shading: Is it Localized or Distributed?

Are there features other than zero-crossings which can account for the shape-from-disparate-shading performance found in our experiments? Possible candidates

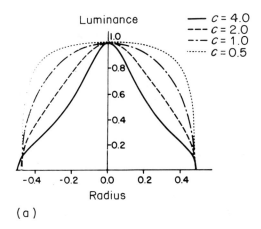

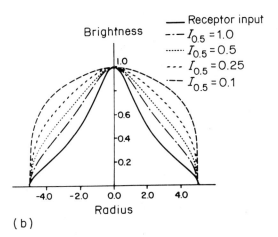

Figure 11. Luminance and simulated brightness profiles. (a) Luminance profiles of ellipsoids with different elongations. Note that for elongations larger than 2.0 inflections occur. (b) Brightness profiles for the ellipsoid with elongation 4.0 (the one with the pronounced inflections in Figure 11a). The non-linear compression (Equation 9) tends to cancel the inflections which might give rise to zero-crossings, rather than to enhance them.

include the intensity peak as proposed by Mayhew & Frisby (1981) and level-crossings in the DOG-filtered image which, according to Hildreth (1983), might account for Mayhew & Frisby's (1981) data as well.

In order to distinguish between a localized (feature-based) and a distributed mechanism for shape-from-disparate-shading we tested the effect of a small disparate token displayed in front of a non-disparate background (Figure 9). Our data show that for large elongations, a single stereo feature (ring) is not sufficient to produce the same percept as full disparate shading [compare Figure 9(a) with Figures 9(b)–(d)]. For small elongations (0.5–2.0; not shown in Figure 9) the differences were not pronounced. We therefore conjecture that disparate shading does not rely on feature matching and thus can be used for surface interpolation when edges are sparse. This view is well in line with the finding that edge information, whenever present, overrides shape-from-disparate-shading (Figure 8).

Note, however, that we do not propose the naive idea of pointwise intensity matching as a mechanism for shape-from-disparate-shading because of its sensitivity to noise in both the data and in neural processing. Even in the absence of image noise, intensity-based algorithms (e.g. Gennert, 1987) can lead to severe matching errors when run on our stimuli.

Surface Interpolation and Subjective Surfaces

In the experiments with sparse edge information (Figure 9b-d), an interpolated surface was measured directly with the depth probe technique. If the depth separation between the ring and the shaded ellipsoid was large (elongation 4.0) an ambiguous perception was experienced. One interpretation consisted of a solid base at about the depth perceived from shape-from-shading alone with the ring floating in front of it (Figure 9d). The other interpretation was a transparent subjective surface onto which the ring was drawn (Figure 9c). In this case, the depth of the entire surface was pulled towards the ring. Surprisingly, a subjective surface could also be perceived when the token was floating in front of a uniformly grey disk (Figure 9b). An interaction between shape-from-shading and edge-based stereo is therefore not necessary to perceive subjective surfaces.

Shape-from-Shading: Algorithms and Psychophysics

A computational theory for shape-from-shading is presented by Ikeuchi & Horn (1981). As an example, they discuss the image of a sphere with Lambertian reflectance function, illuminated by parallel light from the viewing direction. This example can be directly compared to our Experiment 1 (D^-E^-) where about 25% of the correct depth was perceived by the observers. Interestingly, the algorithm of Ikeuchi & Horn underestimates depth if the input data are noisy. The distortion of shape in their algorithm depends on a regularization parameter λ. For a large value of λ, which would be appropriate for noisy image data, the smoothing of the surface leads to a considerable underestimation of depth. On the other hand, the iterative scheme becomes unstable if the value of λ is reduced too much. For an approach which avoids smoothing by a regularization term, see Horn and Brooks (1985).

The algorithm of Ikeuchi & Horn also shows other types of errors when the light source position and the reflectance properties of the surface are not known exactly. The types of errors reported from numerical experiments are asymmetric distortions for false assumptions of the light source position and overestimation of depth when false reflectance functions are assumed. In our psychophysical studies, these errors did not occur. Asymmetric deformations as reported by Ikeuchi & Horn are not present even for the obliquely illuminated objects (Figure 7). Whether this corresponds to a correct judgement of the illuminant direction by the human observer is currently under investigation. Also, varying the reflectance function did not change the shape-from-shading performance as measured with our depth probe technique in Experiment 1 (Figure 6, dashed lines).

How Useful is Shading as a Cue for Depth?

Todd & Mingolla (1983) and Mingolla & Todd (1986) used psychophysical techniques to investigate how observers analyze shape by use of shading cues. According to their results, the human observer underestimates surface curvature by over 50% when using shading information. A similar result has been reported by Barrow & Tenenbaum (1978), showing that shading of a cylindrical surface can deviate substantially from natural shading before a change in the perceived shape can be detected. This is well in line with our psychophysical findings which suggest that non-disparate shading is a poor cue to depth. It is, however, in contrast to the intuition of artists who use shading as a primary tool to depict objects in depth.

Is it possible that we are not asking the right question when we try to analyze shape with the local depth probe? Obviously everybody can describe the shape of a vase in a photograph even without any texture on it. In principle, the information that can be obtained from shape-from-shading is surface orientation rather than absolute depth. However, as Todd and Mingolla have shown, the surface normal on simply shaded bodies is difficult to estimate in psychophysical experiments, and even after a training phase subjects make a lot of errors. A precise measurement of surface slant and tilt does not seem to be necessary for shape perception.

In the study reported here, we tried to measure the perceived depth directly with a stereoscopically viewed depth probe. This seems to be a much simpler task for the subjects, and indeed we did not need a long training phase to obtain consistent depth measurements. It is not obvious that this method worked for shading cues alone, since it involves a cross-comparison of supposedly more or less independent modules as well as a comparison of local (depth probe) and global (shading) information. Since our depth probe is defined by stereopsis it requires binocular viewing even for non-disparate images (pure shape-from-shading). To avoid this, we developed a paradigm to measure shape-from-shading monocularly (Bülthoff & Mallot, 1988). With this paradigm we can also analyze other cues, e.g. texture gradients and occluding contours, which would show similar problems with a local stereo depth probe.

Integration of Depth Modules

Concrete predictions of the types of interactions that should occur between different depth cues are still difficult to obtain from computational theory. Therefore, we hope that psychophysical studies will in turn provide useful hints for computational investigations into the integration of depth information.

Accumulation is a simple type of interaction that can be implemented in a number of different ways. Depth information can be collected from different cues and performance should improve as more information becomes available. Our data show that it is not the reliability which improves, but the perceived depth which increases. This result hints at regularization as the mechanism for the observed accumulation. Given a stereo contour surrounding a surface patch, the most conservative estimate would be a smooth interpolation as performed by computer vision algorithms (Grimson, 1982; Marroquin, 1984; Terzopoulos, 1986).

In our stimuli, the smoothest interpolation is a flat disk. In a tradeoff with the smoothness constraint, the visual system seems to use the available information to the extent of its reliability. This might explain why depth perception increases as more information becomes available.

Conflicting cues were presented in Experiments 1 and 3. Whenever visible, edge-based disparities were decisive for the perceived depth (Figure 5, $D^- E^+$, Figures 8 and 9). Except for the subjective surface (see the section on "Surface interpolation and subjective surfaces") the "veto effect" was restricted to a vicinity of the edge as can be seen from the sparse edge data in Figures 8 and 9. Edge-based stereo thus overrides both shape-from-shading and shape-from-disparate-shading. It is possible, however, that this veto relationship occurs only in the locally derived depth map. The global percept of the polyhedral ellipsoid in Experiment 1 ($D^- E^+$) is not flat but convex. A conflicting cue combination of shape-from-shading and shape-from-disparate-shading was presented in the experiment with smooth-shaded non-disparate images ($D^- E^-$). In this case, shape-from-shading is not vetoed by the lack of shading disparities but leads to a reduced depth perception of about 25%. An inhibitory interaction between the two cues may account for this poor shape-from-shading performance and the ceiling effect in Figure 6.

Asymmetric types of interaction, such as veto or disambiguation, can be expected from models of surface interpolation that start with reliable but sparse depth information typically obtained from disparate edges or occluding contours. Interpolation between the sites of the edges could rely on a smoothness constraint

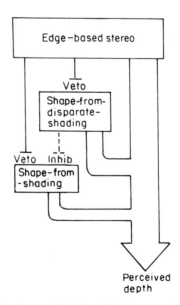

Figure 12.   Integration of depth cues. The size of the boxes and interaction channels reflects the contribution of the different depth cues for the overall perceived depth (accumulation). In contradictory cases, shape from both disparate and non-disparate shading is vetoed by edge-based stereo. An inhibitory influence of shape-from-disparate-shading on shape-from-shading is discussed in "Integration of depth modules".

(Grimson, 1982) or on additional cues such as shading (Ikeuchi & Horn, 1981; Blake *et al.*, 1985) and binocular shading of specular surfaces (Grimson, 1984). Its distributed mechanism and the veto relationship to edge-based stereo make shape-from-disparate-shading especially suitable for surface interpolation in human vision. The interactions of different depth cues (as derived from our depth probe experiments) in consistent and contradictory cases are summarized in Figure 12. Another summary of our data which includes both depth probe and shape comparison techniques is shown in Figure 13. This representation is based on the idea (sketched in Figure 2) that the integration of different 3D-cues can lead to the perception of different 3D-descriptors (range, shape, orientation). The contribution of single monocular cues is different for the 3D-descriptors. Object orientation is best recovered from texture cues (Bülthoff & Mallot, 1988) while surface curvature (shape) can be inferred more easily from shading. With binocular shading (Lambertian or Phong shading) range perception is rather strong (70%). It is even stronger for the perception of shape (100%). The addition of a highlight to a shaded surface has no effect in the range matching task while a strong effect was found in the shape comparison task. Highlights always led to an overestimate of shape while dull surfaces (Lambertain shading) were judged to be flat.

Recently, Poggio (1985) proposed a new formalism for the integration of different vision modules, based on a probabilistic approach (Marroquin, 1984; Marroquin *et al.*, 1987). The advantage of this coupled Markov random fields

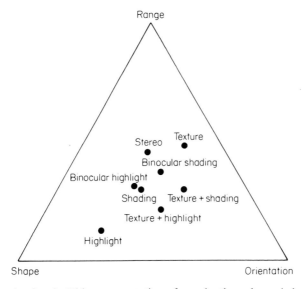

Figure 13. Depth triangle. This representation of our depth probe and shape comparison data shows the relative importance of depth cues (stereo, shading, texture) for different 3D-descriptors (range, shape, orientation); see also Figure 2. Shading has a stronger influence on the perceived shape, while texture seems to be more important for orientation (compare with Figure 1). Stereo is of equal importance for all 3D-descriptors because the shape, orientation and distance to an object (range) can be easily derived from a complete depth map.

approach over regularization theory lies in the possibility of simultaneous segmentation and (piecewise) smoothing of the image. As far as the experiments discussed here are concerned, the results should not be significantly different from those of regularization. However, if other cues such as occlusion are considered, more complex types of interaction are to be expected from the coupled Markov random field approach.

ACKNOWLEDGEMENTS

We are grateful to A. Blake, E. Hildreth, D. Kersten, B. Saxberg and T. Poggio for helpful discussions and I. Bülthoff for going through long and tedious experimental sessions.

This report describes research done within the Center for Biological Information Processing (Whitaker College) at the Massachusetts Institute of Technology. Support for this work is provided by a grant from the Office of Naval Research, Engineering Psychology Division and a NATO Collaborative Grant No. 0403/87. One of us (HAM) was supported by a grant from the Deutsche Forschungsgemeinschaft (Ma 1038/1-1,2).

REFERENCES

Ardity, A. (1986). Review of "Binocular Vision". In K. R. Boff, L. Kaufman & J. P. Thomas (Eds) *Handbook of Perception and Human Performance*, Vol. I, *Sensory Processes and Perception*, Chapter 23. John Wiley, New York.

Bajcsy, R. & Lieberman, L. (1976). Texture gradient as a depth cue. *Computer Vision Graphics and Image Processing*, **5**, 52–67.

Barrow, H. G. & Tenenbaum, J. M. (1978). Recovering intrinsic scene characteristics from images. In A. Hanson & E. Riseman (Eds) *Computer Vision Systems*, pp. 3–26. Academic Press, New York.

Barrow, H. G. & Tenenbaum, J. M. (1981). Interpreting line drawings as three-dimensional surfaces. *Artificial Intelligence*, **17**, 75–116.

Blake, A. & Bülthoff, H. H. (1989). Does the brain know the physics of specular reflection? *Nature* (in press).

Blake, A. & Zisserman, A. (1987). *Visual Reconstruction*. MIT Press, Cambridge, Mass.

Blake, A., Zisserman, A. & Knowles, G. (1985). Surface description from stereo and shading. *Image and Vision Computing*, **3**, 183–191.

Braunstein, M. L., Andersen, G. J., Rouse, M. W. & Tittle, J. S. (1986). Recovering viewer-centered depth from disparity, occlusion, and velocity gradients. *Perception and Psychophysics*, **40**, 216–224.

Bülthoff, H. H. & Götz, K. G. (1979). Analogous motion illusion in man and fly. *Nature*, **278**, 636–638.

Bülthoff, H. H. & Mallot, H. A. (1988). Integration of depth modules: local and global depth measurements. *Investigative Ophthalmology and Visual Science*, **29** (Suppl.), 400.

Daugman, J. (1985). Uncertainty relation for resolution in space, spatial frequency, and orientation optimized by two-dimensional visual cortical filters. *Journal of the Optical Society of America*, **2**, 1160–1169.

Dosher, B. A., Sperling, G. & Wurst, S. (1986). Tradeoffs between stereopsis and proximity luminance covariance as determinants of perceived 3D structure. *Vision Research*, **26**, 973–990.

Gennert, M. A. (1987). A computational framework for understanding problems in stereo vision. MIT Artificial Intelligence Laboratory Thesis.

Gregory, R. L. (1966). *Eye and Brain.* McGraw-Hill, New York.

Grimson, W. E. L. (1982). A computational theory of visual surface interpolation. *Philoscophical Transactions of the Royal Society (London) Series B,* **298,** 395–427.

Grimson, W. E. L. (1984). Binocular shading and visual surface reconstruction. *Computer Vision Graphics and Image Processing,* **28,** 19–43.

Grzywacz, N. M. & Hildreth, E. C. (1987). Incremental rigidity scheme for recovering structure from motion: position-based versus velocity-based formulations. *Journal of the Optical Society of America,* **A4,** 503–518.

Hemilä, S. (1987). The stimulus–response functions of visual systems. *Vision Research,* **27,** 1253–1261.

Hildreth, E. C. (1983). The detection of intensity changes by computer and biological vision systems. *Computer Vision Graphics and Image Processing,* **22,** 1–27.

Horn, B. K. P. & Brooks, M. J. (1985). The variational approach to shape from shading, MIT Artificial Intelligence Laboratory Memo, No. 813, pp. 1–32.

Ikeuchi, K. & Horn, B. K. P. (1981). Numerical shape from shading and occluding boundaries. *Artificial Intelligence,* **17,** 141–184.

Julesz, B. (1971). *Foundations of Cyclopean Perception.* University of Chicago Press, Chicago.

Kender, J. R. (1979). Shape from texture: an aggregation transform that maps a class of textures into surface orientation. In *Proceedings of the International Joint Conference on Artificial Intelligence,* Tokyo, Japan.

Kramer, L. (1975). Interpretation of invertebrate photoreceptor potentials in terms of a quantitative model. *Biophysics of Structure and Mechanism,* **1,** 239–257.

Longuet-Higgins, H. C. & Prazdny, K. (1981). The interpretation of moving retinal image. *Proceedings of the Royal Society (London) Series B,* **208,** 385–397.

Marr, D. & Hildreth, E. (1980). Theory of edge detection. *Proceedings of the Royal Society (London) Series B,* **207,** 187–217.

Marr, D. & Nishihara, H. (1978). Representation and recognition of the spatial organization of three-dimensional shapes. *Proceedings of the Royal Society (London) Series B,* **200,** 269–294.

Marr, D. & Poggio, T. (1979). A computational theory of human stereo vision. *Proceedings of the Royal Society (London) Series B,* **204,** 301–328.

Marroquin, J. L. (1984). Surface reconstruction preserving discontinuities. MIT Artificial Intelligence Laboratory Memo, No. 792.

Marroquin, J. L., Mitter, S. K. & Poggio, T. (1987). Probabilistic solution of ill-posed problems in computational vision. *Journal of the American Statistical Association,* **82,** 76–89.

Mayhew, J. E. W. & Frisby, J. P. (1981). Psychophysical and computational studies towards a theory of human stereopsis. *Artificial Intelligence,* **17,** 349–386.

Mingolla, E. & Todd, J. T. (1986). Perception of solid shape from shading. *Biological Cybernetics,* **53,** 137–151.

Naka, K. I. & Rushton, W. A. H. (1966). S-potentials from color units in the retina of fish (*Cyprinidae*). *Journal of Physiology (London),* **185,** 536–555.

Pentland, A. P. (1984). Local shading analysis. *IEEE Transactions, Pattern Analysis and Machine Intelligence,* **6,** 170–187.

Pentland, A. P. (1986). Shading into texture. *Artificial Intelligence,* **29,** 147–170.

Phong, B. T. (1975). Illumination for computer generated pictures. *Communications of the ACM,* **18,** 311–317.

Poggio, G. & Poggio, T. (1984). The analysis of stereopsis. *Annual Reviews of Neuroscience,* **7,** 379–412.

Poggio, T. (1985). Integrating vision modules with coupled MRFs. MIT Artificial Intelligence Laboratory Working Paper, No. 285.

Poggio, T., Torre, V. & Koch, C. (1985). Computational vision and regularization theory. *Nature,* **317,** 314–319.

Stevens, K. A. (1981). The visual interpretation of surface contours. *Artificial Intelligence*, **17**, 17–45.
Stevens, K. A. & Brooks, A. (1987). Probing depth in monocular images. *Biological Cybernetics*, **56**, 355–366.
Terzopoulos, D. (1986). Integrating visual information from multiple sources. In: A. P. Pentland (Ed.) *From Pixels to Predicates*, pp. 111–142. Ablex, Norwood, NJ.
Todd, J. T. & Mingolla, E. (1983). Perception of surface curvature and direction of illumination from patterns of shading. *Journal of Experimental Psychology: Human Perception and Performance*, **9**, 583–595.
Ullman, S. (1979). *The Interpretation of Visual Motion*. MIT Press, Cambridge MA.
Witkin, A. P. (1981). Recovering surface shape and orientation from texture. *Artificial Intelligence*, **17**, 17–47.

7 The Primal Sketch in Human Vision

Roger J. Watt

Centre for Cognitive and Computational Neuroscience and Department of Psychology, Stirling University, Stirling FK9 4LA, UK

INTRODUCTION

One of the most important practical lessons learnt from machine vision over the last decade is that any system needs to have a first class primal sketch stage if it is not going to be seriously restricted. For example, it is widely accepted that sub-pixel accuracy for edge locations is necessary in order to achieve an acceptable level of stereoscopic depth information. Great sensitivity to edges is another requisite, particularly if the resultant edge map is to have a useful degree of connectivity along the edges that are marked. Speed is a further important consideration: on standard machinery the primal sketch convolutions can be by far the slowest processes in a system, and speed is then severely restricted.

As well as considerations of precision, stability, sensitivity and general computational efficiency, the primal sketch has to deliver information that is appropriate for subsequent stages of visual processing. Generally, this means that the primal sketch is required to locate all the points on "edges" in the image. An "edge" means a step change in image intensity and is supposed to correspond to the occluding contours in the scene, amongst other physical causes. The set of points, or edge elements (edgels) so created, is then often structured, by grouping together connected points, into a set of lines.

In this chapter, I shall examine what is known about the equivalent stages in human visual processing. Much of what is known is derived from psychophysical techniques that, of necessity, assess performance of the human visual system as a whole. The knowledge is necessarily indirect and therefore I give a brief introduction to psychophysical techniques. Before doing or interpreting any experiment, however, we have to have a clear idea of what we should be expecting to find.

AI and the Eye   Edited by A. Blake and T. Troscianko
© 1990 John Wiley & Sons Ltd.

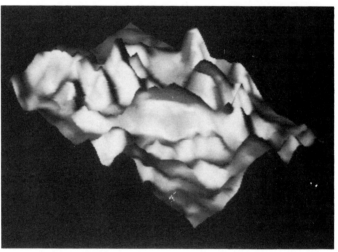

Figure 1. This shows a typical image displayed pictorially (top) and as a 2D intensity function (bottom). The latter gives a better impression of what the primal sketch has to deal with.

COMPUTATIONAL THEORY

Any information-processing system has an associated computational theory. This is essentially an analysis of what the system is required to achieve and what information is available so that it can achieve it. In its barest form the computational theory is a job specification. It is not part of the computational theory to specify how the tasks are split down into modules and how the modules are implemented. Given this rarefied definition, it is nonsense to discuss the computational theory of the primal sketch because the primal sketch is only a module within a system. However, by relaxing the concept of a system so that we can regard the primal sketch as a complete system, it is then possible to create a computational theory.

Visual information can support a great many different activities ranging from locomotion, through recognition to reading. For each of these there is a flow of information from the optical image to the command and control machinery. This means that each of them is essentially a system with its own computational theory. However, it is generally supposed that all of these activities can use the same common initial information path. The primal sketch is very largely this common path, and we can specify the requirements of the primal sketch with this in mind.

Marr (1976) defined the goal of the primal sketch to be the creation of an explicit description of significant grey-level changes in the optical image. Of course, without knowing what the description is being created for, it is difficult to know what particular attributes and grey-level relationships should be explicit and are significant. To Marr the ultimate aim was a volumetric description of the objects within sight, reached via surface-based descriptions. Although this places an undue emphasis on depth estimation and on recognition, it is adequate. It assumes that the scene is filled with distinct things with significant volume and therefore possessing surfaces. This in turn places constraints on the types of structure that optical images can exhibit, and provides a key to what might be significant.

Any one thing projects a region in an optical image; this region has a definite outline boundary and can be described by its outline and the quality of the image within the outline. When there is more than one thing in sight, then some of the projected images may be superimposed when the things occlude each other. This may result in one of the things actually projecting to more than one enclosed region of the image, although when this happens the various regions will have many properties in common. In particular, their outlines will contain abrupt corners which are in reality part of a T junction.

Occluding Contours

For an organism living in a three-dimensional world it is very useful to be able to recognize or interpret the cause of two-dimensional projections in optical images. This is, in principle, impossible because any 2D image could have arisen from very many structurally different layouts. However, matter is constrained in the way in which it fills space and this serves to simplify the visual recognition problem considerably. Matter tends to be clumped into permanent, continuous, compact structures with discrete surfaces that tend to scatter and reflect light. The consequence of this is that things project an occluding contour into optical images and this contour is generally closed. Whilst there are many other sources of 3D information for actions, the occluding contour is a powerful indicator of the shape of something.

How can we use different 2D line shape measurements for the interpretation of 3D surface shape? A single isolated thing will give rise to one or more closed occluding contours, some of which may have branches extending out and then terminating. For each closed contour we can define an inside and an outside as a reference direction for measuring its shape. In a more typical scene with many things occluding each other, there are still one or more closed occluding contours, but for each it is necessary to decide whether the contour in question belongs in whole or in part to the surface itself or to the surface in front. If it belongs to the surface in front then it should not be used to describe the surface behind.

Generally, an occluding contour causes a luminance change in the image because the two surfaces either side are likely to have different reflectances or illuminations. This means that, at least in an ideal world, we could define an occluding contour as being the locus of all points where luminance changes abruptly. For the moment, I shall assume that this definition is acceptable and propose that we can take the optical image and replace it by a new image which has a value of 1 wherever there is an occluding contour, and a value of 0 elsewhere. How do we use this edge map to create the primal sketch?

Finally, we can consider the area of the image enclosed by the occluding contour boundary. This has a spectral character that is a consequence of the reflectance properties of the surface and the spectral nature of the illuminant: it is partly characteristic of the surface. The area has an intensity distribution that is a consequence of the shape of the surface variations in its reflectance and the direction and distance of the illuminant. This is also, therefore, partly characteristic of the surface.

Let us start with the corners of lines or edges as in L junctions. If we suppose that the lines themselves could indicate occluding contours, then the L must arise because of a vertex or a sharp crease in the occluding surface. A line orientation discontinuity in an occluding contour must be projected from a surface orientation discontinuity. The two lines meeting at a corner are very likely to be projected from two different smooth facets of the surface and it is most sensible to segment the line representation at such points. Turning to T junctions, the two lines, if they correspond to occluding contours, are most likely to belong to different, unconnected occluding contours, and thus to two different surfaces. Alternatively they could arise when a surface occludes itself. The sensible course under such circumstances is to treat the figure as two lines, one continuous across the junction and one terminating at the junction, instead of treating it as three lines meeting at a point.

The curvature of an occluding contour is related to the shape of the body from which it is derived. It has been shown that where an occluding contour is concave, the surface must have negative Gaussian curvature (i.e. it is saddle shaped). Where an occluding contour is convex, the surface must have positive Gaussian curvature (i.e. it is ovoid in shape). It is obvious that measurements of the contour curvature can be very informative in respect of the underlying 3D shape of the surface.

Bulges in an occluding contour also bear a relationship to the 3D shape of the surface. There are two points to make. Firstly, the same geometric properties hold as before, so that where a bulge actually changes the sign of contour curvature, the sign of the surface Gaussian curvature is also changed. Moreover, the magnitude of surface curvature is monotonically related to the magnitude of contour curvature, and so bulges in the contour correspond to knobs or flatter sections of the surface. The second point is that the distribution of bulges along a contour gives a good indication of how rough or smooth the surface itself is. This is obviously important for picking the surface-object up.

Texture and Spatial Scale

Whilst reading this, you will have looked up from a page covered in high contrast edges and lines and looked around to see many textured surfaces such as carpets, woodgrain, wallpaper. As I write this, I can look up and see mountainsides that are dusted with snow. The problem with all of these textures is that the luminance changes arising from them are not easily distinguished in the image from those arising from occluding contours. Textures are all pervasive and exist in many different domains. A flat surface can have a texture pattern; a surface itself can be textured and rough; an occluding contour can be jagged and serrated. There are even things that are best regarded as volumetric textures, such as trees.

What are textures? Texture is a word with an ordinary colloquial meaning which is rather tactile; it is concerned with the way things feel. To apply it to vision, one might perhaps be discussing the visual correlates of the way things feel. If the visual texture of the surface of an object is a guide to the way it would feel, it is also a guide to the way in which the surface will react to forces, for instance those generated by gripping. A rough textured surface may provide a good grip so long as the texturing has a typical sizing that is of the same order of magnitude as the device that is gripping; e.g. fingers or walking boots. This leads us to another view of texture as detail at fine scales relative to the action being undertaken. It is important to know something about the texture because it can affect the success of our proposed action. However, all we need to know is the typical statistical character of the texture. The degree of friction offered by a rough surface depends greatly on how rough it is, how spiky, whether it is anisotropic, but depends very little on the exact details. A statistical description will provide nearly all the most useful information.

If this is the computational value of textures, then it is easier to understand how texture in an image should be treated. Suppose that our image is made up of a mosaic of partly overlapping regions, each projecting from a distinct surface with its own pattern of texture. These regions have boundaries which can be treated in exactly the manner that I outlined in the previous section. Moreover, the image statistics within each region are a consequence of the surface texture, shape and the illumination, and are thus partly characteristic of the surface.

Texture patterns on a surface are usually distributed homogeneously so that their statistics are the same at all regions on the surface. There are many statistics which are potentially useful, particularly the means and standard deviations of the distributions of luminances and the spatial correlations of luminance at different spatial distances and directions. For example, given a set of particular points $x_i y_i$ with a particular luminance, what is the distribution of luminance values for the set of points at $x_i + \Delta x$, $y_i + \Delta y$, where x and y are specific increments. If, for some values of these increments the distributions of luminances or contrasts are different from those for the pattern as a whole, then the texture has a spatial structure. These are the second-order statistics.

When the surface is projected onto a two-dimensional image, then the texture pattern statistics are no longer uniform. Those parts of the surface that are furthest away from the image are isotropically shrunk in all their spatial dimensions. The patterns and their spacings are all decreased in every direction by the same amount. Where the surface normal is oriented away from the observer the spatial dimensions of the pattern are decreased, but only in the direction of the tilt. Where the surface's principal curvatures change, some bending and twisting of the pattern elements occurs. This will be particularly noticeable if they are elongated.

It will be very useful for any texture characterization to record how the texture is varying over the surface. This allows some degree of interpretation of the three-dimensional shape of the surface.

How can texture statistics be computed? A mean is calculated by summing all the values and dividing by the number of values. The only difficulty in using this lies in knowing the size of area that should be used, and this has already been provided by the scale definition of texture. For each point in the image we calculate the local mean centred at that point by adding all the values within a distance that is given by the scale of the task. This gives a new image which has been obtained from the original but has much of the irrelevant detail removed and replaced by its mean value. For a variety of reasons, both numerical and computational, it is advantageous to weight the values nearer the centre more than those that are further away from that point. A Gaussian weighting function is most suitable. When this is done for a linear quantity like the mean, the operation is convolution and is variously known as smoothing or filtering. There is an analogous operation to calculate the local standard deviation, although this is not linear and cannot be accomplished by convolution.

PSYCHOPHYSICS

The human observer is a programmable black box. One can program or instruct the box to make a particular mapping between an input pattern, the visual stimulus, and a set of discrete output responses. Provided that the input pattern can be well specified and the output responses recorded, then it is feasible to discover what mappings are possible. Whilst this has some qualitative benefit, one usually learns little by enquiring what mappings are possible. It is preferable to suppose that the black box registers and processes the stimulus with some random, variable error and perhaps some systematic, constant error. These two error components then specify the tolerance with which the box has been constructed. The most useful knowledge about human vision is obtained by measuring how the tolerance varies with continuous changes in the input stimulus. I shall give some examples below, but first let me explain the general logic.

Figure 2 shows a mapping function from the physical measure of a stimulus to some internal measure of activity in the black box. The mapping is subject to some uncertainty, as suggested in the figure, so that any one point on the continuum of physical measure gives rise to a distribution of possible internal measures that have

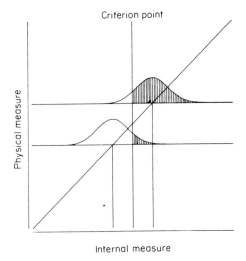

Figure 2. An illustration of the logic behind psychophysical technique. A fixed physical measure gives rise to a probability density function on the associated internal measure. This is compared with a criterion. The hatched area is the probability of a positive response.

a, say, Gaussian probability density function. We have specified a criterion point on the internal scale to partition the continuum into two responses, say, plus and minus.

Suppose that a stimulus A is presented to the black box. The probability of various internal measures is shown in the figure, and the probability that a measure greater than the criterion is the area of the shaded portion. If a greater physical measure, B, is presented, then this area is larger, and a positive response more probable. It can be seen that the function relating the probability of a positive response to the physical measure is then the cumulative Gaussian function, shown in Figure 3.

Figure 3, a plot of probability of positive response as a function of physical measure, is what is typically obtained in a psychophysical experiment. This function can be characterized by two parameters: its location and its spread, which correspond to the constant and variable errors of the black box, on the one hand, and the mean and standard deviation of the uncertainty distributions in Figure 2, on the other.

Initial Image Filtering Stages

In common with most machine vision systems, the initial processes in human vision are approximated well by convolutions between the image and a range of filters (e.g. Wilson & Bergen, 1979; Watson, 1983). Unlike most vision systems, in human vision the filters have various sizes and may be elongated to give a range of orientation selectivities. There may be a number of non-linearities, but none of these are essential non-linearities (Legge & Kersten, 1983).

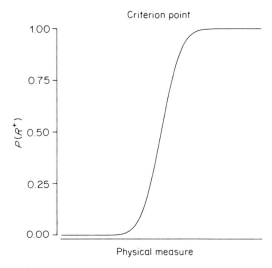

Figure 3.   A psychometric function resulting from the process described in Figure 2.

Combining the outputs of filters of different sizes is a problem that has been investigated a little. In practice, it is often possible to use only one spatial scale for analysing the restricted set of images that robotics applications are interested in. As a result there is little experience in this problem to date. Ideally any combination process should meet these two criteria:

1. Where any filter response has evidence for a line or edge, this must be preserved in the combination.
2. Where more than one filter response has evidence for the same line or edge, then the combination should only preserve one item of evidence.

The original idea came from Marr & Hildreth (1980), who suggested that where evidence for an edge was found in different filters but at the same place in the image, then all the filters would be responding to the same physical feature. The problem with this approach is that the edges found by different filters are rarely at exactly the same place in the image. Where they are not it is often very unclear how many physical features there are and where those features might be.

A similar approach has been proposed by Canny (1983). His proposal was that the finest scale be taken first; its output should be characterized in terms of edges and lines; and then the response of the next finest scale could be predicted. This is compared with the actual response at that scale, and the edge/line characterization revised to take any mismatch into account. This cycle is repeated until all the required spatial scales have been examined.

Each of these techniques analyses the output of each filter separately. An alternative idea, derived from studies of human vision, has been suggested by Watt & Morgan (1985). They proposed that the filter outputs could be combined before any analysis takes place. In particular they suggested that the filter outputs should

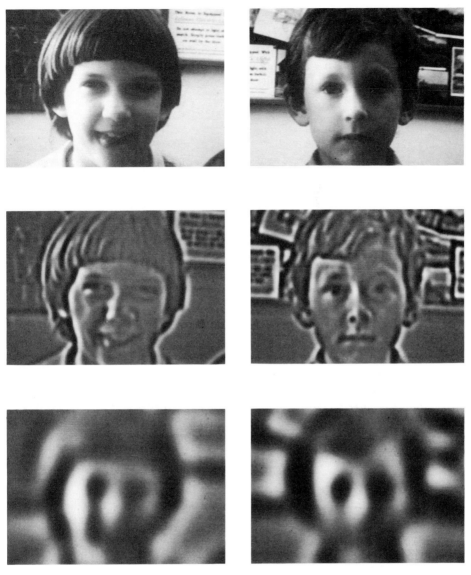

Figure 4. Two images and fine- and coarse-scale-filtered (Laplacian and Gaussian) versions.

just be added together wherever they have the same sign. The result is two signals: one with all the various positive responses added together; one with all the various negative responses added together.

Where filters have the same sign of response, they are likely to be providing evidence concerning the same physical feature. Adding the responses together at these places satisfies criterion 2 by reducing the evidence to one item. However, where the filters have opposite signs of response, they are most likely to be responding to different physical features, and so by keeping their responses separate at such points, criterion 1 is implemented.

This operation, which is called MIRAGE by its inventors, can be written down very simply. Suppose that we have an image $I(x, y)$, and a set of filters $\nabla^2 G(s)$, for a range of s. Then we have a set of filter responses $R(x, y, s)$:

$$R(x, y, s) = I(x, y)*\nabla^2 G(s).$$

We can introduce an intermediate set of paired responses, $R^+(x, y, s)$ and $R^-(x, y, s)$ to hold all the positive response values and the negative response values respectively:

$$R^+(x, y, s) = \begin{cases} R(x, y, s) & \text{if } R(x, y, s) > 0 \\ 0 & \text{otherwise} \end{cases}$$

and

$$R^-(x, y, s) = \begin{cases} R(x, y, s) & \text{if } R(x, y, s) < 0 \\ 0 & \text{otherwise.} \end{cases}$$

Finally, for each (x, y) point we add all the values of R^+ corresponding to different space constants s, to make a new signal $T^+(x, y)$, which is not now a function of s:

$$T^+(x, y) = \sum_s R^+(x, y, s)$$

and similarly:

$$T^-(x, y) = \sum_s R^-(x, y, s).$$

The MIRAGE operation can be regarded as a compound second-derivative filter that is freed from some of the spatial scale restrictions that simple filters possess.

The response of MIRAGE to texture variations is interesting. Figure 6 shows a one-dimensional slice through a texture and the effects of the MIRAGE operation. The response of MIRAGE contains the response of the larger filters that are only sensitive to the overall structure, but it also contains the response of the smaller filters to the texture elements.

Edges, Lines or Regions

Following a widely used practice, the initial convolution stages of image processing are followed by the identification of edge points and the creation of an edge map. The general assumption that is made here is that images contain mostly step edges and impulse function lines that are distorted by various artefacts. It is often further assumed that the appropriate way to treat lines is as two edges back-to-back. The

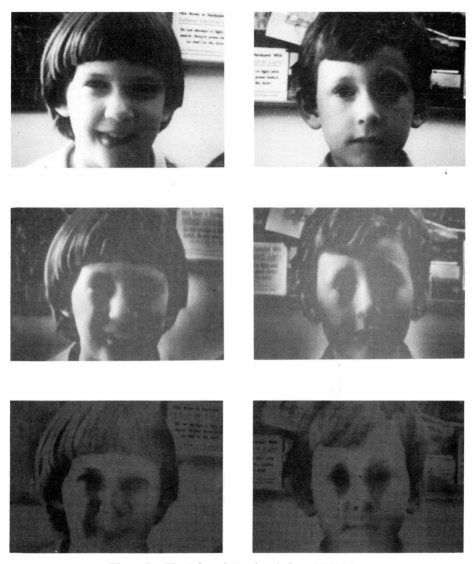

Figure 5. The T^+ and T^- signals from MIRAGE.

usual technique is to identify the location of zero-crossings, if second-derivative filters have been used (e.g. Marr & Hildreth, 1980), or the location of peaks, if first-derivative filters have been used (e.g. Canny, 1983). It was natural to investigate whether human vision uses either of these two or some other alternative. Westheimer & McKee (1977) suggested that the visual system actually locates the intensity centroid of line-like stimuli. The centroid is given by

$$\frac{\int I(x)x\,dx}{\int x\,dx}$$

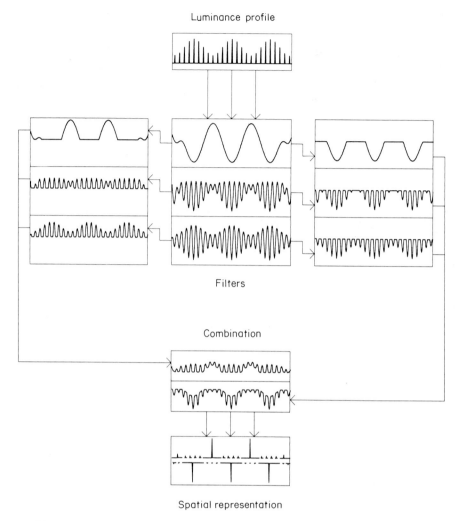

Figure 6.   A schematic illustration of MIRAGE working on a texture stimulus.

where $I(x)$ is the image and x is taken over some finite region across the line. It is not clear how this suggestion could be extended to a luminance edge.

Watt & Morgan (1983a) showed that the centroid of these line-like stimuli was indistinguishable from the mid-point between the two zero-crossings in the second derivative of the image after the optics of the eye were taken account of. However, Watt & Morgan (1983b) then proceeded to show that the zero-crossing could not account for the ability of observers to compare the blurs of two edges, but that peaks or centroids of the zero-bounded regions of response in the second derivative (mildly smoothed) could account for the data. The next stage was to demonstrate that the way in which edge localization accuracy varied with edge blur and edge

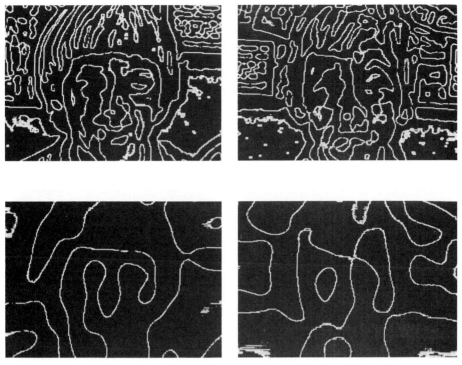

Figure 7. Zero-crossings at fine and coarse spatial scales from the images in Figure 4. Some of these correspond, approximately, to edges.

contrast was most consistent with the centroids of the zero-bounded regions of response (Watt & Morgan, 1984).

There are two difficulties that arise from this suggestion, however. The first is that centroids will rarely correspond to either edges or lines directly. Watt & Morgan (1985) proposed that a set of rules be used to determine whether an edge or line caused the response. Essentially, these rules are based on the symmetry or antisymmetry of the situation (lines are symmetric, edges are antisymmetric). After these rules have been used, the edge or line location can be computed from the centroids.

The second difficulty with centroids is a conceptual problem. In one dimension, the centroids can be easily defined and, more importantly, can be easily used to identify and localize edges and lines. In two dimensions, the centroid can still be defined, but for a zero-bounded region of response there is only one centroid, a point, no matter how elongated the region is. The centroid is not useful in two dimensions as an edge finder. There are two possible ways of reconciling this problem. On the one hand, there are several alternative edge finders that would behave rather like the centroid. A variant on the medial axis transform, weighted by local response, for example, would meet this requirement.

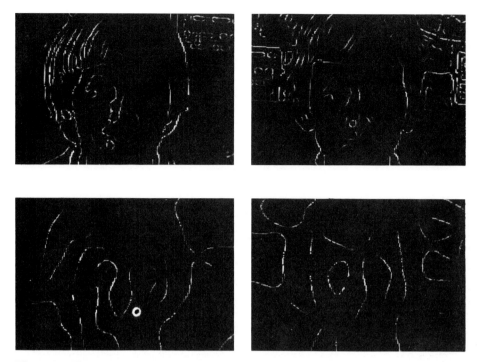

Figure 8.   The same zero-crossings as Figure 7, but with intensity coding zero-crossing slope to make the more significant ones more conspicuous.

The alternative is to abandon the idea that edge finding is an essential function of the primal sketch. Each zero-bounded island of response can be regarded as a region of the image that is consistent at some spatial scale. A perfectly good description of the image can then be created by characterizing these regions. Recent work in my laboratory at Stirling has shown that such a technique is adequate for creating descriptions of images of faces that allow neural networks to discriminate between the owners of the faces. The benefits of this approach are severalfold. Zero-crossings and peaks are prone to noise, which although not a serious problem in digital machinery would be a difficulty with analogue machinery such as neurons. The edge finding approach is only as valid as its initial assumptions that edges and lines in images are the predominant significant features and are all just distorted versions of the impulse and step functions. It is far from clear how valid these assumptions would be for images of natural scenes. Finally, the regions approach can easily be generalized to colour and texture because the boundaries of regions, which in these cases are poorly defined, are not critical to the description that is produced.

2D Shape

I now turn to show psychophysical examinations of how our human visual system analyses the curvature of lines. A straightforward starting point is to consider the

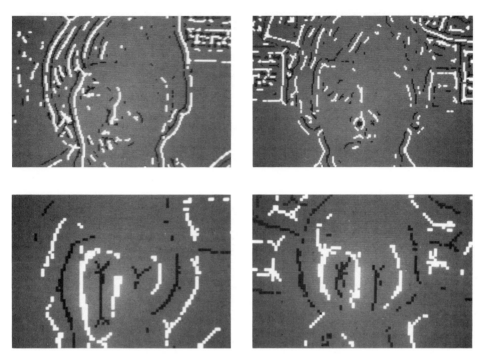

Figure 9. Peaks (ridges) and troughs (valleys) in the fine- and coarse-scale images of Figure 4.

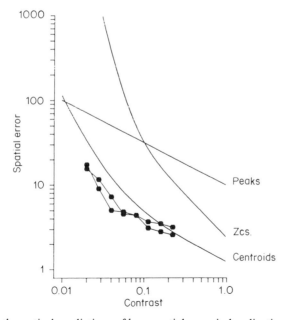

Figure 10. The theoretical predictions of how spatial error in localization varies with edge contrast plus some typical data from Watt & Morgan (1984).

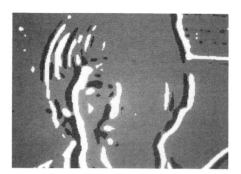

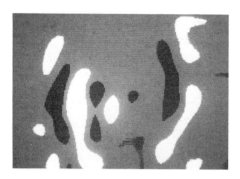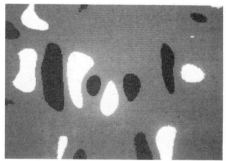

Figure 11.   For two spatial scales taken from Figure 4, the blobs are shown. It is interesting that, for these images at least, the blobs all have relatively simple shapes. Experiments have shown that images such as the lower pair have sufficient information for discrimination between two sets of face images.

detection of non-collinearity in lines. How sensitive are we to departures from straightness in a line, how does it depend on the way in which a line is bent, and how is it related to the information available in the retinal response to the line?

This question was exhaustively examined by Watt *et al.* (1987). Suppose that we show a subject two lines, one absolutely straight, and one that has a slight wiggle in it, like in Figure 14. We can ask the subject to report which is the curved line and thence collect a psychometric function. The probability of reporting "left stimulus" as a function of the amplitude of the wiggle cue that is obtained is shown in Figure 15. Clearly we are sensitive to the presence of the cue, and are quite reliable even for wiggles as small as a few arc seconds. The general finding about detecting bulges can be stated as a simple rule. The area of the bulge should exceed some critical quantity (0.3 square arc minutes). One of the basic findings that led to this conclusion was that as the space constant of the bulge (its length along the line) is increased, sensitivity also increases in direct proportion (Watt *et al.*, 1987). Changes in sensitivity were also found for changes in the shape of the bulge, according to the same rule. It certainly is not the case that the bulge should reach some critical amplitude.

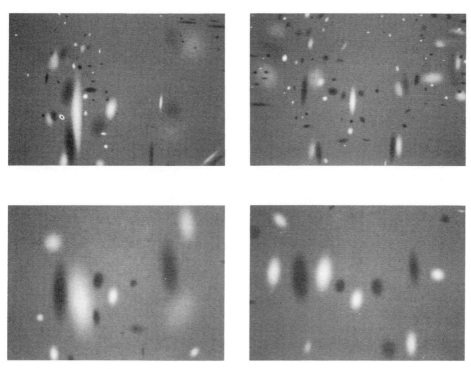

Figure 12. These show synthetic blobs (elongated Gaussians) derived from symbolic descriptions of the actual blobs in Figure 11. Although virtually unrecognizable because of the way in which the images have been manipulated, the important point is that much useful structure has been encapsulated.

The probable reason for this is that the area of the bulge depends on the bulge being a systematic departure from collinearity. As Figure 16 shows, the length of the bulge is important in determining whether the area or amplitude of the bulge is the most appropriate cue. From the figure it can be seen that for all bulges except the very smallest in length, the area is a better, more sensitive, measure. This is because it reflects the positive serial correlations in the signal.

Next we can turn to line curvature itself. Rather little is known about how contour information is integrated to estimate curvature. Wilson (1986) has shown that the outputs of spatial filters can be used to obtain the necessary high sensitivities and has suggested an orientation domain mechanism. Watt & Andrews (1982) and Watt (1984) found that the integration of curvature information conforms to two rules. Firstly, precision improves with the second power of the length of the line. This is what would be expected of a mechanism that was measuring curvature by some form of quadratic regression procedure rather than some form of orientational mechanism. Watt & Andrews (1982) were able to support this finding further by measuring the relative efficiencies of curvature judgements and orientation judgements. Curvature judgements were the more

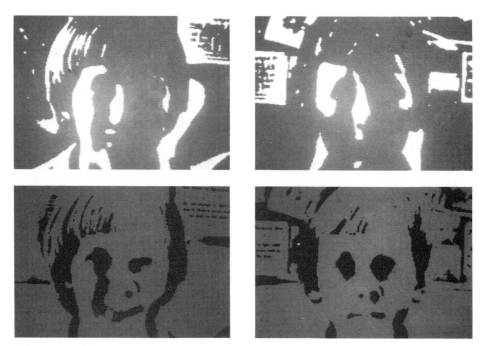

Figure 13. These show the blobs from the MIRAGE-processed images of Figure 5. Note how a wide range of spatial scales has been captured by the MIRAGE process and yet the blob shapes and structures remain relatively simple.

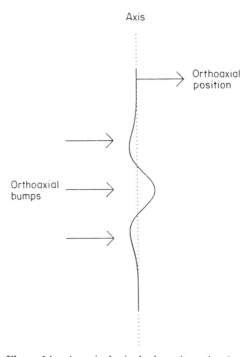

Figure 14. A typical wiggle detection stimulus.

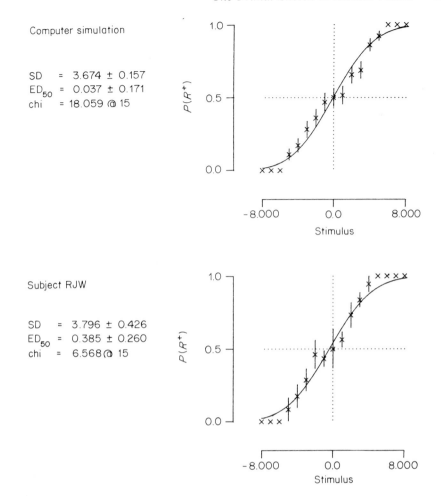

Computer simulation

SD   = 3.674 ± 0.157
ED_{50} = 0.037 ± 0.171
chi   = 18.059 @ 15

Subject RJW

SD   = 3.796 ± 0.426
ED_{50} = 0.385 ± 0.260
chi   = 6.568 @ 15

Figure 15. Psychometric functions for the detection of a wiggle as in Figure 14. The computer simulation is based on an area cue as described in the text and matches the data well. Taken from Watt *et al.* (1987).

efficient, leading to the conclusion that they cannot be based on orientation. Secondly, the integration process is restricted to a fixed range of orientations of 40°. Little else is known about the measurement of line curvature by the human visual system. In general, the human visual system is very sensitive to the curvature of lines, being able to reliably discriminate spatial differences of a few arc seconds. This is impressive for a system which has an effective pixel size of a few tens of arc seconds. However, in order to achieve this precision, the visual system integrates curvature information along a considerable length of line.

The manner in which sensitivity to line curvature improves with the length of the line is an important clue about the mechanism involved. It provides a test between two plausible models. The first is a general model-fitting approach, where one seeks to find the best-fitting one-parameter curve to the set of points. The parameter could

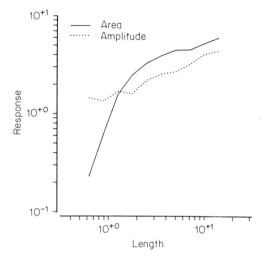

Figure 16. The size of area and amplitude cues for a wiggle stimulus, as a function of its length (relative to a spatial sampling distance or noise bandwidth). Notice the superiority of area cues.

be the quadratic term in an orthogonal polynomial regression, or it could be the radius of a circular arc. In either case, the general principle is to find a value of the parameter that minimizes the mean squared deviation. The second method is to take a line second derivative and average this. Although this sounds very similar to the model-fitting technique it is statistically very different, not least because computing the line second derivative relies on determining an order for the samples and then introduces high serial correlations into the noise. Figure 19 shows the effect of line length of these two alternatives. It is clear that the model-fitting approach gives the inverse square law that was measured psychophysically.

Finally, we turn to consider corners. From both pragmatic and computational points of view it is natural to expect that this high-efficiency integration of line curvature might be blocked at contour corners and intersections. That it indeed can, by several different image features such as corners and intersections or a gap in the line, has been established (Watt, 1985, 1986; Watt & Campbell, 1985). The basic finding in these studies is that the presence of one of these segmentation

Figure 17. A curvature discrimination stimulus.

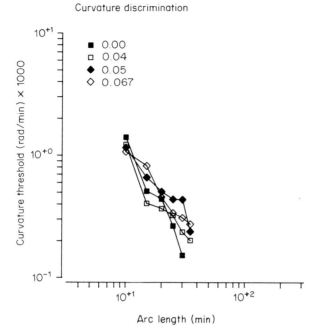

Figure 18. The effects of arc length on curvature discrimination thresholds. The parameters are arc curvatures. The functions all lie close to an inverse square relationship as described in the text. The data are taken from Watt & Andrews (1982).

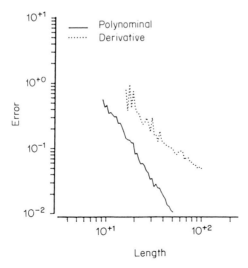

Figure 19. The predicted variations in curvature error or threshold as a function of arc length. The polynomial model provides a close fit to the psychophysical data from Figure 18.

features has the same effect as a complete break in the target at the same place. Breaking a line into several pieces forces the visual system to assess the curvature of each independently and therefore allows considerably less scope for information integration along the line. The same appears to be true of corners, intersections, etc. This result holds quite generally true, irrespective of where the segmentation features are placed. In the same studies it was found that smooth corners and curvature do not segment lines. Segmentation only occurs where there are discontinuities in lines or their first derivative. Interestingly, it does not occur for the continuous cross-line in a T junction, but does for both lines in an X junction.

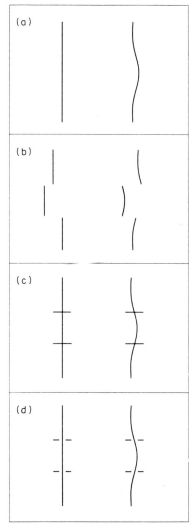

Figure 20.   Some sample stimuli from the corners experiment. The (b) stimuli precipitate segmentation, as do the (c) stimuli but not (d).

The mechanism whereby these features are located remains unknown, although there are at least three possibilities.

The first is to seek distinct local summits and/or pits in the response of isotropic second-derivative filters. This could be accomplished by, for example, taking the second derivative of the filter output. The second technique for finding corners involves the use of a range of differently oriented filters. Along a smooth continuous contour, the distribution of response values across orientations will be narrower than it is at luminance corners. We can construct a kind of orientation map in three dimensions: two for spatial position and a third dimension for orientation. At each point in the image the response of a range of differently oriented filters is calculated. At a corner this distribution may be actually bimodal, although it is more likely just to be fairly broad. The advantage of this technique is that the histogram of orientations produced at the corner is, in its own right, a characterization of the corner.

The third technique is essentially analytic. An edge map is created with each pixel in the map set to true or false depending on the presence or absence of a luminance feature that could be due to an edge or line in the image. This edge map can then be converted into a two-dimensional function recording the local edge orientation at each pixel where there actually is an edge. This would be obtained from the edge map by analysis of neighbouring edge points. The orientation of closed contours can be extracted from such maps as a one-dimensional bounded function of position along the contour. If such functions plot orientation as a function of line position, then a corner corresponds to a discontinuity. Of course,

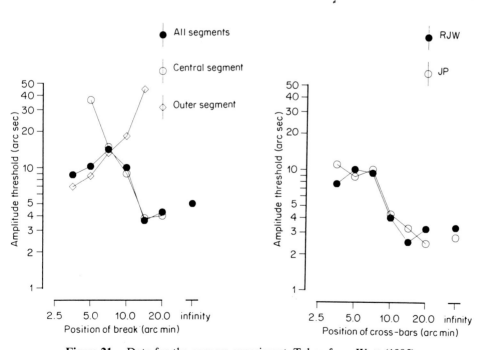

Figure 21.   Data for the corners experiment. Taken from Watt (1985).

where contours are not closed or intersect or overlap, slightly different techniques will be required.

Texture

There has been a great deal of psychophysical research but much of it has been phenomenally rather than computationally planned. This makes it very difficult to interpret. Moreover much of the research has involved relatively regularly spaced repeated binary images of simple shapes such as X, T, L and the regular spacing plus the lack of variation between the elements make for a degenerate texture.

The simplest account of texture discrimination results is that offered by Julesz (1981) who has hypothesized that two texture patterns may be rapidly distinguished if they differ in their first- or second-order moments, or if they contain different densities of critical features such as line ends, corners and intersections.

Geometry and Spatial Metrics

The human visual system has many sources of geometric distortion: imperfect optics; hemispherical retina; relatively scrambled connections in the optic nerve; and many others. These distortions can be compensated for by the use of error-correcting metrics or codes (cf. Andrews, 1964).

An error-correcting code is one which utilizes a presumed fixed statistical distribution of input values to correct for drifts in its output. For instance, Andrews cites the example of line curvature. On average, over the image and over time at any one place in the image, the mean contour curvature can be expected to be zero. If curvature is coded with respect to the mean value that is actually found, then any distortions will be corrected. This is generally reliable but will obviously fail if the visual diet is indeed biased. An example of this has been studied by Craven & Watt (1989). Figure 22 shows a well-documented visual illusion where empty spaces

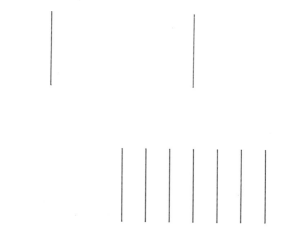

Figure 22.   The Oppel–Kundt illusion. The two intervals are physically the same length, but the empty one appears narrower in width than the filled one.

appear narrower than filled spaces. The essential argument of Craven and Watt is that if distance is computed on the presumption of an average contour density, then indeed empty spaces will be measured as narrower than they really are. The question of what in an ordinary image would correspond to contour density has not been fully answered, but Craven and Watt showed that zero-crossing numbers within a range of spatial scales are adequate and do account quantitatively for the illusion.

The illusion makes the point clear that a consequence of using error-correcting codes can be a non-Euclidean representation of retinal image. If Euclidean geometry is a constraint, then an iterative relaxation type of process is required to find a minimum adjustment to the various measurements. Iteration is inherently time consuming, which leads to a consideration of the dynamics of the primal sketch.

Dynamics

Recent experiments (Watt, 1987a) have shown that for some tasks the visual system scans, over a period of at least 1000 ms, from a spatial scale with a standard deviation of approximately 2 arc degrees down to a scale of approximately 1 arc minute. The experiments all involved judgements of simple attributes of single isolated lines, such as orientation, length or curvature. Take the orientation case as an example of the logic employed. Before spatial filtering, a vertical line (length L and negligible width) has a vertical luminance dispersion of standard deviation:

$$\sigma_v = \frac{L}{2\sqrt{3}}$$

and a horizontal dispersion of standard deviation:

$$\sigma_h = 0.$$

Filtering at a spatial scale of standard deviation s, leads to a more dispersed distribution with:

$$\sigma_v = \left(\frac{L^2}{12} + s^2\right)^{1/2}$$

$$\sigma_h = s.$$

In judging the orientation of the line, it is the ratio of these two that will determine the level of performance:

$$\frac{\sigma_v}{\sigma_h} = \frac{1}{s}\left(\frac{L^2}{12} + s^2\right)^{1/2}$$

This factor ranges from 1, when $L = 0$ to infinity when $s = 0$. If sensitivity, dσ, is defined to lie in the range 0 to infinity, then:

$$\mathrm{d}\sigma = \frac{\sigma_{\mathrm{v}} - \sigma_{\mathrm{h}}}{h} = \frac{(L^2/12 + s^2)^{1/2} - s}{s}.$$

This parameter is dependent on both L and s. It follows that s can be estimated by measuring dσ as a function of L. This was done at a variety of different exposure

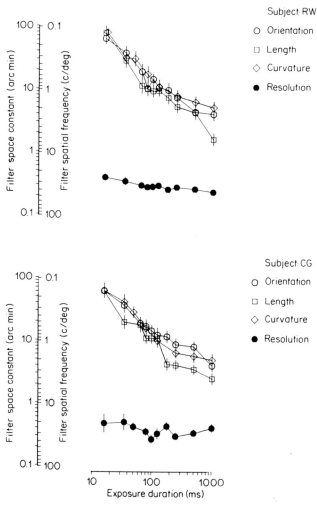

Figure 23.   The effects of exposure duration on the effective spatial scale of the visual system for a range of different tasks. For geometric judgements the human visual system scans from coarse to fine in an inverse function. (From Watt, 1987a, with permission.)

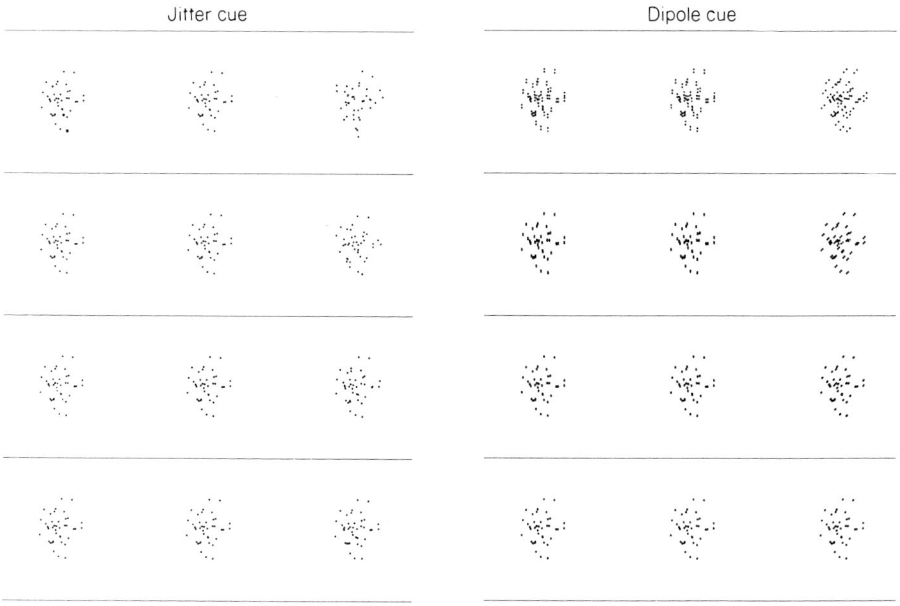

Jitter cue	Dipole cue

Figure 24.   Two types of texture discrimination. On the left each dot is randomly displaced in the odd pattern out. On the right there is a statistically consistent pattern. The latter is discriminated much faster.

durations and it was found that the spatial scale, *s*, is reciprocally related to exposure duration, *t*:

$$s = \frac{k}{t}.$$

Experiments reported in Watt (1987b) have examined the nature of this scanning process. Subjects were asked to examine three patches of randomly distributed dots and to identify the odd one out. The odd one out was distinguished by its statistics or only by its exact geometry. The general finding was that scanning was only found in the latter case, indicating that the computation of geometry is time consuming and involves a coarse-to-fine strategy, whereas texture statistics can be computed rapidly.

That the scanning scale is reciprocal to time is also worthy of comment. To investigate this question I have examined synthentic fractal, one-dimensional functions. Natural images are thought to be fractal, at least over a wide range of spatial scales (Pentland, 1984). It would have been impractical to examine several thousand real images. In some respects it would be more generally interesting to use surface fractals, but there are three comments to make concerning the use of line fractals. First, line fractals are computationally cheaper. Second, the interest lies in the number of intervals found at each scale: it is plausible that dividing a line

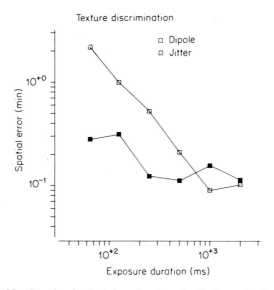

Figure 25.   Psychophysical data for the stimuli shown in Figure 24.

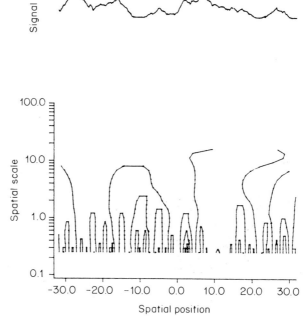

Figure 26.   A Brownian fractal pattern (top) and its scale-space diagram which plots the location of zero-crossings as a function of spatial scale and position.

signal into distances is analogous to dividing a surface signal into areas ("blobs"). Third, so far as human vision is concerned, it remains an open question whether isotropic filters or one-dimensional filters are the more appropriate mode of analysis.

Fractal patterns vary in their fractional dimension, which corresponds to the jaggedness of the pattern. This covaries exactly with the slope of the log power spectrum, and is a measure of the relative energies at large and fine spatial scales.

For each function, a space-scale diagram (cf. Witkin, 1986) was computed (see Figure 26). At each spatial scale the number of zero-crossings was then counted. This is plotted as a function of spatial scale in Figure 27. Note that both axes are logarithmic. The panel in Figure 27 labelled "Change in zero-crossings" is a plot of

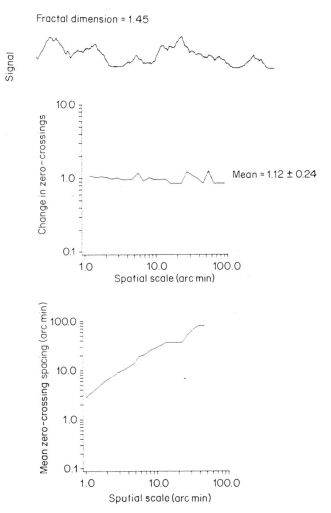

Figure 27. The Brownian fractal pattern (top) and the relationship between spatial scale and number of zero-crossings.

the derivative of the log/log plot of the number of zero-crossings. The mean of this derivative is approximately -1.0, indicating an exponent of -1 in the spatial scale versus number of zero-crossings function. After many such calculations, each with a fresh fractal function, the grand mean exponent was found to be -1.032. Interestingly, the correlation between fractal dimension and exponent was nearly zero at 0.106.

The consequence of this for a visual system which exhibits the scanning behaviour illustrated in Figure 23 is straightforward. As the visual system reduces

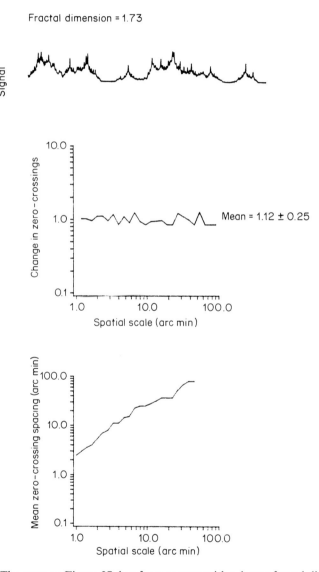

Figure 28.   The same as Figure 27, but for a pattern with a larger fractal dimension.

spatial scale by a factor of two (for example) the number of elements in the representation is approximately doubled. There is not, of course, a particular scale at which all the number of elements suddenly doubles. As scale is increased an adjacent pair of zero-crossings appear: this corresponds to the creation of a new zero-bounded distribution of response. The original has been replaced by three.

Analysis of the space-scale diagram suggests that this tends to occur at a spatial scale that is one third of the scale at which the original distribution itself appeared.

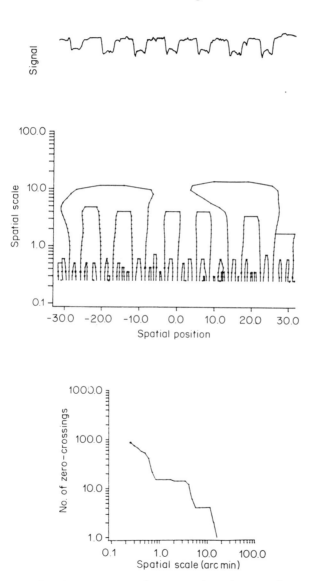

Figure 29. A vertical line through a page of text (top), its scale-space diagram (centre) and the relationship between scale and number of zero-crossings (bottom). The pattern is not like that obtained for fractal patterns.

Since we have the number of zero-crossings inversely proportional to spatial scale, which is itself inversely proportional to time (in the human visual system) we then have the relationship that number of zero-crossings is proportional to time. It then follows that the rate of increase of number of zero-crossings does not alter with time. If the visual system were limited in speed at any one instant by the number of zero-crossings, then the scanning behaviour would not help; if it is limited by the increase in zero-crossings then the scanning behaviour is a sound and rational strategy. This latter is believed to be the case (Watt, 1988).

For an interesting contrast to this behaviour of fractal patterns, Figure 29 shows the one-dimensional luminance pattern down a page of text. Notice that number of zero-crossings alternates between being independent of spatial scale and being a very steep function of spatial scale. The page of text is curious in that the zero-bounded distributions of response all divide at very nearly the same spatial scale.

I conclude that the representation of position is hierarchical, with position for zero-bounded distributions being calculated when they appear and added to an already existent primal sketch representation.

The primal sketch in human vision is dynamic, structured and has memory. This stands in contrast to most machine vision approaches to edge finding.

Figure 30.   This shows how the MIRAGE blobs change as the coarsest scale filters are turned off in the scale scanning process.

SUMMARY

How can we formalize the representation of the image at this level of analysis? There are three basic *primitives*: corners (and intersections, line ends); connections (lines and edges); and regions of texture. We start by defining a *sentence* for each:

⟨CORNER; name; list of attributes; set of relations.⟩
⟨CONNECTIONS; name, list of attributes; set of relations.⟩
⟨REGION; name; list of attributes; set of relations.⟩

Each sentence is enclosed in angle brackets ⟨ and ⟩; these mean that the order of the items within is to be preserved. The first such item is an identifier, to say what type or primitive is being used. The second item is a name, which is unique to each instance of each primitive. The purpose of a name is to allow cross-references, as we shall see shortly. The third item is a list of attributes. This list will have a different form or *grammar* for the three primitives, it is a list because the order of the attributes is important. The final item is a set of relations. This set is an unordered list of, for example, all the connections and regions that are attached to a particular corner. The elements of the set will be the unique names of other sentences.

The description of an image is then a set of such sentences. Notice that, unlike conventional language, the order of the sentences in a description of this type is not important. Even if it were desirable to give the sentences a specific linear order this would be rather arbitrary. Each connection sentence will refer to two corner sentences: which sentence should come first in the order of the description? An ordering according to some anticipated access route used by subsequent processes might be more fruitful. Those sentences obtained at coarser scales would then naturally occupy an earlier place in the description list than those at the finest scales. Corner sentences might precede connection sentences.

The type of grammar that evolves following considerations of this sort is multi-dimensional. The set of corner sentences might be placed in a two-dimensional order according to the topology of their occurrence in the image. This would allow the searching of neighbourhoods more easily than if the sentences were not ordered. A third dimension for ordering according to spatial scale would have like benefits. It is critical to be quite clear that, for the purposes of our understanding of vision, the function of such ordering and dimensionality is not a reconstruction of the image, but a way of making explicit some of its structure.

ACKNOWLEDGEMENT

Some of the work described in this chapter was supported by a grant from the SERC Image Interpretation Initiative.

REFERENCES

Andrews, D. P. (1964). Error-correcting perceptual mechanisms. *Quarterly Journal of Experimental Psychology*, **16**, 104–115.

Canny, J. (1983). Finding edges and lines in images. MIT Artificial Intelligence Laboratory Technical Report, No. 720.

Craven, B. J. & Watt, R. J. (1989). The use of natural image statistics in the estimation of spatial extent. *Spatial Vision*, in press.

Julesz, B. (1981). Textons, the elements of texture perception and their interactions. *Nature*, **290**, 91–97.

Legge, G. E. & Kersten, D. (1983). Light and dark bars: contrast discrimination. *Vision Research*, **23**, 473–483.

Marr, D. C. (1976). Early processing of visual information. *Philosophical Transactions of the Royal Society (London) Series B*, **275**, 483–524.

Marr, D. C. & Hildreth, E. (1980). A theory of edge detection. *Proceedings of the Royal Society (London) Series B*, **207**, 187–217.

Pentland, A. (1984). Fractal-based description of natural scenes. *IEEE Transactions, Pattern Analysis and Machine Intelligence*, **6**, 661–675.

Watson, A. B. (1983). Detection and recognition of simple spatial forms. In O. Braddick and A. Sleigh (Eds) *Physical and Biological Processing of Images*. Springer, Berlin.

Watt, R. J. (1984). Further evidence concerning the analysis of curvature in human foveal vision. *Vision Research*, **24**, 251–253.

Watt, R. J. (1985). Image segmentation at contour intersections in human focal. *Journal of the Optical Society of America*, **A2**, 1200–1204.

Watt, R. J. (1986). Feature-based image segmentation in human vision. *Spatial Vision*, **1**, 243–256.

Watt, R. J. (1987). Scanning from coarse to fine spatial scales in the human visual system after the onset of a stimulus. *Journal of the Optical Society of America*, **4A**, 2006–2021.

Watt, R. J. (1987b). Space-scale analysis in the human primal sketch. *Proc. AVCC*, **87**.

Watt, R. J. (1988). *Visual Processing: Computational, Psychophysical and Cognitive Research*. Erlbaum, Hove.

Watt, R. J. & Andrews, D. P. (1982). Contour curvature analysis: hyperacuities in the discrimination of detailed shape. *Vision Research*, **22**, 449–460.

Watt, R. J., & Campbell, F. W. (1985). Vernier acuity: interactions between length effects and gaps when orientation cues are eliminated. *Spatial Vision*, **1**, 31–38.

Watt, R. J. & Morgan, M. J. (1983a). Mechanisms responsible for the assessment of visual location: theory and evidence. *Vision Research*, **23**, 97–109.

Watt, R. J. & Morgan, M. J. (1983b). The recognition and representation of edge blur: evidence for spatial primitives in human vision. *Vision Research*, **23**, 1457–1477.

Watt, R. J. & Morgan, M. J. (1984). Spatial filters and the localization of luminance changes in human vision. *Vision Research*, **24**, 1387–1397.

Watt, R. J. & Morgan, M. J. (1985). A theory of the primitive spatial code in human vision. *Vision Research*, **25**, 1661–1674.

Watt, R. J., Ward, R. M. & Casco, C. (1987). The detection of deviation from straightness in lines. *Vision Research*, **27**, 1659–1678.

Westheimer, G. & McKee, S. P. (1977). Integration regions for visual hyperacuity. *Vision Research*, **17**, 89–93.

Wilson, H. R. (1986). Discrimination of contour curvature: data and theory. *Journal of the Optical Society of America*, **A3**, 1191–1199.

Wilson, H. R. & Bergen, J. R. (1979). A four mechanism model for threshold spatial vision. *Vision Research*, **19**, 19–32.

Witkin, A. P. (1986). Scale space filtering. In A. Pentland (Ed.) *From Pixels to Predicates*. Ablex, Norwood, NJ.

8 Retrieval of Structure from Rigid and Biological Motion: An Analysis of the Visual Responses of Neurones in the Macaque Temporal Cortex

D. I. Perrett, M. H. Harries, P. J. Benson, A. J. Chitty and A. J. Mistlin

Psychological Laboratory, University of St Andrews, Fife, KY16 9JU, UK

INTRODUCTION

This book concerns the relationship between artificial intelligence and the eye. We describe here the properties of cells in a region of the brain responsive to visual stimuli which is very far removed from the eye. In this region one can get insights into the workings of "natural intelligence" in image processing. That is, one can observe the way a neural system computes the structure of objects from the visual image. We will describe the properties of cells in one region of the temporal association cortex which respond to body movements. We will also describe how different populations of neurones utilize different types of dynamic information to discriminate the structure of the body.

Figure 1 (upper left) illustrates the side of the monkey brain. Visual information arrives at the back of the brain (extreme right) and is highly processed by the time it reaches the area of study in the temporal association cortex. The area of study (dotted box Figure 1, upper right) lies between 6 and 17 mm anterior to the interaural plane in the superior temporal sulcus which runs diagonally from the tip of the temporal lobe (ventral and anterior) to the middle of the parietal lobe (dorsal and posterior). Cells sensitive to body movements within the upper bank of the sulcus (areas PGa and TPO; Seltzer & Pandya, 1978) share several properties with cells responsive to static images of the body and face (Bruce *et al.*, 1981; Perrett *et*

AI and the Eye   Edited by A. Blake and T. Troscianko
© 1990 John Wiley & Sons Ltd.

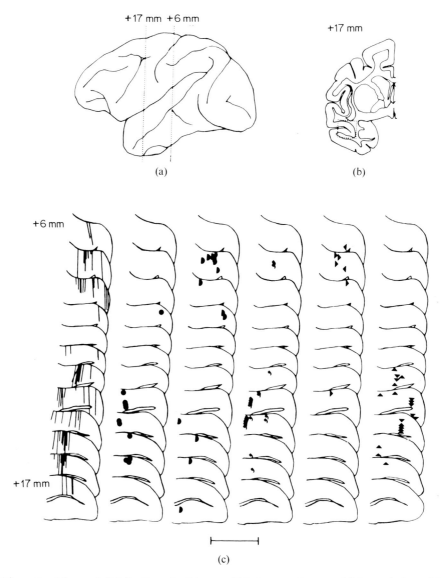

Figure 1.   Clumped distribution of cell types within temporal cortex. (a) Lateral view of the monkey brain with the orientation of sections. (b) Outline of brain structures evident in a coronal section through the left hemisphere at $+17$ mm anterior to the interaural plane. The dotted box bounds the recording area within the superior temporal sulcus. (c) Enlargement of recording area visualized in serial sections (from $+6$ to $+17$ mm anterior). From left to right position of cell recording tracks; location of cells selective for faces (●); profiles (◗); rotation of the head (,); movement left (◀) and right (▶); up (▲) down (▼). Scale bar = 5 mm.

al., 1984, 1985a, b). The major similarity is that both cell types are usually selective for specific views. For example, cells responsive to the static face respond only to the front view of the head and not to other perspective views, e.g. profile. Similarly, some cells selective for body movements will respond to the front view of the moving body and not to the side or back views.

To collect quantitative data from cells which are sensitive to static or dynamic visual information, stimuli are presented from behind a large-aperture shutter for 1 s. Responses are then measured to the first 250 ms of presentation before the monkey has had time to move its eyes. (Responses are actually measured during

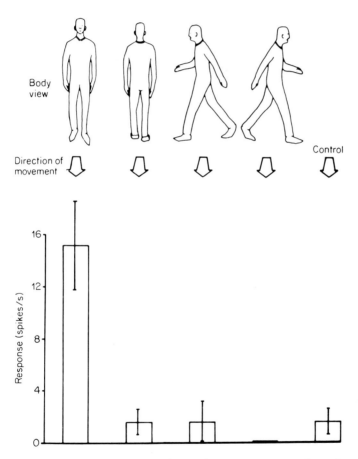

Figure 2. Neuronal sensitivity to views of a moving body. Upper: schematic representations of four body views used for stimuli. Lower: the histogram bars present the mean and standard error of response from randomly ordered trials with one stimulus type. The cell gave a significantly greater ($P < 0.0005$) response to the front view of the body when walking towards the observing monkey compared with the other body views and controls moving towards the monkey. [Overall effect of conditions—$F = 11.81$; df 4, 16; $P < 0.0002$ (number of trials per condition $N = 5$ for each).]

the period 100–350 ms after stimulus onset because cells have a minimum latency to respond of 100 ms.)

Figure 1 indicates the location within the cortex of cells that respond to static images, faces and other stimuli. The study region is visible in the cross-section on the right of the figure and has been enlarged and stacked as a series of sections running from posterior to anterior in the lower columns. Cells responsive to specific static views of the head/body are found in a series of anatomically discrete clumps within the same brain area.

In the same brain region we find many cells sensitive to movements. These cells are unresponsive to static stimuli. Many, but not all, respond only to a particular body movement and are, thus, selective for the form of the stimulus. Figure 1 shows that cells responsive to head rotation and cells responsive to movement left, right, up and down are all found in clumps intermixed with cells responding to static views of the body. Cells selective for body movements can be either selective for the view of the body, responding to one body view independent of its direction of movement, or they can be additionally selective for the direction of movement, responding only to one body view moving in one direction (Figures 2 and 3). Cells selective for direction and view are most commonly found to prefer compatible

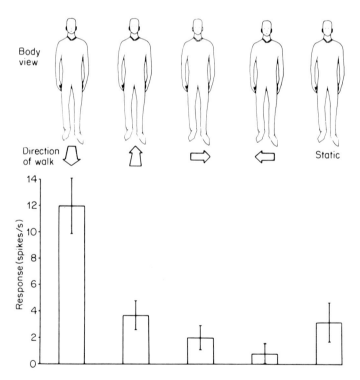

Figure 3. Neuronal sensitivity to direction of body movements. Upper: schematic representations of the front view of a body. Lower: the histogram illustrates a significantly greater ($P < 0.002$) neuronal response to the front view of a body when approaching the observing monkey compared with the same body views when moving away, to the right, to the left and static. [Overall effect of conditions—$N = 11, 12, 6, 5, 10$; $F = 7.06$; $df\ 4, 39$; $P < 0.0005$.]

movements (e.g. left profile view, walking left) but some 30% are selective for incompatible movements (e.g. left profile view, walking right) (Perrett *et al.*, 1985b).

EYE MOVEMENTS

One might ask whether the monkey looks at the different moving stimuli equivalently. A differential response could arise simply because the monkey looks at one stimulus and not at the second. Figure 4 demonstrates, however, that eye

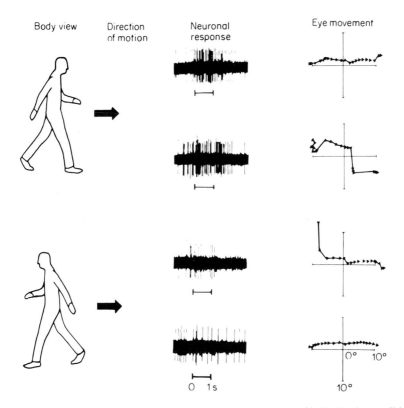

Figure 4. Activity of a cell selectively responsive to the right profile body view walking to the right. Upper left: two trials with an effective stimulus, a human walking to the right with right profile body view. Right: scan path of monkey's eyes during the first 1.0 s of stimulus presentation, (▶) indicates the eye position and direction of movement every 50 ms. Both trials showed strong neuronal discharges despite quite different paths of tracking eye movements. Lower: responses of the same cell on two trials with an ineffective stimulus, walking to the right but with left profile. The difference in neuronal response to the left and right body view cannot be accounted for by eye movement patterns. [This cell responded significantly (*P* < 0.001, Tukey test) more to the right profile (16.5 ± 2.3 mean response ± 1 SE spikes/s) than to left profile moving right (3.2 ± 0.9), right profile static (2.0 ± 0.9), body-sized control objects moving right (6.7 ± 1.4) and spontaneous activity (3.0 ± 0.9); number of trials randomly interleaved per condition, *N* = 6; *F* = 16.5; *df* 4, 20; *P* < 0.0001.] Calibration bar for neuronal response denotes the first 1.0 s of stimulus presentation (stimulus duration 1.0–1.5 s). Calibration axes for eye movements define 10° of visual angle (left, right, up and down) relative to a position directly in front of the monkey's eyes.

movements recorded during the presentation of different stimuli cannot account for the differences in responsiveness, since the monkey tracks both stimuli evoking response and stimuli failing to evoke response. Furthermore, the pattern of saccades and tracking eye movements has little correlation with discharge.

It should be noted that cells selective for the form of the moving body are activated 100–150 ms after stimulus onset. Thus, cells are responsive at a very early latency and at a time before the onset of tracking eye movements. Thus, in one brain area neuronal populations are sensitive to static and dynamic information about the body. Their responses cannot be accounted for in terms of arousal because the cells (or their responses) discriminate stimuli, such as left and right profile, which presumably elicit equivalent emotional responses.

TRANSLATION

We have been studying the different ways in which movement information is utilized by cells to enable them to respond selectively to one view. As a body walks from A to B there is a displacement or translation of the whole body from A to B and there is internal articulation of the limbs relative to one another.

One can arrange for viewing conditions to isolate these two types of movement. The translation component can be isolated simply by displacing a photographic or video image of a body across a screen. With 3D stimuli the same effect can be achieved by a static person being moved on a trolley.

We have tested the effectiveness of translating stimuli for 32 cells which were found to be selective for body view during normal walking movement but unresponsive to static stimuli. Of the cells tested 75% continued to discriminate body view with translating stimuli. Equivalent results were obtained either with the translation of 2D stimuli or with the movement of 3D bodies on a trolley. Thus a large number of cells selective for the form of a walking body are able to detect form from translation. They appear to be able to utilize the translation component in particular directions for either pure translation stimuli or the more natural, complex and uneven movements normally made during ambulation.

Why should such a specific neural system exist for detecting form from translation, since in nature one rarely encounters objects moving with pure translation? One answer to this question is that the system remains form sensitive with either pure translation or with translation combined with irregular movement such as that which occurs with bodies walking normally. The question, we think, reflects the blinkering effect of our own technology. Our familiarity with cameras and photographs makes us well aware that we can see form from static information but it blinds us to the possibility that dynamic visual information might also support perception of form.

The Gestalt psychologists noted that the 'common fate' of image elements moving with the same trajectory was sufficient for these elements to be grouped together (Wertheimer, 1922; Woodworth, 1938). Once grouped together, elements can be perceived as a meaningful form in much the same way as static elements. If a series of random marks is placed on a transparent sheet as a background, and on a second sheet a target is constructed out of the same type of marks then when the sheets are static the target can be completely camouflaged. Yet the gentle translation of one sheet over the second should make the target "pop out". With this stimulus situation there is insufficient information to interpret/discriminate the form of the target at any single moment in time, perceptual understanding of form is only attainable with translation of the foreground relative to the background. Recently, using this type of stimulus, we have been able to demonstrate that some cells sensitive to form from translation continue to discriminate body view even when static cues to form are camouflaged in any single frame.

Julesz (1988) argued that evolution has only recently allowed cortical mechanisms to employ stereopsis to break camouflage, it is quite possible that visual systems have been using common fate to break camouflage for a lot longer since it could have evolved in animals without overlapping binocular vision.

ARTICULATION

A second type of movement information is available for cells to discriminate the form of the body, this is the non-rigid articulation of the body limbs relative to one another. Johansson (1973) termed this type of movement "biological motion". He demonstrated the sufficiency of biological motion for form perception by placing lights on the points of articulation of a human actor. The form of such an actor remains obscure while the person is static or even while they translate, but as they articulate their shape becomes immediately obvious.

Not only is the general shape of the body visible but it is easy with such stimuli to tell which way around the body is facing as it moves relative to the camera (Woolford, Benson & Perrett, unpublished studies; Perrett, Catty & Harries, in preparation). Thus, body view can be discriminated from biological motion.

Biological motion stimuli are important because they offer an opportunity to simplify stimuli and to exert a quantitative control over them. We have used a computer-based animation system to simulate the appearance of a walking person. With such a system it is possible to jumble an array by displacing the limb points at a fixed distance in an arbitrary direction from their normal positions; one can then compare neuronal responses to normal and jumbled arrays. We have used biological motion stimuli manufactured either by placing luminous spots on live actors or by computer-controlled animation displays to examine whether cells can detect body form from articulatory cues alone.

SEPARATE NEURAL CHANNELS FOR COMPUTING FORM FROM TRANSLATION AND ARTICULATION

Figure 5 illustrates data from one cell sensitive to the left profile, walking left. This cell continued to discriminate body form for stimuli translating to the left. Responses to biological motion stimuli, in either dot or stick form (where

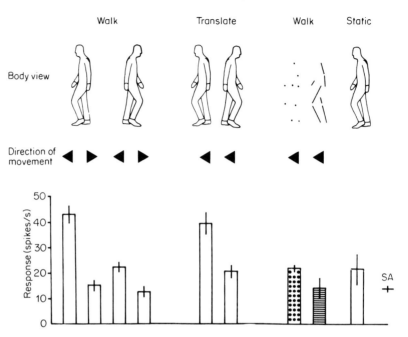

Figure 5.   Upper: schematic representations of right and left profile views of a body walking or translating in the direction given by the arrows seen under normal illumination. The dots represent patches of light-reflecting material which are attached to the points of articulation (e.g. shoulder, elbow, wrist). The stripes represent strips of light-reflecting material which connect points of articulation (e.g. shoulder to elbow). Dot and stripe patterns were viewed under reduced illumination so that no other information about body form was available. Lower: the histogram illustrates that under normal illumination the cell was more responsive to a left profile body view walking or translating to the left (than to other conditions—$P < 0.0001$, each comparison). The cell was unresponsive to the left profile view when information was provided only by means of articulation of the limbs (dot and stick figures) or when a static view was presented. [Overall effect of conditions—$N = 10, 10, 10, 5, 6, 6, 10, 8, 4, 10$; $F = 11.59$; df 9, 69; $P < 0.0001$.]

individual limb articulation points are connected) and to static stimuli, were not significantly greater than spontaneous activity.

We have studied 14 cells (out of 26 tested) which were selective for body form during translation but were unselective for biological motion stimuli. Thus, the neuronal mechanisms for analysing form from rigid translation are dissociable from those responsible for the analysis of non-rigid articulation.

In contrast, Figure 6 illustrates the responses of a cell that, under normal light, is selective to the front view of the body when approaching the observing subject. This cell discriminates both direction and form since it is unresponsive to the back view approaching the observer or to any stimulus retreating. Under low light conditions, with only illuminated dots visible on the surface of an actor, an identical pattern of results is found with the cell again being selective for the front view of the body approaching the observer.

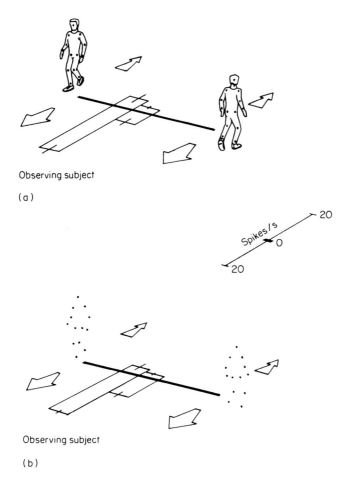

Observing subject

(a)

Observing subject

(b)

Figure 6.   Sensitivity to body view through biological motion. (a) The schematic characters represent a human body who faced towards and away from the monkey under normal lighting conditions. The arrows indicate the direction the body moved. The cell's response to each combination of body view and direction of motion is represented as a histogram bar ($\pm$ 1 SE). The length of each bar is proportional to the mean response. The response to a body-sized control object translating towards the monkey was 6.2 $\pm$ 1.5 spikes/s and the spontaneous activity (SA) of the cell was 1.4 $\pm$ 0.5 spikes/s (not illustrated). The cell fired at a significantly ($P < 0.05$) greater rate when the body both faced and walked towards the monkey than in any of the other conditions (including a control object moving towards the monkey) or SA. [Overall effect of conditions—$N = 5$; $F = 11.12$, df 5, 20; $P < 0.0001$.] (b) The dots represent the pattern of luminous patch lights on the actor that was seen by the monkey under reduced lighting conditions. The response to a body-sized display of dots moving towards the monkey was 4.5 $\pm$ 0.8 spikes/s. Again, the response to the approaching front view of the body was significantly ($P < 0.01$) greater than the responses to the other conditions [$N = 15$; $F = 59.21$; df 5, 70; $P < 0.0001$].

There are several visual cues which change between the back and front views of the body approaching the observer, the most obvious being the details of the face. Indeed, many of the cells sensitive to body form through translation utilize the pattern cues present in the face, but cells discriminating body view with biological motion stimuli cannot be relying on the pattern of the face as the head is represented only as a single dot. It is more likely that these cells are using the patterns of articulation and occlusions of marker points. For the front view, the knee leads the hip and foot markers as the body walks towards the observer. For the back view of the body walking towards the observer, the knee lags behind the hip and foot markers and is often occluded from sight when the leg is flexed.

In all, we have studied 63 cells sensitive to the whole or part of the body moving with biological motion stimuli. Of these 30% continued to discriminate form since they were selective for one body view compared with either a second view or control arrays of moving dots. These cells were, thus, able to compute structure on the basis of non-rigid articulations alone.

The mechanisms for analysing the two types of motion (articulation and translation) are, thus, dissociable since it is possible to find cells which are selective for one type but not for the other. Within the temporal cortex there is, however, a considerable interaction and convergence of information-processing streams, and while there is evidence for a separation between two types of movement there is also evidence for convergence of analysed structure. Six cells have been found to be selective for form using either translation or articulation. These cells discriminated body forms for both biological motion and pure translation stimuli when these were tested separately.

CONVERGENCE OF STATIC AND DYNAMIC CHANNELS OF PROCESSING

While the physiological recordings reveal the existence of different populations of cells processing static and two types of dynamic information, there is evidence for a convergence or cross-communication between channels of processing (Zeki & Ship, 1988).

The upper half of Figure 7 illustrates the responses for one cell that was selective for the back view of a static body. In the lower half of the figure, testing with biological motion stimuli revealed that this cell is again selective for the back view of the body while it is retreating from the observer. This cell, then, prefers the back view from either static or biological motion information.

Research in the early stages of visual processing has increasingly emphasized the segmentation of systems which process static and dynamic channels of information. The present data indicate that dynamic visual information processing can also be separated into different channels (that of translation and articulation), but more importantly the data indicate that information about form or structure computed by the separate analyses of early vision converge on to the same neuronal mechanisms within the temporal association cortex.

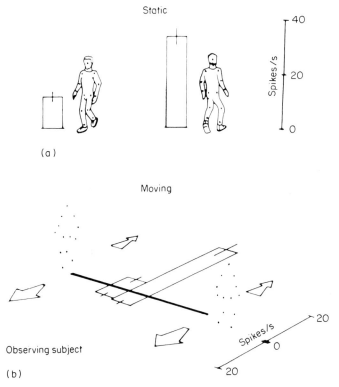

Figure 7. Integration of static and dynamic information. Conventions for stimulus representations and histograms illustrating responses are as in Figure 6. (a) Responses to static stimuli. Under normal lighting conditions the cell's response to the rear view was significantly ($P < 0.01$) greater than to the front view or to SA (SA = 12.4 ± 4.2 spikes/s) [$N = 10, 10, 12$; $F = 16.74$; $df\ 2, 29$; $P < 0.0001$]. (b) Responses to moving stimuli under patch light conditions. Under patch light conditions the cell responded significantly more to the back view of the body when the actor walked away from the monkey than to the other conditions or SA [$N = 10, 12, 12, 12, 10, 12$; $F = 14.8$; $df\ 4, 51$; $P < 0.0001$]. This response indicates that the cell could respond to form derived solely from the dynamic information of biological motion.

COMPARING THE NATURAL AND ARTIFICIAL SYSTEMS FOR RETRIEVING STRUCTURE FROM NON-RIGID MOTION

Johansson (Johansson, 1973, 1975, 1976; Johansson *et al.*, 1980) has described the perception of biological motion stimuli as immediate and compelling. In formal attempts to assess the efficiency of human observers' perception, Johansson (1976) found that exposure durations of between 0.1 and 0.2 s are sufficient for naïve observers to correctly label a film of a biological motion stimulus depicting a human actor walking from left to right with ten light markers attached to the major points of limb articulation. Similar temporal requirements for perception were found by Lappin *et al.* (1980). The efficiency of perception here suggests that visual analysis is fairly automatic and that it proceeds from early stages of, say, encoding of spot movement to later stages of form recognition without guidance from "higher centres" or learned strategies. The processing can thus be termed "bottom-up".

Several attempts have been made to produce a computational model of the process underlying the retrieval of structure from biological motion stimuli. The problems in retrieving form are unlike those associated with rigid motion because the limb elements move relative to one another making the whole display non-rigid (Ullman, 1979). Locally rigid solutions could be sought but Ullman's algorithm requires four non-coplanar points on each rigid element, not two as is the case with Johansson's stimuli.

For a computational model the actual time taken to perform computations depends on the particular computer on which calculations are performed. The efficiency of computational models and the psychophysical observers can be related, however, by comparing the number of frames required to reach a correct solution. The earliest computational model of Rashid (1980) used the correlation of dot marker position (in two dimensions x and y) and velocity (dx/dt and dy/dt) between frames to postulate links between these points in the biological motion stimuli. Points persistently close to one another, and moving with similar trajectories, are likely to be linked. This simple procedure, although slow, produced reasonable solutions for simple stimuli (a walking man). For complex stimuli (e.g. two men walking around one another) the procedure was slow and inaccurate (after 30 successive frames, incorrect links between hands and knees were suggested by the model).

The performance of Rashid's computational model appears poor in comparison with human performance requiring only 0.2 s (5–10 frames) and single cells which respond selectively to body form in biological motion stimuli within 0.2 s of stimulus onset. The more recent computational approach of Sugie & Kato (1987) utilized a physical constraint to interpret the displays. They assumed that the axis of rotation of a rigid element remains fixed during the rotation. With this constraint a solution can be deduced as to the 3D trajectory of a rod element with only three successive frames and two points marked along the length of the rod. For multiply connected rods, such as the body, the resolved trajectory for one rod element can be used as a frame of reference for defining the trajectory of the next linked rod element, and so on until all element trajectories are defined. This model resolves the correct linkage in biological stimuli extremely efficiently, indeed performance is at the theoretical limit of three successive frames. The model would seem to outperform the human observer.

We have recently re-examined the duration of stimuli necessary for human subjects to discriminate the form of a walking human figure in computer animated biological motion displays (Woolford, Benson & Perrett, unpublished studies). The subjects' task was to discriminate normal figures walking on the spot (viewed from the front, side or back) from jumbled figures where the position of marker points had been moved by a fixed distance (30% of the head to toe height) in a random direction. Additionally, to eliminate any static cues to form we tested subjects with both conventional displays (no-mask) and in displays where the walking dot figure was seen against a background mask of 100 randomly placed static dots.

We found that naïve subjects performed rather poorly and required more than eight frames (0.3 s) to perceive the figures, but after 30 trials of practice their performance was improved remarkably. Without the mask we found that subjects could discriminate body form with only a single frame of exposure! Without the mask subjects were able to join up the dots using purely static information and hence were effectively performing a static pattern discrimination. With the mask static cues were essentially eliminated and subjects' performance was at chance levels with one frame. Performance was better than chance with two or three frames' exposure.

We learn from these studies that the biological motion stimuli contain multiple cues on which form perception can be based and that when subjects are forced to use purely dynamic cues to retrieve structure they can perform extremely efficiently. A second lesson from the psychophysics comes from the improvement with practice. This indicates that the perception of biological motion stimuli is not entirely automatic but must in some way involve additional "top-down" influences where expectations for the form of the moving object are used in some way to compare against visual input. The appropriate computational model for processing would appear to be one in which input data is checked against specific models stored in memory and the results of the matching used to guide subsequent predictions (see Lee & Chen, 1985; Leung & Yang, 1987).

Computational models derived so far, however, have two properties that make them inadequate for accounting for human and single-cell data. The first property is that the models are general purpose. The perceptual system, however, appears to employ specific mechanisms rather than a general purpose analysis. Sumi (1984) found that normally oriented biological motion stimuli were more accurately perceived than inverted stimuli, which were often incorrectly perceived for very extended periods of time. The physiological data indicate again that many special-purpose and view-specific mechanisms are employed in the analysis of a walking body.

The second difference between natural and artificial systems is that most of the computational models achieve a less complete description of the visual input compared with natural recognition systems. The computational systems only retrieve the linkage structure (which elements connect with which) whereas natural systems additionally inform us as to the nature of the linked stimuli, identifying it as a walking body and more specifically as a left profile view of a body walking to the left. What is needed is a hybrid model which finds potential links and then checks these against specific models of the static or articulating body (see Lee & Chen, 1985; Leung & Yang, 1987).

FRAMES OF REFERENCE

It is important to consider the frames of reference in which the analysis of body motion is performed; different frameworks are useful for making explicit different types of information.

Viewer-centred Coordinates

For the majority of cells which we have studied, the viewer forms the frame of reference (Perrett *et al.*, 1985b, 1989). Cells are selective, for example, for the body moving to the viewer's right or the body facing the viewer's right. Changing the viewer's vantage point would change the cells' responses to the same movement.

This type of analysis is useful in guiding the viewer's reactions. To run away or to chase another, a viewer must specify the movements of the other with respect to him/herself.

Object-centred Coordinates

By contrast, Marr (Marr, 1982; Marr & Nishihara, 1978; Marr & Vaina, 1982) emphasized the importance of describing parts of an object or movements relative to the main axis of the object rather than relative to the viewer. Such object-centred descriptions have the advantage that they do not change with changes in the viewer's vantage point. To describe an object completely requires only a single object-centred description to be stored in memory.

We have found that cells displaying object-centred coding of movement are far less numerous in the temporal cortex than viewer-centred cells. Figure 8 illustrates the responses of one such cell. One can only understand the coding of this cell by relating the arm movements to the torso of the body. All movements bringing the arm in front of the chest produce an effective response (dark arrows). The direction of effective movements, with respect to the viewer, changes for different views of the body but remain constant with respect to the torso.

We have argued that such object-centred coding can be derived by adding together the outputs of appropriate viewer-centred descriptions. For the above cell the combined outputs would be face viewer and rotate arm towards viewer; face away and rotate arm away from viewer, etc.

Cells displaying object-centred analyses are also found for whole body movements, not just the movement of individual limbs. Figure 9 illustrates data from a cell responsive to the front view of the body approaching the monkey and to the back view retreating. Again there is a constant relationship between the direction of movement and the body itself. The cell fires whenever the body "walks forward" in a direction following its nose. As we have just noted, an object-centred description of the body walking forward can be manufactured by appropriate combinations of viewer-centred descriptions "face left and walk left; face towards and approach; face away and retreat; face right and walk right".

Goal-centred Coordinates

Cells displaying object-centred coding of body movements are, however, fairly rare and this may well reflect the lack of general utility of such descriptions. Object-centred coding neither helps the viewer to determine how to react nor does it specify much about what the body is doing. A far more important and pervasive type of coding is one in which the movements of the body are related to the spatial

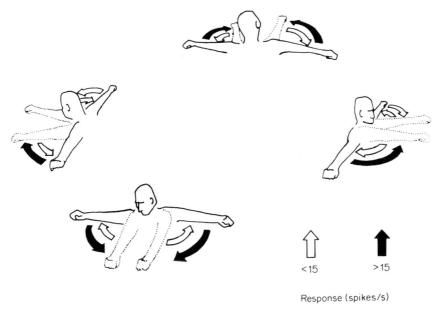

<15   >15

Response (spikes/s)

Observing monkey

Figure 8. Object-centred coding of arm movement. Neuronal responses to different directions of arm rotation and to different views of an actor. The direction of rotation of a laterally extended arm is indicated by the direction of the arrowhead. The monkey's vantage point is indicated at the base of the figure. The directional selectivity relative to the monkey changes for different views of the actor. For the front view of the body, movements of either arm towards the monkey were significantly ($P < 0.01$ each comparison) greater than spontaneous activity (1.2 ± 0.5) and movements away ($F = 43.0$; $df\,4, 21$; $P < 0.01$). For the back view of the body, movements of either arm away from the monkey were significantly ($P < 0.01$ each comparison) greater than movements towards and spontaneous activity ($F = 13.0$; $df\,4, 21$; $P < 0.01$). The directional sensitivity relative to the actor's body remains constant since the cell always responds to movements which bring the arm in front of the actor's chest.

position of a second object in the environment. We have labelled such coding as "goal centred" because it makes explicit the goal or purpose of the movement.

An example of goal-centred coding is illustrated in Figure 10 (see figure legend for details). The cell responds to movement of the experimenter but only when these movements lead him to the exit door of the laboratory. One can make sense of the directional selectivity of the cell only by relating the movements of the experimenter to the external door. Even when the monkey's chair was rotated, so that it faced a different direction (Figure 10b), only movements which were directed towards the external door of the laboratory produced large responses.

For this cell the goal of the preferred action appears to have a learned significance. (This is the only position in the local environment through which the experimenters go out of sight for long periods of time.) One might speculate that the cell's activity reflects an emotional response to the event rather than a visual

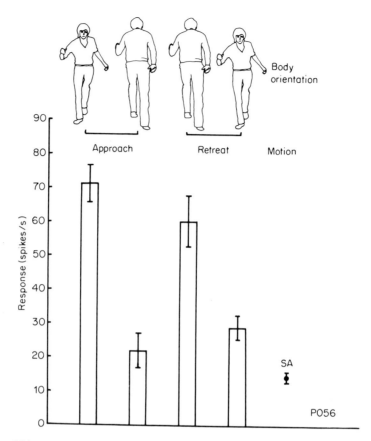

Figure 9. Object-centred coding of a body walking forwards. The mean and standard error of the responses (spikes/s) to different views of the body when approaching and retreating from the monkey are shown for cell P056. The cell responded most to the body moving in a direction compatible with its orientation (i.e. in the direction it was facing). The cell responded more to the front view than to the back view of the body when it moved towards the monkey ($P < 0.01$). The response to the back view was greater than the front view, however, when it moved away from the monkey ($P < 0.01$). (Number of trials per condition: $N = 8, 5, 4, 8$; SA $= 15 \pm 4.0$ ($N = 8$). Overall effect of conditions—$F = 15.9$, df 4, 28, $P < 0.0001$.)

analysis of the event. The particular significance of long-term disappearance of an experimenter, however, varies with circumstance. Usually leaving is of no consequence, but sometimes leaving may provoke disappointment and isolation calls, other times it provokes threats. It would, therefore, appear that it is the visual event of leaving the laboratory that is important rather than any emotional or behavioural response. In general, cells in the temporal cortex appear to code visual objects and events independent of emotional consequences and resulting behaviour. It may be a good strategy of coding to attempt a visual recognition of significant objects and actions without reference to emotional or behavioural

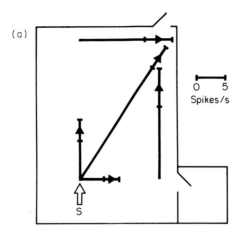

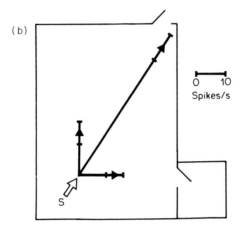

Figure 10.   Goal-centred coding of whole body movement. (a) Neuronal response to the sight of an actor walking in different directions in the laboratory. The length of each line represents the magnitude of neuronal response (mean ± 1 SE for five trials) for one direction of movement. The external boundary of the figure gives the plan view of the laboratory with an indication of the position of the external door and an internal door to a small preparation room. The direction of walking is given by the filled arrowheads and the starting position by the origin of the lines. The vantage point and orientation of the monkey (S) is given at the base of the figure. From a starting position close to the monkey, movement towards the external door produces a significantly larger response ($P < 0.05$ each comparison) than the other two directions of movement ($F = 16.6$; $df 2, 8$; $P < 0.01$). (b) The same conventions as (a) but the monkey's orientation in the room was modified. The triggering level, which is used to isolate a single cell's response, was changed slightly to prevent the slowly changing activity of background cells influencing the results. With the monkey's vantage point changed the cell still gave a significantly larger response ($P < 0.01$ each comparison) to movement towards the external door than to other directions ($F = 19.8$; df 2, 8; $P < 0.01$).

context. In this way recognition could act like a consultation of an unbiased visual encyclopedia; the behaviour which ensues after recognition can then be flexible and guided by the environmental context or mood of the observer.

SUMMARY

Figure 11 summarizes the different levels of representation of static and dynamic information about objects. The three levels discussed here that are appropriate for neurones in the temporal cortex utilize viewer-, object- and goal-centred coordinates. Viewer-centred representations are prevalent in the temporal cortex, perhaps because they provide a basis on which the viewer can organize behavioural reactions in social encounters and/or predator–prey interactions. One needs to know which way a lion is moving with respect to oneself if one wants to escape rather than jump into its mouth. Object-centred descriptions may have a role in recognizing what an object is, but the utility of object-centred descriptions for understanding body movements is probably much smaller. Goal-centred descriptions, on the other hand, are particularly useful for describing actions, since they make explicit the relationship between an agent performing an action and the goal of that act.

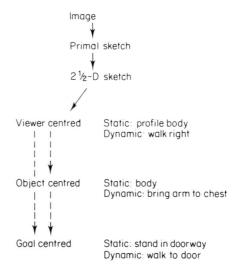

Figure 11. Levels of representation of information during visual processing. The initial stages of processing follow Marr's scheme whereby the image is first broken down into component local orientations (the primal sketch) then synthesized to make explicit surfaces, their orientation and boundaries (the 2 + 1/2D sketch). High-level descriptions of objects are then built for static and dynamic information from particular vantage points (viewer-centred descriptions). These descriptions hold for changes in retinal position, orientation and size but do not generalize over changes in perspective as the object is rotated > 45°. Viewer-centred descriptions are combined to form object-centred descriptions which are independent of vantage point. Goal-centred descriptions specify the movements of an animate object (agent) relative to part of the environment (the goal of the action).

ACKNOWLEDGEMENTS

This work was supported by grants from the MRC (G8427112N), SERC Image Interpretation Initiative (GR/E 8825.7) and a Royal Society University Research Fellowship to D. I. Perrett. P. J. Benson was supported by the St Andrews University Free Endowment Fund. A. J. Chitty and A. J. Mistlin were supported by SERC Information Technology Postgraduate Studentships.

REFERENCES

Bruce, C. J., Desimone, R. & Gross, C. G. (1981). Visual properties of neurones in a polysensory area in superior temporal sulcus of macaque. *Journal of Neurophysiology*, **46**, 369–384.

Johansson, G. (1973). Visual perception of biological motion and a model for its analysis. *Perception and Psychophysics*, **14**, 201–211.

Johansson, G. (1975). Visual motion perception. *Scientific American*, **232**(6), 76–88.

Johansson, G. (1976). Spatio-temporal differentiation and integration in visual motion perception. *Psychological Research*, **38**, 379–393.

Johansson, G., von Hofsten, C. & Jansson, G. (1980). Event perception. *Annual Review of Psychology*, **31**, 27–63.

Julesz, B. (1988). In the last minutes of the evolution of life, stereoscopic depth perception captured the input layer of the visual cortex to break camouflage. *Proceedings of the 11th European Conference of Visual Perception*, Bristol, Perception A3.

Lappin, J. S., Doner, J. F. & Kottas, B. (1980). Minimal conditions for the visual detection of structure and motion in three dimensions. *Science*, **209**, 717–719.

Lee, H. J. & Chen, Z. (1985). Determination of 3D human body postures from a single view. *Computer Vision, Graphics and Image Processing*, **30**, 148–168.

Leung, M. K. & Yang, Y. H. (1987). A region-based approach for human body motion analysis. *Pattern Recognition*, **20**, 321–339.

Marr, D. (1982). *Vision: A Computational Investigation into the Human Representation and Processing of Visual Information*. Freeman, San Francisco.

Marr, D. & Nishihara, H. K. (1978). Representation and recognition of the spatial organization of three-dimensional shapes. *Proceedings of the Royal Society (London)*, Series B, **200**, 269–294.

Marr, D. & Vaina, L. (1982). Representation and recognition of the movements of shapes. *Proceedings of the Royal Society (London)*, Series B, **214**, 501–524.

Perrett, D. I., Smith, P. A. J., Potter, D. D., Mistlin, A. J., Head, A. S., Milner, A. D. & Jeeves, M. A. (1984). Neurones responsive to faces in the temporal cortex: studies of functional organization sensitivity and relation to perception. *Human Neurobiology*, **3**, 197–208.

Perrett, D. I., Smith, P. A. J., Potter, D. D., Mistlin, A. J., Head, A. S., Milner, A. D. & Jeeves, M. A. (1985a). Visual cells in the temporal cortex sensitive to face view and gaze direction. *Proceedings of the Royal Society (London)*, Series B, **223**, 293–317.

Perrett, D. I., Smith, P. A. J., Mistlin, A. J., Chitty, A. J., Head, A. S., Potter, D. D., Broennimann, R., Milner, A. D. & Jeeves, M. A. (1985b). Visual analysis of body movements by neurones in the temporal cortex of the macaque monkey. A preliminary report. *Behaviour and Brain Research*, **16**, 153–170.

Perrett, D. I., Harries, M. H., Mistlin, A. J. & Chitty, A. J. (1989). Three stages in the classification of body movements by visual neurones. In H. Barlow, C. Blakemore & M. Weston-Smith (Eds) *Images and Understanding*. Cambridge University Press, Cambridge.

Rashid, R. F. (1980). Towards a system for the interpretation of moving light displays. *IEEE Transactions: Pattern Analysis and Machine Intelligence*, **2**, 574–581.

Seltzer, B. & Pandya, D. N. (1978). Afferent cortical connections and architectonics of the superior temporal sulcus and surrounding cortex in the rhesus monkey. *Brain Research*, **149**, 1–24.

Sugie, N. & Kato, K. (1987). A computational model for biological motion perception. *IEEE Montech, Conference on Biomedical Technologies*, November 1987, 140–143.

Sumi, S. (1984). Upside-down presentation of the Johansson moving light-spot pattern. *Perception*, **13**, 283–286.

Ullman, S. (1979). The interpretation of structure from motion. *Proceedings of the Royal Society (London), Series B*, **203**, 405–426.

Wertheimer, H. (1922). Untersuchungen zur Lehre von Gestalt. *Psychologische Forschung*, **1**, 47–58.

Woodworth, R. S. (1938). *Experimental Psychology*. Holt, New York.

Zeki, S. & Ship, S. (1988). The functional logic of cortical connections. *Nature*, **335**, 311–317.

9 Colour Constancy

D. A. Forsyth

Robotics Research Group, Department of Engineering Science, University of Oxford, OX1 3PJ, UK

INTRODUCTION

The fact that we can talk about objects having a colour illustrates the pervasive nature of a remarkable human skill: people are able to describe the colour of an object in a way that is largely independent of the lighting in which they find it. This skill is referred to as colour constancy. Although convincing psychophysical evidence for colour constancy is sparse, it is a skill that is potentially very useful to machines. Its uses extend from such simple tasks as sorting fruit or improving holiday photographs to improving the performance of machine vision programs that must generate descriptions of objects from pictures. Examples of potential applications of colour constancy in machine vision include the following.

1. To construct object descriptions from images, we must collect those parts of an image which arise from a single object. Colour can contribute to this decision because it is a surface property. Grouping tasks of this sort will not, in general, require surface colour information if we assume that the illuminant changes slowly over space, and if we wish to group only in small neighbourhoods. However, where the illuminant changes quickly, or when we wish to group over larger neighbourhoods, we must decide whether a difference in the colour observed can be ascribed to a change in the illuminant, or must be put down to a change in surface colour. This requires colour constancy.
2. It is possible to recover some information about three-dimensional surface shape from images by using shading patterns. To do this, however, it is necessary to distinguish changes in the image that arise from shading from those that arise from changes in surface lightness or in illumination. Thus,

AI and the Eye   Edited by A. Blake and T. Troscianko
© 1990 John Wiley & Sons Ltd.

surface colour information can benefit shape processes, and recovering three-dimensional surface shape information from shading should proceed in concert with recovering surface colour information and with recovering information about the scene illuminant.

3. If a program describes an object using the colours observed in an image of that object, then it cannot normally use that description to recognize the object reliably in other images, because these colours will change as the illuminant changes. Colour constancy, by greatly reducing the effects of changes in the illuminant colour, makes it possible to use colour information in such recognition tasks.

In the following section, I review briefly the evidence for human competence at colour constancy, and discuss the algorithms that have been proposed for achieving colour constancy to date. In "A novel algorithm for colour constancy", I describe a new algorithm for colour constancy that I have designed and implemented. In "Experimental results", I show results for my algorithm working on real pictures, and compare it to a model of another popular algorithm. Finally, in the discussion, I explain why I think that programs that have colour and lightness constancy skills are crucial to building advanced machine vision systems.

REVIEW

Psychophysical Results

Colour constancy has been considered at least since Helmholtz (1962), who appears to have believed that it arose from cognitive interactions. Ewald Hering demonstrated in an elegant experiment, described by Barlow & Mollon (1982), that the colour reports of an observer were mediated by more complicated factors than just the output of the photoreceptors alone. Recent studies using collages of coloured papers, known as Mondrians after the art of Piet Mondrian, have indicated that humans exhibit colour constancy to some extent. Mondrians have the advantage that changes in image brightness due to shape and shadowing effects are avoided, and that they do not contain cognitive cues to surface colour.

A study by McCann *et al.* (1976) is often quoted as showing that humans display colour constancy, but has been cast in doubt by recent work of Young (1987), which indicates that the study did not completely eliminate cues to the chromaticity of papers used as stimuli. More recent work of Arend & Reeves (1986), Benzschawel *et al.* (1987), Blackwell & Buchsbaum (1988) and Brainard & Wandell (1988) further encourages a belief in colour constancy in people. Much of this evidence also suggests that there may be a fast mechanism in part underlying constancy. This is in accord with the work of Land and Daw (1962) which, despite its poor experimental procedures, has been used as an argument against models of constancy that require adaptation over some period of time, such as that of Judd (1940). It is clear, however, that a slow process is involved in colour constancy—one can see this by spending some time in strong daylight and then walking into a poorly lit room. The fact that both fast and slow interactions appear to be involved has led to some confusion and to sharp exchanges (Judd, 1960; Land, 1960).

There is a body of evidence that people perform surprisingly well at complex lightness constancy tasks (Katz, 1935; Beck, 1972; Gilchrist, 1979). Lightness constancy is a more difficult task than colour constancy, because changes in surface orientation can change the magnitude of the light reflected without changing its spectral composition, and can mimic changes in lightness as a result.

Thus, there is a shortage of conclusive evidence as to just how effective human colour constancy mechanisms are. However, we need not allow this point to deter us from attempting to build programs that display constancy, as their potential value is enormous.

Early Algorithms for Colour Constancy

Judd (1960) describes extensive early work, including propositions that surface colour was recovered from receptor output by estimating the colour of the illuminant, perhaps from light scattered into the eyeball by dust, from scattering within the eyeball itself, or from highlights. Other early models considered constancy to be an effect of adaptation over some not clearly specified period of time (for example, the work of Judd, 1940).

Perhaps the earliest and simplest algorithm for colour constancy is the coefficient rule, which is normally attributed to von Kries (1878). The coefficient rule involves computing a coefficient separately for each class of receptor, usually by some form of local averaging process. The colour descriptor is then computed by multiplying the output of each receptor by its coefficient. This technique appears to have been intended as a model of adaptational effects, which at that time were commonly viewed as the source of colour constancy. It appears to be deficient as a model of the human visual system (McAdam, 1946; Jameson & Hurvich, 1972; Wyszecki & Stiles, 1980).

The Retinex School

As a result of a number of experiments in colour perception (Land, 1959a, b; Land & Daw, 1962) which convinced him that contemporary models of colorimetry did not describe human experience well, Land proposed an algorithm for colour constancy in the Mondrian world, which he called the Retinex (Land *et al.*, 1971). In this paper, the Retinex is reported as describing surface colour without needing to know the illuminant cast on a particular scene, by using the coefficient rule and a contrast process to compute coefficients. This contrast process remains poorly understood. Unfortunately, although Land has described and modified this algorithm a number of times (Land, 1977, 1983, 1985, 1986), it is difficult to be certain how effective the algorithm is at achieving constancy, as he has not published details of any tests. Furthermore, the algorithm is difficult to analyse.

Brainard & Wandell (1986) have published a result for a simple case, which shows that the contrast process is equivalent to a form of averaging process, but no other rigorous results exist.

Clearly, if an algorithm computes coefficients using an averaging process, some form of local average of surface reflectance must be constant for it to display constancy. Unfortunately, we can disturb any average, either local or global, by changing the spatial arrangement or extent of surfaces present in the image. Thus, no such algorithm can display acceptable colour constancy.

Both Horn (1974) and Blake (Blake, 1985; Brelstaff & Blake, 1987) have constructed algorithms that were intended to mimic the Retinex algorithm, but are not rigorously equivalent to it. Their proposals have the advantage that they can more easily be analysed. Hurlbert (1986) demonstrates some formal links between these two algorithms, and a third described to her in a personal communication by Crick. She claims, but does not prove rigorously, that the Retinex algorithm is also a member of this class.

It is clear that both Horn's algorithm and Blake's algorithm are capable of recovering relative lightness information for Mondrian images where the illuminant changes slowly over space. The assumptions involved in both algorithms, that surface lightness changes only fast spatially and that illumination changes only slowly spatially, are clearly shown in these formulations. Unfortunately, in the real world illumination can have fast spatial changes (Gilchrist, 1979; Gilchrist *et al.*, 1983). Furthermore, for the purposes of machine vision, we require absolute rather than relative reports of both colour and lightness, which neither algorithm is capable of providing.

Algorithms Based on Finite-dimensional Linear Models

Using finite-dimensional linear models of lights and of surface reflectances to build colour constancy algorithms has become popular in recent years. This class of model simplifies building algorithms, because one can represent surface reflectances and illuminants as vectors and use the machinery of linear algebra to describe their interactions. However, it involves potentially misleading assumptions about surface reflectance.

One constructs a finite-dimensional model of surface reflectances by requiring or assuming that every surface reflectance in the world in which our algorithm lives can be accurately represented by a weighted sum of a finite number of distinct functions, which we call basis functions. A similar construction may be applied to illuminant functions. A typical example of a set of basis functions is the set used in Fourier analysis. We will use this set to illustrate a number of points throughout this chapter.

In Figure 1 I have shown the first three functions of the Fourier basis. If, for example, we were to represent surface reflectances using these three functions, the coefficients of each of the three functions would be sufficient to specify a surface reflectance. Thus, in this representation we can write a surface reflectance function as a three-vector of coefficients (see Figure 2).

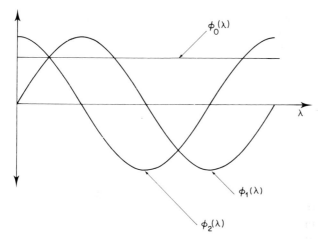

Figure 1. The first three functions of the Fourier basis, shown over a single period. I have not labelled the horizontal axis because the relative magnitude of the functions is unimportant for our purposes. These functions form a three-dimensional basis.

The first use of such models in colour vision applications is normally attributed to Sallstrom (1973). Recent publications have employed the statistical work of Cohen (1964) and the measurements of Krinov (1947) to justify using low-dimensional models of surface reflectance. Unfortunately, issues of sampling bias make it difficult to evaluate evidence that a low-dimensional model is valid. Maloney (1986) discusses this point in greater detail.

Buchsbaum (1980) and more recently Gershon (1987), constructed colour constancy algorithms by assuming that a spatial average of surface reflectance was constant for all images. We have already seen that algorithms based on this

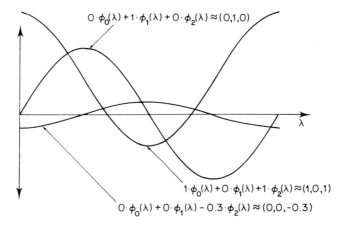

Figure 2. Some examples of functions that we can construct using the basis of Figure 1. Notice that none of these functions could be surface reflectance functions, because they have negative values.

assumption cannot display robust colour constancy. A more sophisticated algorithm is described by Maloney and Wandell (Maloney, 1984; Maloney & Wandell, 1986; Wandell, 1987). They assume that surface reflectances belong to an N-dimensional space. They assume that there are M receptors, $M > N$, and that the sensor is linear. Let us consider the case for $M = 3$ and $N = 2$, that is, three receptors and two degrees of freedom in surface reflectance. In this case, if we image a set of surfaces, there will in general be two degrees of freedom in the gamut we observe, and because the sensor is linear this gamut will be a plane in three-space. If we insist that to each different illuminant there corresponds a distinct plane, we can see that we can identify the illuminant by observing the gamut. This algorithm will fail if the number of degrees of freedom in the surface reflectances observed is not exactly two, because there will not be a unique plane containing the gamut. The geometric object underlying this algorithm is known as a Grassmann manifold* (Boothby, 1986). Unfortunately, this approach cannot recover absolute surface lightness information. Furthermore, to recover the two remaining degrees of freedom in surface colour requires four photoreceptors, making it an unattractive model of human colour constancy.

A NOVEL ALGORITHM FOR COLOUR CONSTANCY

Basic assumptions

In both the theoretical work and the experimental work that follows, I make a number of important assumptions.

1. I assume that surfaces are Lambertian, and have a property which I call surface reflectance, which is independent of viewing geometry and adequately describes the different amounts of light reflected at different wavelengths. This is an enormous assumption. However, this assumption is well entrenched in the literature (McAdam, 1982; Wyszecki & Stiles, 1982), sufficiently so that in many publications (Buchsbaum, 1980; Maloney, 1984; Maloney & Wandell, 1986, Wandell, 1987; Gershon, 1987; to name a few examples) it receives no comment.
2. I assume that each image contains a variety of different coloured objects. The colours of these objects must not be "unreasonably" distributed (that is, we do not have only shades of some colours, for example), and there must be "sufficient" different colours. Neither term can be made precise at this stage.
3. All reflection considered is diffuse. Either no specularities occur, or all patches of specular reflection have been isolated as such.
4. Changes in the image due to changes in surface colour can be distinguished from those due to changes in lighting or in surface orientation.

---

* Felicitously, it is named after a pioneer in colour vision, Hermann Grassmann.

These assumptions are universal in the colour constancy literature to date, although some authors believe that colour constancy may be performed on the properties of specularly reflected light alone (D'Zmura & Lennie, 1986; Lee, 1986; Klinker *et al.*, 1987). Assumption 4 appears in a stronger form in the literature of the Retinex school (Land *et al.*, 1971; Horn, 1974; Blake, 1985, for example), who assume that all edges in images are due to changes in surface reflectance. In real images this assumption is violated (Gilchrist, 1979; Gershon *et al.*, 1986). However, in the Mondrian world this assumption holds unless we specifically construct the illuminant to violate it.

Overview of Theory

It should be obvious that it is not possible to recover surface reflectance from a picture. We can hope only to recover a small set of the properties of a surface reflectance function. We will therefore attempt to build an algorithm that should make a picture look as though it had been taken under some canonical light. We will refer to the receptor responses that a patch evokes under the canonical light as that patch's *colour descriptor*.

Intuitively, one can then model the effects of a coloured illuminant on a scene by a mapping that maps a patch's colour descriptor to the receptor responses observed for that patch under that particular illuminant. In the mathematics that follows, I investigate the circumstances under which such mappings are invertible, and the conditions necessary to ensure that one may identify the mapping that produced a particular picture simply by looking at the picture.

Recall that the value of any surface reflectance function is never greater than one, nor less than zero. Now if we attempt to construct a surface reflectance function using the first three functions of the Fourier basis (see Figure 1), we see that only a certain three vectors of coefficients are acceptable. For example, $(0, 1, 0)$ does not represent a surface reflectance function, because the function is negative for some wavelengths (see Figure 2). The set of acceptable representations is easily seen to be *bounded*; it does not go off to infinity in any direction. This property is well known (see Koenderink, 1987).

The second thing we notice is that if (a, b, c) and (d, e, f) represent acceptable surface reflectance functions, then so does $\mu(a, b, c) + (1 - \mu)(d, e, f)$, for any μ between 0 and 1. This property is referred to as convexity, and again remains true however many functions we use to represent surface reflectances. The fact that the set of acceptable surface reflectance functions is convex is valuable in actually building an algorithm, as we shall see.

The first property implies that if we were to image every possible surface reflectance under some light, we would obtain a bounded gamut. In particular, there are receptor responses that could *not* have arisen from an acceptable representation of surface reflectance under this light. We can turn this argument about, and say that if we *do* observe these receptor reponses, then the picture could *not* have been taken under that particular light. It follows that if we have a picture taken under an unknown light, we can use the gamut of that picture to state under which lights the picture *was not* taken.

We use this approach to construct a set, which we call the *feasible set*. The feasible set consists of all those lights under which the image could have been taken. In fact, since we are identifying lights with mappings, the feasible set can also be defined as consisting of all those mappings that could produce the image taken under the canonical light from the image we observe. We shall use this second definition below.

The generic algorithm for colour constancy

Let us assume that we are in a world where exact colour constancy is possible. In Appendices A and B, I show the conditions under which this is the case. In particular, to be able to do exact colour constancy, we must require that either only one receptor sensitivity function is non-zero for any wavelength, or that we may obtain a set of functions with this property by applying some linear map to the receptor sensitivity functions. If photoreceptors with these independence properties are not available, then we need strong restrictions on surface reflectances and on illuminants. Determining the extent to which constancy will fail when these conditions are not satisfied is beyond the scope of this chapter.

Surprisingly, we need never in fact construct the set of acceptable representations of surface reflectances explicitly. If we image a very large number of surfaces under the canonical illuminant, the gamut of this image will be effectively identical to the acceptable representations, and we may work with that (given some caution about the canonical light; if this is, for example, total blackness, we cannot expect useful information from a constancy algorithm).

Given that one has L receptors, an algorithm for performing colour constancy has this form:

1. Construct the gamut under the canonical illuminant, by imaging a very large number of surfaces. Call this D.
2. To construct the feasible set for any patch imaged under a constant illuminant:
   (i) Form the convex hull of the gamut observed. Call this C. We can use this convex hull to represent the gamut precisely because we know that the set of acceptable representations of surface colour is convex.
   (ii) The feasible set is now that set of $L \times L$ linear maps, M, such that $M(<)CD$, that is, the set of linear maps that take the gamut we observe to a subset of the gamut under the canonical illuminant. This implies that any receptor response that we observe in C corresponds to a real surface reflectance.
3. Within this feasible set, use some estimator to choose that map most likely to correspond to the illuminant.
4. Apply the map so chosen, to obtain the colour descriptors.

We can construct the gamut under the canonical light by observing as many surfaces as possible under that light. One may ensure that this light is the same between observations by employing a number of differently coloured objects, and insisting that, for valid observations of the world, these objects each retain the colour that they had for the first observations. If two such observations actually occurred under different illuminants, then *per se* the world is too perverse for one to be able to do colour constancy. No algorithm, however constructed, can succeed in a world where, under one illuminant two objects have the same colour, and under another they differ in colour. We simply assume that this has not happened, and proceed. If we have been incorrect assuming that the world is well behaved, it will soon become apparent as familiar objects change colour. Finally, since the gamut is convex, one may construct an approximation to the gamut under the canonical illuminant by taking the convex hull of the union of the gamuts obtained by these observations.

In fact, we cannot choose arbitrarily from the $L \times L$ matrices of full rank, but must choose from some subset of this set. Once we have specified which subset, the algorithm is completely specified. In Appendix B, I show that if we use photoreceptors with the independence properties shown above, we need consider only an L-dimensional subset of this space, and that the resulting algorithm works for an infinite dimensional space of surface reflectances. This corresponds to a form of the coefficient rule, and for this reason I call this algorithm *Crule*.

EXPERIMENTAL RESULTS

Very few acceptable demonstrations of colour constant algorithms exist in the literature. Published texts exist for Maloney and Wandell's algorithm working on synthetic images only (Maloney, 1984). With the exception of results published on one Mondrian image by McCann *et al.* (1976), there exists no published account of the colour constancy performance of the Retinex algorithm on real data. Gershon's (1987) algorithm has been demonstrated on a single real image. This result is flawed by the fact that there was only a single object in the image. Brill (1979) submitted an abstract to the OSA meeting in 1979 which implied that he had a colour constancy algorithm that worked on real pictures.

This shortage of careful experimentation has led to a failure to recognize an important point. A change in the illuminant may seriously impair the accuracy of measurement of the receptors themselves. Therefore, accurate surface colour perception requires that the operating points of the receptors themselves be manipulated.

Preliminary Information

All images were taken with a monochrome CCD camera (National Panasonic type WV-CD 50) with its gain control defeated. Three separate exposures of each image were made using Kodak Wratten filters (numbers 29, 47B and 58) for colour separation, and a sharp near infrared cut filter, which is essential as a result of the pronounced near infrared sensitivity of CCD cameras. I used conventional photographic lenses. The CCD camera appears to measure no chromatic aberration, probably because its pixels are large with respect to any fringes. I used two

500 W photographer's lamps (Photoflood Pearl bulbs) of unknown colour temperature and a warm white apperance, as illuminants. I coloured the illuminants by hanging translucent coloured plastic filters in front of the bulbs (these were "Powerflash" filters, from the warm effects set and the cold effects set. These are available from most photographic equipment stockists in the UK). At no stage have the properties of these filters been measured, so it was not possible to build models of the filters into the algorithm. I refer to the light provided by the bulbs alone lamps as "white light", and to coloured illuminants by the conventional colour names of the plastic filters used.

Neutral density filters were used to weight the separation filters so that the aperture of the lens did not need to be adjusted between exposing each colour separation. This involved an adjustment, performed once only, so that images taken *under the canonical illuminant* appeared in colour most like the objects imaged when displayed on the screen of a Sun workstation. This approach introduces an unknown mapping between the receptor responses recorded and the colour appearance to a neutrally adapted human observer of the scene. Since we are attempting to recover colour descriptors rather than human responses, this mapping is of little consequence for our theories at this stage, as long as one remembers that it exists.

We require that the algorithm produce near constant, non-trivial, colour descriptors for objects, when presented with well-populated scenes imaged under widely varying lights, given that one does not claim constancy when a change in illuminant does not produce a change in the receptor responses. This competence is recognizable without possessing any information about the spectral properties of illuminants or of surface reflectances. It is particularly important to notice that I am not quoting inferred surface reflectances for objects because doing so would imply either a restriction on the properties of surface reflectances, or that it is possible to recover a function uniquely from a finite number of projections. Since I wish to avoid the first implication, and since the second implication is clearly incorrect, I quote instead the colour descriptors obtained. This information is sufficient because colour constancy, or any lack of it, is easily recognized from these data.

For these experiments, I used Mondrians made of Color Aid papers (a set of 202 papers, with standard colours, available from the Color Aid Corporation, 37 East 18th St, New York, NY 10003, USA). The 60 patches that comprised each test Mondriaan were chosen from a shaken bag, to provide some randomness in the structure of their gamut.

Implementation Details

For the experiments I describe, I formed the canonical hull by imaging 180 of the set of 202 Color Aid papers under white light. The *feasible set* for any image will then consist of all those diagonal maps that take the hull of the image we observe to a subset of the canonical hull. In particular, because the sensitivities of the filters used hardly overlap at all, it is possible to use the identity matrix for the matrix of eigenvectors described in Appendix B.

Although a vector of receptor responses all of which are zero is a completely legitimate observation, it will clearly be difficult to make any inference about surface colour from this measurement. We therefore treat this as a special case, and do not admit it to our discussion. Thus, the diagonal terms in these maps will be positive.

Associated with each receptor response is a feasible set of illuminants. It is easy to see that we obtain the feasible set for the whole image by intersecting the feasible sets associated with all the receptor responses. In fact, it can be shown that we need intersect only the feasible sets associated with the hull points of the image gamut. Since the feasible set is convex (Appendix C), we can represent it by a set of hull points. In general, the more points the more accurate the representation will be, but the representation will converge to the set. A set of hull points for the feasible set is easily found (Appendix C).

However, if there are insufficient colours in the image or if the colours are unreasonably distributed, the hull points of the image gamut may not in fact lie on the boundary of the largest gamut that one could obtain under the given light. Under these circumstances the algorithm may obtain a very large (and hence unhelpful) feasible set. There is no requirement that the spatial extent of each colour be constant, just that there should be patches of each of many colours. This means that this algorithm is not dependent on strong assumptions about spatial averages of surface reflectance.

Crule is relatively simple to implement, but intersecting the convex hulls requires care. I used an elegant and simple technique for intersecting hulls, which results from work of Woodwark *et al.* (1984), and which was first employed for computing hull intersections by Cameron (1989). This involves iteratively refining a cuboidal approximation to the intersected hull.

RESULTS

Statistical Analysis

Figures 3–8 show the performance of this algorithm on a typical set of ten chips selected from a Mondrian. We need, however, a more manageable technique for measuring the degree of constancy that this algorithm displays and comparing it with the Retinex algorithm. This involves computing some measure of the spread of the colour descriptors computed for a chip from pictures taken under different lights. Although at first a principal components analysis suggests itself, this method is inappropriate given the small number (12) of data points for each chip, and the fact that it is difficult to guarantee a Gaussian spread of points.

Because there is an arbitrary constant involved in the colour descriptors, it is important, too, that this statistic measures relative, rather than absolute, spread. We do not wish an algorithm to appear to perform well simply by multiplying its descriptors by a small quantity. Thus, we compute the mean distance of the outputs from the mean (over the different lights) descriptor for each chip. This mean is then

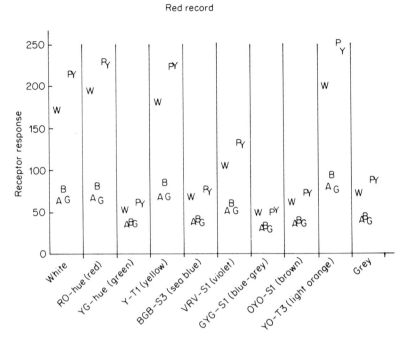

Figure 3. This and the next five figures demonstrate the performance of Crule for ten chips, selected to give a fair impression. This, and the next two figures show the receptor responses for ten chips, under six different lights. Each column represents a chip: the colour name, in the Color Aid corporation's scheme, of the chip is at the base of the column. Under this is a colour name for each chip under incandescent light in brackets. This figure shows the responses for the camera's red channel. The response under white light is plotted as a "W", under blue-green light as an "A", under blue light as a "B", under green light as a "G", under purple light as a "P", and under yellow light as a "Y". The meaning of the colour names for the illuminants is given in the text. Note the wide spread of responses, which will make it difficult to use these values to describe chips.

normalized by the magnitude (in a Euclidean sense) of the outputs. This statistic is zero for a perfectly constant algorithm, increases as constancy fails and is unaffected by scaling descriptors.

The graphs show the cumulative distribution for this statistic, measured for the 60 different chips in a Mondrian under six different lights. In Figure 9, I show the cumulative distribution of this statistic for the receptor responses engendered by each chip, and in Figure 10, I show the cumulative distribution for the output of Crule. It is very clear that Crule is significantly reducing the spread of the descriptors. Figure 11 shows the performance of an implementation (after Brainard & Wandell, 1986) of the Retinex algorithm on the same scene. As one can see, on a single image with an unchanging average surface reflectance, the Retinex algorithm performs very well, and its failure is a measure of the failure of the camera and lighting set-up to conform to the assumptions necessary for a coefficient rule to work (which are explained in Appendices A and B).

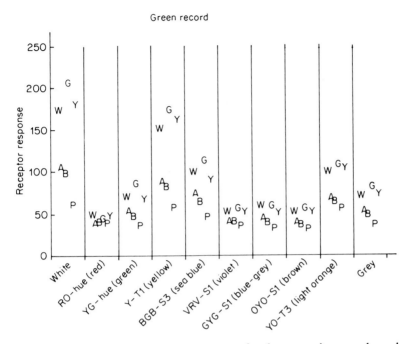

Figure 4. This figure shows the receptor responses for the camera's green channel, using the same conventions as Figure 3.

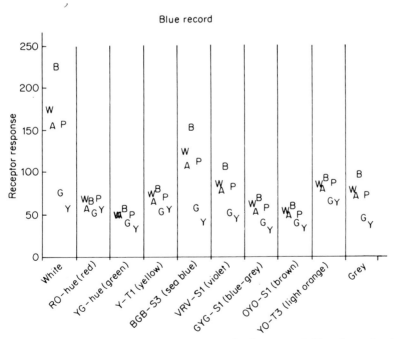

Figure 5. This figure shows the receptor responses for the camera's blue channel, using the same conventions as Figure 3.

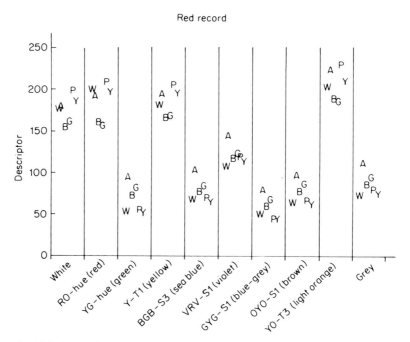

Figure 6. This figure shows the descriptors in the red channel, output by Crule, using the same conventions as Figure 3. Notice that the descriptors are clustered, indicating a high degree of colour constancy.

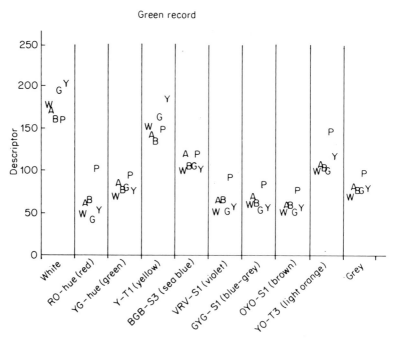

Figure 7. This figure shows the descriptors in the green channel, output by Crule, using the same conventions as Figure 3.

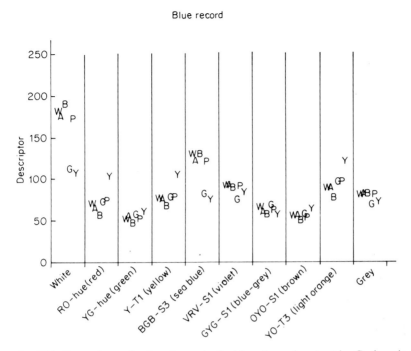

Figure 8. This figure shows the descriptors in the blue channel, output by Crule, using the same conventions as Figure 3.

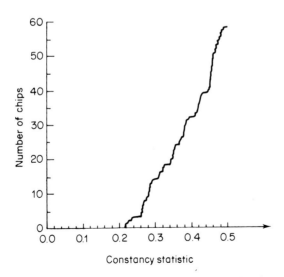

Figure 9. Cumulative distribution of the statistic, computed for the camera outputs.

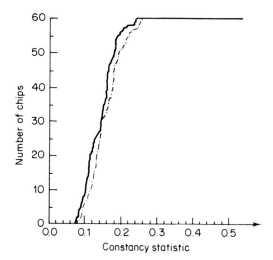

Figure 10. Cumulative distribution of the statistic, computed for the descriptors' output by Crule for a 60-element Mondrian under six lights (solid line), and for both that Mondrian and that Mondrian with a large red border (dashed line). Notice the small size of the error balls, which indicates good constancy, for both cases. In particular, the fact that the plots are similar indicates that a change in the average surface reflectance of a scene will not cause Crule to perform poorly.

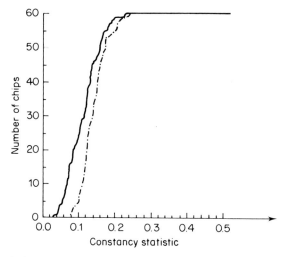

Figure 11. Cumulative distribution of the statistic, computed for the descriptors' output by Retinex for a 60-element Mondrian under six lights (solid line), and for both that Mondrian and that Mondrian with a large red border (dashed line). Notice the small size of the error balls, which indicates good constancy, in the first case. In the second case, we see that the error balls are larger, which indicates that the descriptors computed have varied as we changed the average surface reflectance of the scene.

We know, however, that we can disturb the constancy of the Retinex algorithm by running it on a series of images that contain the same chips, but with a different average surface reflectance. Crule should not have this characteristic. I demonstrated this effect by taking images under six different lights of the Mondrian used for the first experiment, but with a border of red paper attached. If we form the cumulative distribution of the constancy statistic for the outputs for the Mondrian both with and without a border, we expect that this distribution will be similar to the first distribution for Crule, and will reflect poorer performance for Retinex. Figures 10 and 11 show that this is indeed the case.

Adaptation and Imaging Effects

An informal look at the output images of Crule and of Retinex indicates that under certain circumstances both algorithms fail badly. The pictures where this occurred involved very strongly saturated lights; in particular, in the case of pictures taken under a deep red light, there was very little information in either the green or the blue channels, because the constancy algorithm is connected to its receptors by a quantizing system with constant quantization thresholds. As a result, under red light, the signal on the green channel has a dynamic range of slightly fewer than three bits. The algorithm is thus more ignorant about what the green transducer is measuring than it is about what the red transducer is measuring, and its constancy is therefore impaired.

The solution is simple. Since a constancy algorithm wants a good measurement of the stimulus at the transducers, it should control the gain of the transducers to be consistent with its estimates of the illuminant colour. If the world is illuminated with a deep red light, and we do not increase the gain of the blue and green transducers (or adjust the thresholds of the quantizer), then the constancy of the system will fall off as the light becomes more strongly coloured. For a system to be able to do proper, robust and accurate colour constancy requires that it manipulate either transducer gain or detection thresholds so that it uses the dynamic range of the signalling channel in the best possible way.

The human vision system faces a similar problem, in that the operating range of human photoreceptors is very much greater than the signalling capacity of the nerve channels (Barlow & Mollon, 1982). This, to my mind, is the source of the slow process involved in constancy that has caused such confusion. The receptor requires a broad operating range because of the great range in illuminant intensities that is possible, but the dynamic range in a given scene is low. Furthermore, the average brightness of the retinal image will remain nearly constant for fairly long periods of time. Under these circumstances, it is efficient for a photoreceptor to use most of its signalling capacity to indicate the difference between some average brightness (which we shall call its operating point) and its measurement, and to transmit the average signal only slowly.* This slow process

---

* The "average" involved may be a spatial average across the retinal field, or a temporal average over some recent window of the photoreceptor history. I do not wish to commit myself to the suggestion that it is a formal average, as opposed to a measurement of the slowly varying portion of the intensity at the retina.

does not in itself achieve constancy, but is a prerequisite for doing so. This would predict, for example, that one would be able to disrupt the Land & Daw (1962; and see above) experiments by exposing subjects to an inappropriate light field very shortly before the Mondrian is flashed on the screen.

It is possible, therefore, to draw an attractive analogy between the needs of a machine colour constancy system and the human system. Both have to deal with considerations of dynamic range in the channel between their receptors and the simultaneous constancy system. Humans solve this problem using adaptation. We now understand why machines should be built to mimic this human property if we want them to be able to perform colour constancy.

DISCUSSION: COLOUR CONSTANCY IN THE REAL WORLD

Surface colour perception is confounded not only by the colour of the lighting used, but also by the orientation of the surfaces imaged, by spatial changes in the illuminant field and by shadowing and similar effects. Computational approaches to colour constancy have tended to deal with this problem by computing descriptions only for a world of flat, frontally presented surfaces, in which these ambiguities do not arise. Neither humans nor any reasonable robots operate in a world where such simplifying assumptions apply.

There are two difficulties that impede constancy in the real world: surface orientation is an additional confounding effect that must be accounted for in estimating surface lightness, and illuminants may change quickly over space. Gershon *et al.* (1986) show cases where the spectral content of the illuminant changes fast; Gilchrist (1979) has demonstrated many examples where illuminant brightness changes quickly over space. Edge-based surface colour processes must decide which edges contribute to surface colour, and these examples indicate that the decision must be based on more sophisticated cues than gradient magnitude. Proposing that high-level information is involved in rejecting inappropriate edges presupposes that sufficient information is available to construct a cognitive representation of the scene. Were shadows and sharp changes in surface orientation labelled as surface colour changes, it would be difficult to construct such a representation in the first place.

Human photoreceptors do not appear to have the properties required for perfect colour constancy. The support of the receptor sensitivity functions intersects, and they do not appear to be within a linear transformation of a set of functions with non-intersecting support (Appendix B). In a sense, this is not surprising. The human vision system can place only one kind of receptor at each site in the retina, and has a more pressing need for spatial acuity (which would be reduced by employing receptors the support of whose sensitivities did not intersect) than for colour constancy. Furthermore, there are reasons to believe that the transformation that best mimics the effects of the human colour constancy system is not linear (McAdam, 1946; Jameson & Hurvich, 1972; Wyszecki & Stiles, 1980; Bartleson, 1977).

Crule has real advantages as a model of the earliest parts of a surface colour process. The most important aspect of this algorithm is not that it can be made to recover surface colour, but that it recovers a reliable feasible set for the illuminant. This set can be recovered using global support if one believes that there is only one illuminant, or equally simply, using local support. In the case where one uses local support, the feasible set will typically be larger; however, we may now use the feasible set together with the receptor responses to generate a feasible set for surface colour. If we assume that surface colour is nearly constant within regions, we may pool the information in these sets by intersecting them within boundaries. *Prima facie* evidence of spatial changes in illuminant colour will exist, for example, when locally derived feasible sets for the illuminant have an empty intersection. A constraint-based mechanism like this, which represents surface colours as sets of feasible values rather than as fixed entities, allows us to import information from other sources, such as mutual illumination analysis (Gilchrist, 1979; Forsyth & Zisserman, 1989), which may be imprecise. If for some reason we are forced to make up our minds, we may always apply an estimator.

An algorithm based on exploiting illuminant information hidden in the gamut has other advantages. Since it is possible to infer the existence of a constraint on the gamut under a given light inductively from observations of that gamut, one may propose a plausible technique for learning colour constancy, as one does not need to know properties of surface reflectance functions that require measuring the functions themselves. Furthermore, of all those so far proposed this approach places the weakest requirements on the properties of the scene observed. As a result, since it works, it appears to be the most attractive of the techniques proposed to date. Finally, the property that we exploit is always true. As a result, even if the photoreceptors do not admit of full colour constancy, if the illuminant is a member of the set of illuminants that we can represent, its representation will always be within the feasible set.

This is not a claim that humans do use this information to achieve colour constancy, but a suggestion that it would be surprising if they ignored such easily available and useful information. The strongest evidence for the nature of the particular algorithm that humans use would come from a catalogue of errors and failures of the human system. This information does not at present exist.

CONCLUSION

I have demonstrated an algorithm, Crule, that achieves colour constancy on real images of Mondrians. I have compared the performance of this algorithm with that of the Retinex algorithm of Land *et al.* (1971). This experimental work leads us to see chromatic adaptation as a measurement strategy employed by humans, and to realize that machines require a similar strategy to perform accurate constancy.

Although this algorithm gives very good results, one must realize that its success at computing surface colour depends very much on the unrealistic assumptions that underlie the Mondrian world. It is known that in the real world illuminants change quickly spatially. It is clear that surface colour algorithms in vision systems will need to be able to cope with more interesting objects than flat, frontally presented surfaces. There is thus much scope for further work.

APPENDIX A: THE COLOUR CONSTANCY EQUATION

We introduce some notation here:

E	the manifold of observably distinct illuminant functions, parametrized by some parameter vector $\mathbf{t}$, and embedded in a suitable, possibly large, space of functions
λ	the wavelength parameter
$e(\lambda; \mathbf{t})$	a member of E
$e(\lambda; \mathbf{t}^c)$	a particular member of E, known as the canonical illuminant
S	a set of surface reflectance functions
$s(\lambda)$	some member of S
$\rho_k(\lambda)$	the kth receptor sensitivity
L	the number of receptors
$\Phi_k(\lambda; \mathbf{t})$	$\rho_k(\lambda)e(\lambda; \mathbf{t})$ (this is introduced to clarify the development of the theory)
$\boldsymbol{\Phi}(\lambda; \mathbf{t})$	the vector whose components are $\Phi_k(\lambda; \mathbf{t})$, one per receptor.
$\boldsymbol{\Psi}(.; \mathbf{t})$	a function chosen from a set of functions, parametrized by $\mathbf{t}$ which takes the appearance of a surface under the canonical illuminant to its appearance under the light represented by $\mathbf{t}$.

We insist that the set of illuminants be a manifold, and that the parametrization represent some appropiate structure of charts, because we do not wish to waste space dealing with mathematically perverse objects. Two illuminants are "observably distinct" when, if one images all possible surface reflectances under these illuminants, one obtains two gamuts which are not exactly the same set. Vector quantities are denoted by bold type, and vector components by subscripting. The response of the kth receptor to a surface of reflectance $s(\lambda)$ illuminated by a light $e(\lambda; \mathbf{t})$ is

$$\int \rho_k(\lambda)e(\lambda; \mathbf{t})s(\lambda)\,\mathrm{d}\lambda,$$

where the integral is over some appropriate range of wavelengths. For linear receptors such as CCD cameras this is a good model of the response.

Consider a set of surfaces illuminated by some member of E, $e(\lambda; \mathbf{t})$. Our goal is to predict the appearance* of each surface when illuminated by $e(\lambda; \mathbf{t}^c)$, the

---

* This term involves no concept of induction, contrast, assimilation or similar effects; rather, we are considering the appearance of the chip as it would look with a neutral background under a canonical light. In fact we should find that a local version of Crule will have artifacts similar to these effects. We regard them as *interfering* with constancy, and do not build them in explicitly.

canonical illuminant. To do this, we construct a vector-valued function Ψ to predict the receptor responses under coloured lights generated by some surface, given the lighting parameter and the receptor responses generated under the canonical illuminant. Assume for the moment that t is known; we would like to associate with t some function, $\Psi(.; t)$, such that:

$$\Psi\left(\int \Phi(\lambda; t^c)s(\lambda)\, d\lambda; t\right) = \int \Phi(\lambda; t)s(\lambda)\, d\lambda \qquad (1)$$

for all $s(\lambda)$. In this way we associate an operation on surface colour with an illuminant. If we can construct a function $\Psi(.; t)$ with this property, and if we can estimate t for an image, we can perform colour constancy by applying $\Psi^{-1}(.; t)$ to the receptor responses we observe in that image.

Introduce an orthonormal basis $\{\phi_i(\lambda), 0 \le i < L\}$ for the space spanned by the component functions $\Phi_k(\lambda; t^c)$ of $\Phi(\lambda; t^c)$. Without loss of generality, we assume that the L functions $\Phi_k(\lambda; t^c)$ are linearly independent (for if they are not, we may simply ignore one or more of them and proceed). It is clear that such an orthonormal basis exists (we may apply the Gramm–Schmidt algorithm). Then there is a *unique* decomposition of both $\Phi_i(\lambda; t^c)$, and of $\Phi_i(\lambda, t)$ in terms of this orthonormal basis: say,

$$\Phi_i(\lambda; t^c) = \sum_{j=0}^{L-1} a_{ij}\phi_j(\lambda).$$

Since the basis $\{\phi_i(\lambda), 0 \le i < L\}$ was introduced to span the space spanned by the functions $\Phi_i(\lambda; t^c)$, it may be the case that $\Phi_i(\lambda; t)$ do not belong to $\text{Span}\{\phi_i(\lambda)\}$, and there will be a residue in the expansion of this function on this basis. Hence, for some matrix with components $r_{ik}(t)$,

$$\Phi_i(\lambda; t) = \sum_{j=0}^{L-1} \sum_{k=0}^{L-1} r_{ij}(t)a_{jk}\phi_k(\lambda) + F_i(\lambda; t), \qquad (2)$$

where F_i is a residue orthogonal to all the $\phi_i(\lambda)$. Now we see immediately that equation (1) becomes:

$$\Psi_k\left(\int \Phi(\lambda; t^c)s(\lambda)\, d\lambda; t\right) = \sum_{j=0}^{L-1} r_{kj}(t)\int \Phi_j(\lambda; t^c)s(\lambda)\, d\lambda + \int F_i(\lambda; t)s(\lambda)\, d\lambda, \qquad (3)$$

where $\Psi_k(.; t)$ is the kth component function of $\Psi(.; t)$.

We insist only that a surface reflectance function is a non-pathological function from some interval Λ to the closed unit interval. Let us require these functions to be members of $\mathcal{L}^2[\Lambda]$, the space of functions whose squares are integrable. This is a very weak restriction. It is clearly also reasonable to assume that E is some finite-dimensional submanifold of $\mathcal{L}^2[\Lambda]$.

We may expand $s(\lambda)$ in terms of the basis $\{\phi_i(\lambda)\}$, as both E and S are subsets of a space of functions. Thus, we have a *unique* decomposition for any $s(\lambda)$,

$$s(\lambda) = \sum_{i=0}^{L-1} \sigma_i \phi_i(\lambda) + s^*(\lambda),$$

where $s^*(\lambda)$ is a residue orthogonal to each of the ϕ_i. We see that equation (3) becomes:

$$\Psi_k \left(\sum_{j=0}^{L-1} a_{ij}\sigma_j; \mathbf{t} \right) = \sum_{j=0}^{L-1} \sum_{s=0}^{L-1} r_{kj}(\mathbf{t}) a_{js} \sigma_s + \int F_k(\lambda; \mathbf{t}) s^*(\lambda) \, d\lambda. \tag{4}$$

This equation is fundamental to any analysis of colour constancy. We call equation (4) the *colour constancy equation*, and refer to the term $\int F_k(\lambda; \mathbf{t}) s^*(\lambda) \, d\lambda$ as the residual term. This term is the only impediment to success on the part of a colour constancy algorithm. If this term is not constant for every surface under each light, we will need to be able to predict its value. We cannot do this in general, for the term will depend on terms in the expansion of $s(\lambda)$ that we have not observed.

From equation (4) we may also see that constructing some non-linear $\Psi^{-1}(.; \mathbf{t})$ is erroneous. The residual terms cannot be determined, or accounted for by non-linearity in the form of this function without other strong assumptions about the form of surface reflectance functions. Since a colour constancy algorithm can work properly only in a world where the residual term is constant (without loss of generality, assume that this is zero). There are three preconditions that will ensure a zero residual:

1. For any illuminant, parametrized by $\mathbf{t}$, the residual term $F_k(\lambda; \mathbf{t}) = 0$, for all k. There is no condition on surface reflectances.
2. Surface reflectance functions are only L dimensional and in particular are members of the space spanned by $\{\phi_0(\lambda), \ldots, \phi_{L-1}(\lambda)\}$.
3. Surface reflectances are $M > L$ dimensional. In this case, we assume that the space of surface reflectances is spanning by

$$\{\phi_0(\lambda), \ldots, \phi_{L-1}(\lambda), \phi_L(\lambda), \ldots, \phi_{M-1}(\lambda)\},$$

where $\phi_0(\lambda), \ldots, \phi_{L-1}(\lambda)$ are derived from the receptors and the canonical illuminant in the manner indicated. Now we have insisted that the illuminants that we consider be represented by a manifold; we require further that this manifold be embedded in some finite-dimensional subspace of functions which represent illuminants. If we choose this space such that for each $e_i(\lambda)$ in some basis of the space (and hence for any basis)

$$\int \rho_k(\lambda) e_i(\lambda) \phi_j(\lambda) \, d\lambda \quad \text{for } L \leq j < M \quad \text{and} \quad 0 \leq k < L,$$

then the residual terms will be zero for any of the illuminants.

I refer to the first precondition as a minimal assumption of the first kind, and to the second and third preconditions as being minimal assumptions of the second kind. An algorithm based on minimal assumptions of the first kind will work for an infinite-dimensional set of surface reflectances, but requires a restriction on the illuminants which we describe in Appendix B. An algorithm based on minimal assumptions of the second kind, however, will work only on a finite-dimensional set of surface reflectances.

Let us assume that in the world in which our algorithm will work these residual terms are zero, so that equation (4) becomes:

$$\Psi_k\left(\sum_{j=0}^{L-1} a_{ij}\sigma_j; \mathbf{t}\right) = \sum_{j=0}^{L-1}\sum_{s=0}^{L-1} r_{kj}(\mathbf{t})a_{js}\sigma_s. \tag{5}$$

This tells us that the receptor responses we observe under any light are the images in a linear map of the first L coefficients of some expansion of the surface reflectance function. We can now construct an algorithm for estimating $\mathbf{t}$ by exploiting properties of the world.

APPENDIX B: THE STRUCTURE OF THE FEASIBLE SET

Minimal Assumptions of the First Kind

From equation (2) and the assumption that for all $\mathbf{t}$, $F_k(\lambda, \mathbf{t}) = 0$, we have

$$\Phi_i(\lambda; \mathbf{t}) = \sum_{j=0}^{j=L-1} r_{ij}(\mathbf{t})\Phi_j(\lambda; \mathbf{t}^c).$$

We need to consider what this actually means in terms of the illuminant functions. Recall that we defined $\boldsymbol{\Phi}(\lambda; \mathbf{t})$ to have components $\Phi_k(\lambda; \mathbf{t}) = \rho_k(\lambda)e(\lambda; \mathbf{t})$. We can define a vector valued function, $\rho(\lambda)$ such that $\boldsymbol{\Phi}(\lambda; \mathbf{t}) = e(\lambda; \mathbf{t})\rho(\lambda)$. Then for a matrix $R(\mathbf{t})$ having components $r_{ij}(\mathbf{t})$, we have

$$\rho(\lambda)e(\lambda; \mathbf{t}) = R(\mathbf{t})\rho(\lambda)e(\lambda; \mathbf{t}^c).$$

We assume that R has full rank. If $e(\lambda; \mathbf{t}) = 0$, then either $e(\lambda; \mathbf{t}^c) = 0$ or $\rho(\lambda) = 0$. This case is of little interest, so we recall that $e(\lambda; \mathbf{t})$, and $e(\lambda; \mathbf{t}^c)$ are scalar valued functions, and consider

$$\rho(\lambda) = R(\mathbf{t})\rho(\lambda)\frac{e(\lambda; \mathbf{t}^c)}{e(\lambda; \mathbf{t})}.$$

Then this requires for all λ that $\rho(\lambda)$ is an eigenvector of $R(\mathbf{t})$. But $R(\mathbf{t})$ is a function of $\mathbf{t}$ alone and has at most L distinct eigenvectors, so we need to pick the of $\rho(\lambda)$ such that $\rho(\lambda)$ is for any λ an eigenvector of R. This is accomplished by writing

$$\rho(\lambda) = \sum_{j=0}^{L-1} k_j(\lambda)\varepsilon_j,$$

where

$$\text{Support}(k_i(\lambda)) \cap \text{Support}(k_j(\lambda)) = \varnothing, \qquad i \neq j$$

and the ε_j are linearly independent. The terms ε_j, will be the L eigenvectors of $R(t)$. These are a result of the choice of receptor, and that choice represents a constraint on the form of $R(t)$. Notice that if we do not choose the eigenvectors to be linearly independent, then the receptor sensitivities arising will not be linearly independent. Since we have chosen its eigenvectors, we have only L free parameters for R, which are its eigenvalues.

Intuitively, this scheme requires a strong property of the illuminant. Consider some $\lambda = \lambda_0$: we have required that

$$\rho(\lambda_0) = \frac{e(\lambda_0; \mathbf{t}^c)}{e(\lambda_0; \mathbf{t})} R(\mathbf{t})\rho(\lambda_0)$$

in particular, as a result of the expansion of ρ, and the fact that the supports of the coefficient functions are disjoint, there is some $0 \leq i < L$ such that

$$\rho(\lambda_0) = k_i(\lambda_0)\varepsilon_i$$

(no summation over i). Then we have

$$\rho(\lambda_0) = \frac{e(\lambda_0; \mathbf{t}^c)}{e(\lambda_0; \mathbf{t})} R(\mathbf{t})k_i(\lambda_0)\varepsilon_i$$

$$k_i(\lambda_0)\varepsilon_i = \frac{e(\lambda_0; \mathbf{t}^c)}{e(\lambda_0; \mathbf{t})} \mu_i k_i(\lambda_0)\varepsilon_i,$$

where μ_i is the eigenvalue associated with ε_i. One obtains from this equation

$$\frac{e(\lambda_0; \mathbf{t}^c)}{e(\lambda_0; \mathbf{t})} \mu_i = 1.$$

And this is true over the support of $k_i(\lambda)$. Thus, we are requiring that over the support of each $k_i(\lambda)$,

$$\frac{e(\lambda; \mathbf{t}^c)}{e(\lambda; \mathbf{t})}$$

is constant. This is a strong requirement.

The analysis of the case of minimal assumptions of the second kind is more complex. An algorithm based on minimal assumptions of the second kind could recover L surface colour descriptors, and either $L^2 - 1$ or L^2 illuminant parameters, for L receptors. This is rather an embarrassment of parameters for a model of human colour constancy. I believe that an algorithm which can recover these illuminant parameters is at best a novelty. The requirements on surfaces and on lights is stringent, and implementing this algorithm is likely to be difficult. However, as it arises naturally from assumptions of finite dimensionality in surface reflectances, it is worth stating.

APPENDIX C: CONSTRUCTING THE FEASIBLE SET

Proposition: The feasible set is convex.

Proof: Denote by Δ the gamut of all possible surface reflectances imaged under the canonical illuminant, and *Obs* the observed gamut. Now for maps C and D, $C(Obs) \subset \Delta$ and $D(Obs) \subset \Delta$ implies for $0 \leq \mu \leq 1$, $\mu C(Obs) + (1 - \mu)D(Obs) \subset \Delta$ (by the convexity of Δ) and then C and D in the feasible set implies $\mu C + (1 - \mu)D$ is in the feasible set. $\square$

Proposition: The uniquely determined diagonal map taking a hull point $\mathbf{h}$ of *Obs* to a hull point of Δ is on the boundary of the feasible set for an image containing $\mathbf{h}$ alone.

Proof: We can see that an arbitrarily small perturbation of this particular map can take $\mathbf{h}$ to a point outside the canonical gamut. Equally, an arbitrarily small perturbation of this particular map can take $\mathbf{h}$ to a point inside the canonical gamut. Then this map is in the closure of the constraint set, and in the closure of the complement of the feasible set, and is hence on the boundary of the constraint set. $\square$

It is possible to prove that to determine the feasible set, we need only intersect the feasible sets for all the hull points $\mathbf{h}$ of *Obs* (Forsyth, 1989). Thus, to construct the feasible set, we construct the hull points of the feasible sets for each $\mathbf{h}$, and intersect the resulting convex sets. This process is greatly simplified by the convexity properties of the feasible sets. We require that there be many different colours in the image because we are assuming that a hull point of the observed gamut is on the boundary of the gamut that we would observe if the picture contained every possible surface reflectance.

ACKNOWLEDGEMENTS

I thank my supervisor, Michael Brady, for support and encouragement. Larry Arend, Andrew Blake, Margaret Fleck, Tom Troscianko, and Andrew Zisserman have helped me by discussing aspects of this material with me. This work was supported by the Rhodes Trust and Magdalen College, Oxford.

REFERENCES

Arend, L. E. & Reeves, A. (1986). Simultaneous colour constancy. *Journal of the Optical Society of America*, **A3**,1743–1751.

Barlow, H. B. & Mollon, J. D. (1982). *The Senses*. Cambridge University Press, Cambridge.

Bartleson, C. J. (1977). A review of chromatic adaptation. In F. W. Billmeyer & G. Wyszecki (Eds) *Color 77*. Adam Hilger, Bristol.

Beck, J. (1972). *Surface Color Preception*. Cornell University Press, Ithaca, NY.

Benzschawel, T., Walraven, J. & Rogowitz, B. (1987). Studies of colour constancy. *Investigative Ophthalmology and Visual Science*, **28** (Suppl.), 92.

Blackwell, K. T. & Buchsbaum, G. (1988). Quantitative studies of color constancy. *Journal of the Optical Society of America*, **A5**, 1772–1780.

Blake, A. (1985). Boundary conditions for lightness computation in Mondrian world. In D. Ottoson & S. Zeki (Eds.) *Central and Peripheral Mechanisms of Colour Vision*, Macmillan.

Boothby, W. (1986). *An Introduction to Differentiable Manifolds and Riemannian Geometry*. Academic Press, New York

Brainard, D. H. & Wandell, B. A. (1986). Analysis of the Retinex theory of color vision. *Journal of the Optical Society of America*, **A3**, 1651–1661.

Brainard, D. H. & Wandell, B. A. (1988). Classification studies of colour appearance. *Investigative Ophthalmology and Visual Science*, **29** (Suppl.), 162.

Brelstaff, G. & Blake, A. (1987). Computing lightness. *Pattern Recognition Letters*, **5**, 129–138.

Brill, M. H. (1979). Computer simulation of object color recognisers. Abstract submitted to 1979 annual meeting of OSA. *Journal of the Optical Society of America*, **69**, 1405.

Buchsbaum, G. (1980). A spatial processor model for object colour perception. *Journal of the Franklin Institute*, **310**, 1–26.

Cameron, S. A. (1989). Efficient intersection tests for objects defined constructively. *International Journal of Robotics Research*, **8**, 1.

Cohen, J. (1964). Dependency of the spectral reflectance curves of the Munsell color chips. *Psychonomic Science*, **1**, 369–370.

D'Zmura, M. & Lennie, P. (1986). Mechanisms of colour constancy. *Journal of the Optical Society of America*, **A3**, 1662–1672.

Forsyth, D. A. (1989). Colour constancy and its applications in machine vision. D.Phil. thesis, Oxford University.

Forsyth, D. A. & Zisserman, A. (1989). Mutual illumination. *Proceedings of the IEEE Conference on Computer Vision and Pattern Recognition*, IEEE Press, 466–475.

Gershon, R. (1987). The use of colour in computational vision. Ph.D. thesis, University of Toronto.

Gershon, R., Jepson, A. & Tsotsos, J. (1986). Ambient illumination and the determination of material changes. *Journal of the Optical Society of America*, **A3**, 1700–1707.

Gilchrist, A. L. (1979). The perception of surface blacks and whites. *Scientific American*, **240**, 112–124.

Gilchrist, A. L., Delman, S. & Jacobsen, A. (1983). The classification and integration of edges as critical to the perception of reflectance and illumination. *Perception and Psychophysics*, **33**, 425–436.

Helmholtz, H. van (1962). *Treatise on Physiological Optics*, translated by J. P. Southall. Dover, New York.

Horn, B. K. P. (1974). Determining lightness from an image. *Computer Graphics and Image Processing*, **3**, 277–299.

Hurlbert, A. (1986). Formal connections between lightness algorithms. *Journal of the Optical Society of America*, **A3**, 1684–1693.

Jameson, D. & Hurvich, L. M. (1972). Color adaptation: sensitivity, contrast and after-images. In D. Jameson & L. M. Hurvich (Eds) *Handbook of Sensory Physiology*, Vol. VII/4, *Visual Psychophysics*. Springer, Berlin.

Judd, D. B. (1940). Hue, saturation and lightness of surface colors with chromatic illumination. *Journal of the Optical Society of America*, **30**, 2–32.

Judd, D. B. (1960). Appraisal of Land's work on two-primary colour projections. *Journal of the Optical Society of America*, **30**, 254–268.

Katz, D. (1935). *The World of Colour*, translated from the second German edition of 1911 by R. B. Mcleod and C. W. Fox. Kegan Paul, London.

Klinker, G. F., Shafer, S. A. & Kanade, T. (1987). Using a colour reflection model to separate highlights from object colour. *Proceedings ICCV*.

Koenderink, J. J. (1987). Color atlas theory. *Journal of the Optical Society of America*, **A4**, 1314–1321.

Kries, J. von (1878). Beitrag zur Physiologie der Gesichtsempfindung. *Archives of Anatomy and Physiology*, **2**, 505–524.

Krinov, E. L. (1947). *Spectral Reflectance Properties of Natural Formations*. National Research Council of Canada, Technical Translation: TT-439.

Land, E. H. (1959a). Color vision and the natural image. Part I. *Proceedings of the National Academy of Science, USA*, **45**, 115–129.

Land, E. H. (1959b). Color vision and the natural image. Part II. *Proceedings of the National Academy of Science, USA*, **45**, 636–644.

Land, E. H. (1977). The retinex theory of colour vision. *Scientific American*, **237**(6), 108–128.

Land, E. H. (1983). Color vision and the natural image. Part III: Recent advances in Retinex theory and some implications for cortical computations. *Proceedings of the National Academy of Science, USA*, **80**, 5163–5169.

Land, E. H. (1985). Recent advances in Retinex theory. In D. Ottoson and S. Zeki (Eds) *Central and Peripheral Mechanisms of Colour Vision*. Macmillan, London.

Land, E. H. (1986). Recent advances in Retinex theory. *Vision Research*, **26**, 7–21.

Land, E. H. & Daw, N. W. (1962). Colors seen in a flash of light. *Proceedings of the National Academy of Science, USA*, **48**, 1000–1008.

Land, E. H. & McCann, J. J. (1971). Lightness and Retinex theory. *Journal of the Optical Society of America*, **61**, 1–11.

Lee, H.-C. (1986). Method for computing the scene-illuminant chromaticity from specular highlights. *Journal of the Optical Society of America*, **A3**, 1694–1699.

McAdam, D. L. (1946). Chromatic adaptation. *Journal of the Optical Society of America*, **46**, 500–513.

McAdam, D. L. (1982). *Colour Measurement: Theme and Variations*. Springer, Berlin.

McCann, J. J., McKee, S. P. & Taylor, T. H. (1976). Quantitative studies in Retinex theory. *Vision Research*, **16**, 445–458.

Maloney, L. T. (1984). Computational approaches to color constancy. Ph.D. dissertation, Stanford University, Stanford, California.

Maloney, L. T. (1986). Evaluation of linear models of surface spectral reflectance with small numbers of parameters. *Journal of the Optical Society of America*, **A3**, 1673–1683.

Maloney, L. T. & Wandell, B. A. (1986). A computational model of color constancy. *Journal of the Optical Society of America*, **A1**, 29–33.

Sallstrom, P. (1973). Colour and physics: some remarks concerning the physical aspects of human colour vision. University of Stockholm: Institute of Physics Report 73-09.

Wandell, B. A. (1987). The synthesis and analysis of color images. *IEEE Transactions: Pattern Analysis and Machine Intelligence*, **9**, 2–13.

Woodwark, J. R. & Quinlan, K. M. (1984). Reducing the effect of complexity on volume model evaluation. *CAD J.*, **14**, 2.

Wyszecki, G. & Stiles, W. S. (1980). High-level trichromatic colour matching and the pigment bleaching hypothesis. *Vision Research*, **20**, 23–37.

Wyszecki, G. & Stiles, W. S. (1982). *Color Science: Concepts and Methods, Qualitative Data and Formulae*. John Wiley, Chichester.

Young, R. A. (1987). Color vision and the retinex theory. *Science*, **238**, 1731–1732.

10 Scene Structure from a Moving Camera

H. Harlyn Baker

Artificial Intelligence Center, SRI International, 333 Ravenswood Avenue, Menlo Park, CA 94025, USA

INTRODUCTION

Research in using computers to sense and build descriptions of the world has been pursued for several decades, generally in conjunction with efforts to develop a capacity for computer or robot visual perception. Early attempts to develop computer vision systems were handicapped by, among other things, lack of sufficient computer power and memory to make the job feasible. It is only recently, with greatly increased memory capacities and parallel processing that computer vision has been making headway toward the ideal of human performance. Although only a first step in balancing the inequity in the artificial versus the natural mechanism, these new facilities have permitted broader views of the computational issues, and provided some new perspectives on the data and approaches appropriate for this difficult task. In this vein of new perspectives, this chapter describes a robot perception process that integrates spatial and temporal image processing in a novel, powerful and robust way, demonstrating impressive accomplishment and promising considerably more.

DEVELOPING COMPUTER SIGHT

The example of human visual processing has always presented itself as an existence proof that the pursuit of computer sight was a feasible goal. Mimicry of the actual mechanisms involved in the human version, however, has rarely been a concern of those pursuing the computer path. There are several reasons for this, perhaps the most crucial being that an adequate model of the human process has never been

AI and the Eye   Edited by A. Blake and T. Troscianko
© 1990 John Wiley & Sons Ltd.

available. With no human model proposed, it would be somewhat mad either to insist on adherence to one, or to delay development of machine vision systems until one is drafted and accepted. Even if one existed, it is unclear whether it alone should form the basis of a machine duplicate. The evolutionary process was reacting on a scale quite different from ours, with a different set of tools and materials: with our modern devices and egos we may consider ourselves able to choose paths that are more direct. Ignoring for the moment the marvel of its success, we can draw out limitations inherent in the human system when put in comparison with those of a more engineered design, for example: chromatic aberration; sensitivity only to a certain range of energy; the presence of a blind spot; an inability to observe events happening outside a fairly narrow range in time and size scales; and perhaps most significantly, the qualitative rather than metric character of our percepts. Characteristics such as these provide no obvious advantage from an information point of view, and may well argue to us that if the opportunity arises we should develop our own set of plans, and use the human example more as a theme than a model.

Choosing the Approach

On the pragmatic side, the capabilities required of a computer vision system are not necessarily as demanding as those needed to keep us humans alive and working in our environment, full of challenges and dangers. With an extremely limited vocabulary of visual stimulants, and quite simple and obvious discriminations to be made among them, many vision applications can be achieved using almost any old hack—or so it might at times seem. Funding imperatives have also reinforced this, as a requirement for focus on specific applications is often the norm. Another pragmatic reason for the lack of regard for the capabilities or mechanisms of the human system is the vast mismatch between processing and related computing power. In the early days of computer vision we used machines in which finding room to store an image may itself have been an accomplishment, and performing even simple operations on that image took forever. We have not had enormous parallel machines for our experiments: limited to all-too-finite sequential computers, we have developed our ideas and structured our processes within their constraints.

Further contributing to the lack of psychological and physiological relevance in our field (and perhaps to its relative lack of success) has been the general acceptance of a divide-and-conquer approach, where certain parts of a process are studied independently, hopefully to be combined later in delivering the system's full capabilities. This approach may have arisen in computer vision research from observing, for example, the stellar accomplishment of our two-eyed system in making sense out of one-eyed data (such as photographs) or symbolic abstractions (such as line drawings). Capabilities such as these are viewed as providing insight into the mechanism. Developing within this experimental context, individual components of the visual system have been conceptually excised and studied in isolation. Much effort has gone into interpreting single images of scenes, for example, and understanding hand-drawn sketches; researchers have written cube finders, house finders, face finders, tumor finders, etc., interpreted shadows, brightness gradients and two-dimensional outlines in inferring three-dimensional shape. These approaches miss on at least three scores: first, having defined the problem as a sum of *x-finder* processes, the obvious temptation is to develop those processes in the most direct manner, looking at a minimum of the information presented—psychophysical relevance is seldom a consideration; second, focusing on each independently, it is unlikely to be noticed that they have complex interrelationships (including equivalence); third, they ignore the generative issues —if we could enumerate a mimicry of some level of human performance in a certain domain, would that be an answer? What I really question here is whether it is a worthwhile pursuit to build computer programs aimed at specific performance capabilities. We excel at a large variety of specific tasks—recognizing friends, interpreting X-rays, spotting buildings in aerial images, distinguishing subtle texture differences—but will developing each of these lead us closer to the goal of a seeing machine? If a broader view tells us that these are mere projections of, or slices through, the human system's capabilities, then we are unlikely to get very far in covering the *n*-dimensional mosaic with these attempts to paint in specific lower-dimensional functions. (And, despite innumerable efforts, none has as yet come near human competence.)

Developing a Basis for Vision

These criticisms are not, despite the appearance, a call for a back-to-beginnings neural learning program to solve it all. We know in research that, as in the rest of life, it may require getting here to learn what getting here does not give us: standing back a bit can give us a useful perspective. Granted we need some structuring in our approach, but by addressing vision as a set of task-specific, unalterable functional units, we may have divided the task irreparably, and have lost some of the important adaptive characteristics of the human system. Although what is observable about vision is its performance, it comprises much more than this. In fact, the performance part can be viewed as little more than the final stage—the actual putting of a name on some object observed in the stream of sensory information. To recognize an object requires having a description of it stored and a description of it extracted from the current sensory flow. In an adaptable system, the stored descriptions are acquired over time and evolve with experience: they are not cast at birth. To produce a vision system providing this generative aspect may require a refocusing of the research effort: rather than setting out to reproduce visual competence, perhaps we should first develop the representational basis that will later be used in attaining this competence. This is the perspective taken in the research to be presented in this chapter—to process visual information in representing our world and its contents, ignorant from, yet in anticipation of, later use in tasks of scene understanding (for example, recognizing friends, interpreting X-rays, etc.).

Here, we first aim to exploit and develop whatever means are available in building the richest descriptions we can of the three-dimensional world we inhabit. It is only once such a process is understood and operating that we will then turn our attention to *using* the acquired knowledge, perhaps to prime our responsiveness for specific recurring tasks—compiling for efficiency, if you will. Issues such as object recognition will be put on hold, with our primary task being to develop mechanisms for building up and encoding our visual experience—building models of our world. This may be the biggest lesson to be learned from human vision—we need an adaptable system, one which grows with its experience and modifies its representations for, first, expressiveness and discrimination, and only then for task-specific efficiency. (Our effectiveness in dealing with objects depends on our familiarity with them.) Addressing the performance end first with limited information and goals may be both theoretically inappropriate and evolutionarily suicidal.

Data for Building Representations

The world being three-dimensional, single-perspective images would seem to be a somewhat impoverished basis for describing its events. Two images, treated in unison as a stereo pair, provide a much better view of a three-dimensional scene. Computer vision research using this two-image stereo has been studied for the past decade and a half. Some of the computational models developed for this have been meant to mirror theory of human stereo processing, others have been more expediency based. All have been extremely expensive computationally, and none has been what one could call universally successful. Despite the increased dimensionality, the failure could still be in attempting to overextract from inappropriate or impoverished data. The biggest difficulty in stereo processing is what is termed the correspondence problem—matching image elements (the projections of scene elements) in the two views. Many imaging and image-processing factors conspire to make this an ill-posed problem: perspective distorts the shapes of features between viewpoints; occlusion among objects makes it quite possible that a particular feature will not even be visible in a second view; image brightness varies with orientation and surface reflectance properties of objects, and what appears light from one perspective can be dark from another; precision of feature localization is increased with increased separation between the two imaging sites, yet increased separation means greater difference between the images, and therefore increased difficulty in the matching and diminished accuracy. Stereo is difficult, as yet unresolved, and perhaps unresolvable as it is currently addressed.

Recall that our concern is for both the performance aspects of a machine vision system and its generative capability, and from this perspective we must question the appropriateness of stereo as a sole source of three-dimensional analysis. There is no doubt that we see depth in a stereo pair of images of some scene—but is this information adequate for constructing a model of that scene? It might be, if we have knowledge already of everything present and can successfully associate each scene component with its appropriate memory model. If, however, the three-dimensional slice provided by stereo is inadequate (and it will be, in general, if the scene components are novel), then something beyond stereo is needed. In fact, motion is that something. Many of the problems of data sufficiency disappear if a continuum of views is provided, and some of the principal problems in image analysis become considerably more tenable. In sequence analysis, where rapid image sampling produces images that change little from one to the next, matching is less problematic, and, with a much greater range of views of a scene, considerably more complete descriptions of scene objects are attainable. These, image sequences, are the data we choose for our analyses.

Although we diverge considerably from human image processing notions, we capitalize heavily on, or intend to, many of the underlying principles, including the use of a continuous visual flow, the geometry induced by a moving observer, analysis in both spatial and temporal dimensions, and analysis over a range of spatial frequencies. The mechanisms we employ will be from engineering and mathematics; the philosophy will hopefully be more intuitive, and consistent with the human model.

A SPACE-TIME APPROACH TO COMPUTER VISION

The direct focus of our research is on giving a robot the ability to move safely through a scene using its own sight. As in man, the success of the approach depends on its ability to operate explicitly in both space and time, and on exploiting the massive redundancy present in the hundreds of views that can be obtained when moving through a scene.

Spatiotemporal Processing

Our approach involves taking a sequence of images from positions that are very close together—close enough that almost nothing changes from one image to the next. With this capture spacing, none of the features in an image moves more than a few pixels. This sampling frequency guarantees a continuity in the temporal domain similar to the obvious spatial continuity, and lets us avoid the difficult correspondence problem. An edge of an object in one image appears temporally adjacent to (within a pixel or so of) its occurrence in both the preceding and following images. This rapid sampling makes it possible to construct a volume of data in which time is the third dimension and continuity is maintained over all three dimensions (see Figure 2). We refer to this volume as our *spatiotemporal data*.

In our initial implementation, we chose to use a restricted camera arrangement, one whose geometry facilitated the analysis considerably. The camera moved along a *straight path*, acquiring images at *fixed spacings* and looking at *right angles* to its path. In effect, the situation corresponds to looking straight out the side of a train window. Figure 1 shows several frames from a 125-image sequence obtained under these conditions. Figure 2 shows a volume formed by stacking the images together. The front, with (u, v) coordinates, is a regular image—the first in the sequence. The visible side of the volume shows the rightmost column of each image, and gives a (misleading) impression of also being a normal image. The top looks less imagelike, but is a crucial depiction for our processing.

Figure 3 shows the volume sliced horizontally along its middle, cut away to reveal a pattern somewhat like that at the top of the volume to its left. This pattern, showing the temporal continuity of features, is referred to as an *epipolar-plane*

Figure 1. Four frames of a 125-frame sequence from a moving camera.

Figure 2. Spatiotemporal volume formed from 125-image sequence.

image (EPI). By following these paths (which must be straight lines for stationary objects,given our restricted camera geometry) we can establish the position of features in the scene; each linear path is a feature in the scene, and its distance from the camera path depends simply on the slope of the line. Figure 4 shows feature position estimates from one slice of the data shown in Figure 2. Since each path is made up of many observations of a particular feature, these overdetermine its estimate, and the statistical covariance gives us a confidence interval. These confidence intervals are depicted in the figure by ellipses. The coordinate system used here is in units of world inches, with the line at the bottom indicating the camera's path through the scene. Figure 5 is a display created for stereoscopic viewing; it depicts the feature estimates combined from all the slices through the data set shown in Figure 2.

The success of this processing demonstrates that spatiotemporal analysis can be used to great effect in simplifying and making more robust the recovery of scene geometry from images of static scenes. The approach bridges the usual dichotomy of passive depth sensing in that its large number of images leads to a large baseline and thus high precision in our results, while rapid image sampling gives minimal change from frame to frame, eliminating the correspondence problem and increasing the accuracy. Rather than choosing quite disparate views and putting features into correspondence by stereo matching, with this technique we chose to process

Figure 3. Spatiotemporal volume sliced along a scan line.

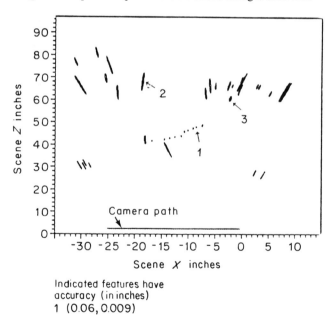

Indicated features have
accuracy (in inches)
1 (0.06, 0.009)
2 (0.86, 0.03)
3 (0.25, 0.04)

Figure 4. Feature estimates from one slice through data set (equivalently, one slice through scene).

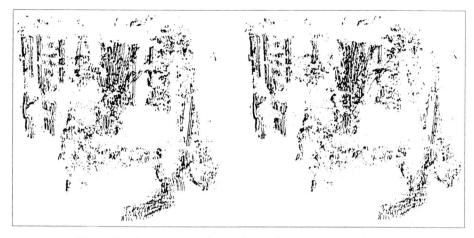

Figure 5.   Cross-eyed stereo display of feature estimates in scene.

massive amounts of similar data, but with much simpler and more robust techniques. Its simplicity, redundancy and inherent parallelism may suggest similarities with the human system.

Extending the Capabilities—Space-Time Surfaces

This early implementation achieved its purpose of demonstrating the feasibility and benefits of the approach, but, with the restriction to a limited camera geometry, brought into question whether it could have any utility for general motion. First, a linear camera path would be an unacceptable or highly improbable trajectory in almost every situation except extended flight. Even accepting a linear path, the orthogonal viewing would preclude many of the camera attitudes necessary for general motion—in particular the important one in which the vehicle is looking where it is going. Furthermore, a constant rate of image acquisition would be both difficult to guarantee and undesirable, while operating in a batch mode, where all the data must be available before scene measurement can begin, would seem to eliminate one of the principal goals of the process—to provide timely spatial information for a vehicle in motion. The analysis really should proceed sequentially, as the imagery is acquired, and be capable of processing at whatever sampling rates are demanded of it, or as dictated by higher-level concerns.

Addressing these issues, we have developed a generalization of the analysis that (a) permits varying view direction, including variation over time, and (b) operates sequentially, allowing initiation and refinement of scene feature estimates while the sensor is in motion. Although not currently implemented, the generalization will also provide for non-linear camera motions. To implement this generalization it was necessary to develop an explicit description of the evolution of images over time. This we have achieved by building a process that creates a set of two-dimensional manifolds defined at the zeros of a three-dimensional spatiotemporal Laplacian. These manifolds represent explicitly both the spatial and temporal structure of the temporally evolving imagery, and we term them *spatiotemporal* *surfaces*. We call the process that builds the surfaces the *weaving wall*, after its action and structure. The surfaces are constructed incrementally, as the images are acquired. A tracking mechanism operates locally on them, using geometric constraints provided by the camera's motion in recovering the three-dimensional scene structure.* These geometric constraints mirror quite precisely the flow lines identified by Gibson in his discussion on ego motion (Gibson, 1950).

Since the surface-construction process maintains both spatial and temporal image relationships, they deliver another special benefit—they provide three-dimensional connectivity information for building coherent spatial descriptions of observed objects. The earlier EPI partitioning, through its selection of the temporal over the spatial analysis of images, could not provide spatially coherent results. It produced point sets, much as the night sky's constellations (Figure 5). We attempted clustering operations on these point sets, but were never satisfied with such a *post hoc* solution. The proper approach to obtaining spatial coherence in our results should begin with not losing it in the first place, and this is what is accomplished by the space–time surfaces.

We still restrict ourselves to static scenes. These may be the *least* likely in any environment, as winds blow, clouds move, and often a moving object in a scene is the one of most interest. But recall our motivation—we wish to build three-dimensional descriptions of scenes. It may be inappropriate to expect this to be possible if our view of the scene is undergoing change unrelated to our active pursuit of that structure. In an earlier publication (Bolles *et al.*, 1987), we discussed this motion issue and suggested means to recognize its presence in a scene. Once distinguished from the static elements, it would be possible to invoke higher-order models and filters to estimate these objects' dynamics (as reported in Gennery, 1982, and Broida & Chellappa, 1986), but our current interest is in modeling static structure, so we leave this for the future.

It is worth repeating this to clarify our goals in the current work. We are not working with changing scenes, nor is our aim to build descriptions of moving or deforming objects. Our camera is all that moves, and any changes in the imagery arise strictly from this movement. Our goal is to model the geometry of a static scene through which the camera is moving. This distinguishes us from most of the current efforts in spatiotemporal analysis that use image-plane velocities for measuring arbitrary flows (for example, Heeger, 1986), or that combine the measured flow with assumptions of constant 3D motion and rigidity for estimating known-order analytic surfaces (i.e. Waxman & Wohn, 1985; Subbarao, 1986; Waxman *et al.*, 1987). Our scenes contain arbitrarily shaped objects, and we wish to exploit all the information available to our sensors, over time, in building the fullest descriptions of them possible.

NEW APPROACH TO EPI ANALYSIS

In common with our earlier work, our new approach involves the processing of a very large number of images acquired by a moving camera. The analysis is based on three constraints.

---

* Details of this analysis are presented in Baker & Bolles (1989).

1. The camera's movement is restricted to lie along a linear path.
2. The camera's position and attitude at each imaging site are known.
3. Image capture is rapid enough with respect to camera movement and scene scale to ensure that the data are, in general, temporally continuous.

Within this framework, we generalize from the traditional notion of epipolar *lines* to that of epipolar *planes*—a set of epipolar lines sharing a property of transitivity (which we discuss below). We formulate a tracking process that exploits this property for determining the position of features in the scene. This tracking occurs on what we term the *spatiotemporal surface*—a surface defining the evolution of a set of scene features over time. Critical to visualizing this space–time approach is obtaining an understanding of the geometry of the sensing situation, and an extremely good depiction of this can be seen in the ego motion studies of Gibson (1950).

Geometric Considerations of Camera Path and Attitude

When an observer (a visual sensor) moves through space along a linear path, the pattern of optic flow it perceives is structured as meridians, initiated ahead at the focus of expansion (FOE) and terminating behind it at the focus of contraction (FOC). Although this has been observed for years (first by Gibson and subsequently by most stereo and motion researchers), it has not been used in a coherent manner in any other computational motion–vision studies. Figure 6 shows this structuring of the visual flow. The meridians are defined, mathematically, by the intersection with a sphere of a pencil of planes that pass through the camera path.

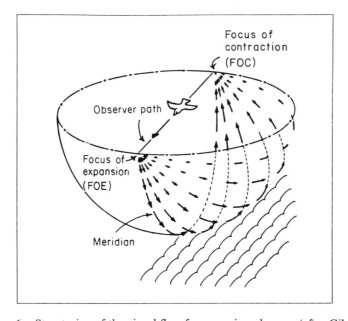

Figure 6.   Structuring of the visual flow for a moving observer (after Gibson).

These meridians form an important constraint, but what is equally important to note is that the visual information is presented in a continuous fashion—it spreads across the view of the observer, constrained by the meridians. Again, this continuity had not been addressed in a coherent manner before our motion–vision studies. Note further that, if the observer turns to look in other directions while continuing in motion, the meridian constraints remain in place and in effect. Now, if the observer sees some object in the scene, say the point P of Figure 7, and attends to it while continuing in motion, then two things may be observed: first, P stays on its meridian; second, the lines of sight from the observer to each observation of P pass through P. The implication of the first point is that all the information pertaining to P is contained in the data collected on that one meridian. The latter point might seem self-evident but in fact is crucial—it will be shown to imply that a linear estimator can be used in determining the 3D position of P relative to the observer (presuming each viewing position of the observer is known). This shows a geometry (the FOE/meridian set), an applicable constraint (the meridians) and a simple estimation procedure for determining the position of viewed features.

Figure 8, indicating several viewing positions and attitudes along a straight path, shows how this geometry pertains to our computer analysis. Our camera is modeled as a pinhole with image plane in front of the lens. The camera moves in a straight line, and its lens centers at the various viewing positions lie along this line. For each feature P in the scene and two viewing positions such as V_1 and V_2, there is an *epipolar plane* that passes through P and the line joining the two lens centers. This plane intersects the two image planes along corresponding *epipolar lines*. The term *epipolar line* comes from *epipole* in photogrammetry, which refers to the

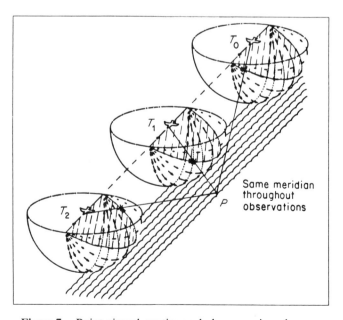

Figure 7.   Point viewed continuously by a moving observer.

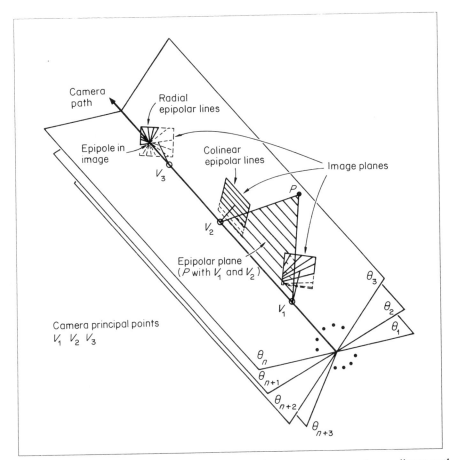

Figure 8. Geometry of general epipolar configuration: camera moves along a linear path, viewing in different directions; the linear path defines a pencil of planes crucial to the analysis.

intersection of an image plane with the line joining the lens centers. In motion work the epipole is known as the focus of expansion (FOE). This epipolar structuring divides the scene into a pencil of planes passing through the camera path, several of which are sketched (θ_1, θ_2, θ_3, θ_n, ..., θ_{n+3}). The pencil is crucial to our analysis —notice its equivalence with the meridians of Figure 6. We view the space as a cylindrical coordinate system with axis the camera path, angle defined by the epipolar plane (meridian) and radius the distance from the axis. As in the meridian discussion, a scene feature is restricted to a single epipolar plane, and any scene features at the same angle (within the discretization) share that plane. This means that, as in our earlier work, the analysis of a scene can be partitioned into a set of analyses, one for each plane, and these planes can be processed independently. In the section on "The Spatiotemporal Surface" (p. 245) we describe how we organize the data to exploit this constraint.

With viewing direction orthogonal to the direction of travel, as depicted at V_2 in Figure 8, the epipolar lines for a feature such as P are horizontal scan lines, and these occur at the same vertical position (scan line) in all the images. This is the camera geometry normally chosen for computer stereo vision work. Each scan line is a projected observation of the features in an epipolar plane. The projection of P onto these epipolar lines moves to the right as the camera moves to the left. If one were to take a single epipolar line (scan line) from each of a series of images obtained with this camera geometry and compose a spatiotemporal image, with horizontal being spatial and vertical being temporal, one would see a pattern as in the EPI of Figure 9. For this type of motion, feature trajectories are straight lines, as can be seen. This is the case handled by our previous analysis. If, on the other hand, the camera were moving with an attitude as shown at V_3 in Figure 8, the set of epipolar lines would form a pattern as shown in Figure 10. For this type of motion, feature trajectories are hyperbolas. Notice that the epipolar lines are no longer scan lines—they are oriented radially and pass through the FOE. Allowing the camera to vary its attitude along the path gives rise to spatiotemporal images as shown in Figure 11. Here, the epipolar line pattern is not fixed from frame to frame, and the paths of features in the EPI are neither linear nor hyperbolic—in fact they are arbitrary curves.

The transitivity property, mentioned in the introduction to this section, arises from the fact that any pair of lines selected from the set form a corresponding pair. That is, for the set of epipolar lines $E^\theta = (e_0^\theta, e_1^\theta, \ldots, e_n^\theta)$ from epipolar plane θ over images I_0 to I_n, any two members comprise a pair of corresponding epipolar lines—e_0^θ with e_1^θ, e_3^θ with e_7^θ, etc. This occurs because the camera's linear path guarantees that a single pencil of planes defines the epipolar mapping over the entire sequence. Thus, any mapping done on the basis of e_0^θ with e_1^θ and then e_1^θ with e_2^θ implies the mapping of e_0^θ with e_2^θ. A similar argument holds for all pairs of mappings in E^θ, and the transitivity follows. If the camera path were nonlinear, no single pencil of planes could be defined, and no such set E^θ could be formed. The only complicating detail with the varying attitude case (as indicated in Figure 11) is that the pattern of epipolar lines changes from image to image: for a fixed camera attitude the pattern is the same for all images in the sequence.

Figure 9. Epipolar plane image from orthogonal viewing: feature paths are straight lines.

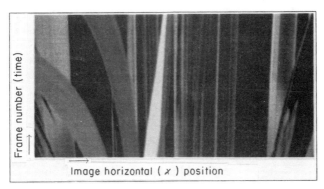

Figure 10. Epipolar plane image from fixed non-orthogonal viewing: feature paths are hyperbolic.

Keeping the Problem Linear

Recall that our goal is to determine the position of stationary features in the scene: we do this by tracking their appearance over time as they project onto these epipolar planes. Obviously in the case of orthogonal viewing (e.g. as in Figure 9 and at V_2 in Figure 8), the tracking is linear. For general camera attitudes, including varying, it is nonlinear. Computational considerations make it extremely advantageous for the tracking to be posed as a linear problem. To maintain the the linearity regardless of viewing direction, we find not linear feature paths in the EPIs (Figures 9–11), but linear paths in a *dual space*. The insight here (described by Marimont, 1986) is that no matter where a camera roams about a scene, for any particular feature, the *lines of sight* from the camera's principal point through that feature in space all intersect at the feature (modulo the measurement error). A line of sight is determined by the line from the principal point through the point in the image plane where the projected feature is observed. From mathematical duality, the duals of these lines of sight lie along a line whose dual is the scene point (see Figure 12); fitting a point to the lines of sight is a linear problem. This, then, gives

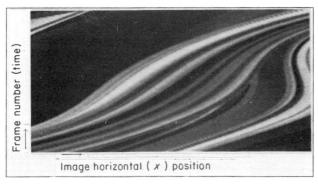

Figure 11. Epipolar plane image from varying view direction: feature paths are arbitrary curves.

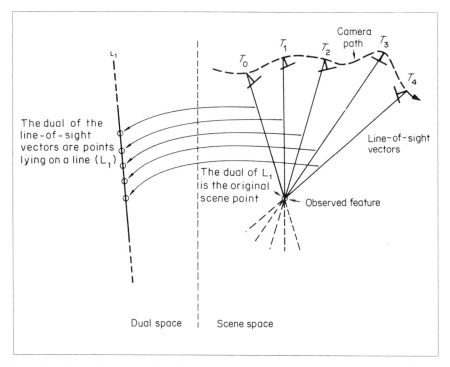

Figure 12. Line-of-sight duality: observations in scene space are lines of sight; these are points in the dual space, which lie along a line whose dual is the feature's original scene point.

us a metric for linear tracking of features: we map feature image coordinates to lines of sight, and use an optimal estimator to determine the point that minimizes the variance from those lines of sight.

Our estimation is done in the scene Cartesian space, not the dual space, because the error metric, nonlinear in the dual space, has more intuitive meaning and better behavior in scene space. The estimated error in each observation is a function of the function of the size of the Gaussian filter employed and the distance of the feature from the camera. We currently model only these uncertainties in image-plane observations, and not others related to the strength of the feature signal or uncertainty in the position of the camera. These others will have to be modeled in a complete solution.

Transformations Required

Having decided on a representation that restores the linearity of our estimator, we must now demonstrate a mechanism for extracting the feature observations from the individual images in which they occur and grouping them by epipolar plane. Only in the case of viewing angle orthogonal to the motion is this grouping simple (Figure 9), and this was the case our earlier work addressed. To obtain this structuring in the general cases, we could take one of two approaches. The first is to *transform the images* from the Cartesian space in which they are sampled to an epipolar representation (as has been done by Baker *et al.*, 1983, and Jain *et al.*, 1987). Because of aliasing effects (particularly on the observation variances) and nonlinearities in the mapping (it is singular when the FOE is in the image, and could require an infinite imaging surface for the reprojection), we prefer to avoid this transformation. Probably the best solution would be to use a sensor that delivers the data directly in the epipolar form—a spherical-retina sensor having meridian scanning would accomplish this. Because such a sensor is not yet available, we choose an alternate approach: to *transform the features* we detect in image space to the desired epipolar space, the cylindrical coordinate system of Figure 8. Here the singularity at the FOE presents no problem, and the observation variances are uniform. The structure we have developed for implementing this transformation brings us several other advantages, as the next section describes.

THE SPATIOTEMPORAL SURFACE

We collect the data as a sequence of images, in fact stacking them up as they are acquired into a spatiotemporal volume, as shown in Figure 2. As each new image is obtained, we construct its *spatial* and *temporal* edge contours. These contours are three-dimensional zeros of the Laplacian of a chosen three-dimensional Gaussian (Buxton & Buxton, 1983, and Heeger, 1986, also describe the use of spatiotemporal convolution over an image sequence), and the construction produces a spatiotemporal *surface* enveloping the signed *volumes* (note that, in two dimensions, edge contours envelop signed *regions*). The *spatial* connectivity in this structure lets us explicitly maintain object coherence between features observed on separate epipolar planes; the *temporal* connectivity gives us, as before, the tracking of features over time. See Baker (1989) for a description of how these surfaces are constructed.

Structuring the Data—Spatiotemporal Connectivity

The need for maintaining this spatial connectivity can be observed by viewing the earlier results presented by Bolles *et al.* (1987), one set of which is shown in Figure 5. There, in processing the EPIs independently, we obtained separate planes of isolated scene feature estimates. Wishing to exploit the fact that there should be some spatial coherence between these sets of points, we used proximity of the resulting estimates on adjacent planes to filter outliers. Features not within the error (covariance) ellipses of those above or below them (i.e. those which could not be joined into a three-space contour) were discarded. The remaining point field (Figure 5) was sparse and fragmented, and not really representative of the continuous solid surfaces visible in the scene. The problem, however, did not lie with this *post hoc* filtering but with the loss of spatial connectivity in the first place. Our separation of the data into EPIs and then subsequent independent processing of these lost the spatial connectivity apparent in the original images. We maintained instead the temporal connectivity that was critical to the feature tracking.

For spatial connectivity in the scene reconstruction, spatial connectivity in the imagery must be preserved. The next two figures present a simplified example of this spatial and temporal connectivity. Figure 13 shows a sequence of simulated images depicting a camera zooming in on a set of rectangles; Figure 14 shows a rendered view of the spatiotemporal surfaces arising from this motion. The spatial and temporal interpretation of these surfaces should be quite apparent.

In our spatiotemporal-surface representation, feature observations bear (u, v, t) coordinates, and are spatiotemporal *voxel facets*. Figure 17 shows a mesh description of the facets for the spatiotemporal surfaces associated with the forward-viewing sequence whose first and last images are depicted in Figure 15. These images are much more complex than those of Figure 13. Let us re-emphasize that the surface is defined at the zeros of a Laplacian of a 3D Gaussian applied over the sequence: there is no thresholding, and the features are simply zero crossings. In the interest of clarity, the surface representations to be shown in the remaining figures are based on a simplified version of this imagery—one-eighth the linear resolution of the originals. Figure 16 shows these two frames at the reduced resolution used for the surface construction of Figure 17.

Others have addressed this problem of combining spatial and temporal information, although no one has either built surfaces such as these or attempted to maintain explicit track of the temporal change. Perhaps the closest is Waxman, who discusses the use of *evolving contours*—isolated 2D contours whose projections over time can be used in deriving the shape of a restricted class of analytic surfaces (Waxman, 1984). He provides no method for tracking the contours through time, however, or for extracting them from real images—nor does he develop a methodology for utilizing the temporal evolution of individual components of the contours over multiple frames. Later work by Waxman and his

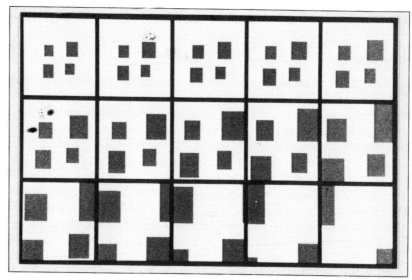

Figure 13.   Simulation: camera moving along a linear path with motion toward rectangles.

Figure 14. Surfaces of motion depicted in Figure 13, rendered for display.

colleagues (Waxman *et al.*, 1988), presenting *convected activation profiles*, involves spatiotemporal convolution of Gaussian gradients applied at features detected in the individual spatial images by a difference-of-Gaussian operator. In this, estimates of image-plane velocities are formed from quotients of the spatiotemporal gradients. There is, however, no estimate of scene motion, and no notion of motion associated with specific objects in the field of view—motion is ascribed to pixels in

Figure 15. Sequence 1st and 128th images at full resolution.

Figure 16. Sequence 1st and 128th images at one-eighth resolution.

the plane. Others, for example Hildreth & Grzywacz (1986), who work with velocity point sets, and Negahdaripour & Horn (1987), who determine relative motion of a plane from image gradients, also do not address these issues of local shape, establishing correspondence over time, associating movement with objects, or extracting the measures from real images. Although we have directed our efforts only at ego motion, our space–time surfaces provide a complete representation of these other projective velocity measures, and maintain a continuous track relating them to their underlying scene features. We are currently looking into using the surface representation for this more general form of motion analysis.

Structuring the Data—Epipolar Plane Representation

As mentioned in the previous section, for non-orthogonal viewing directions, epipolar lines are not distinguished by the spatial v scan-line coordinate. To obtain this necessary structuring we develop within the spatiotemporal-surface representation an *embedded* representation that makes the epipolar organization explicit. Over each of the sequential images, we transform the (u, v, t) coordinates of our

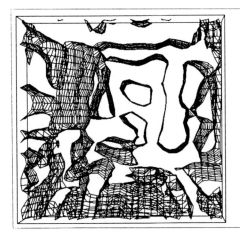

Figure 17. Spatiotemporal-surface representation of image evolution, first ten frames.

spatiotemporal zeros to (r, h, θ) *cylindrical coordinates* (θ indicates the epipolar-plane angle ($\theta \in [0, 2\pi]$); the quantized resolution in θ is a supplied parameter; and the transform for each image is determined by the particular camera parameters). In this new coordinate system, we build a structure similar to our earlier EPI edge contours, but dynamically organized by epipolar plane. This is done by *intersecting* the spatiotemporal surfaces with the pencil of appropriate epipolar planes (as Figure 8). We weave the epipolar connectivity through the spatiotemporal volume, following the known camera viewing direction changes. Figure 18 shows a sampling of the spatiotemporal surfaces as they intersect the pencil of epipolar planes. You will notice the obvious radial flow pattern away from the epipole (FOE). Figure 19 shows seven of these surface/plane intersections, along with the associated bounding planes (refer to Figure 8). The edge that all share is the camera path (the epipole). These seven planes show exactly the contours one would detect in spatiotemporal intensity images such as depicted in Figure 10.

In Figure 20 we isolate a single surface from the top left of Figure 17, and show its spatiotemporal structure. Figure 21 shows the same surface structured by its epipolar-plane components. Baker (1989) gives details of this intersection operation on the spatiotemporal surface.

Recall that the displays are in space–time image coordinates. If the camera had been allowed to vary its attitude, the planes depicted in Figure 19 would appear skewed, perhaps helical, mirroring the migration of epipolar lines as they are projected on the imaging surface. They might vary in a manner similar to that in which Figure 11 varies from Figure 9, and for similar reasons. To facilitate presentation, we have not demonstrated this more general camera movement; it is, however, covered by our analysis and implementation.

Feature Tracking and Estimation

Our approach to scene reconstruction involves tracking scene features as they move in space–time, and to use techniques from estimation theory in approximating and maintaining estimates of their position. This is in distinction with, for

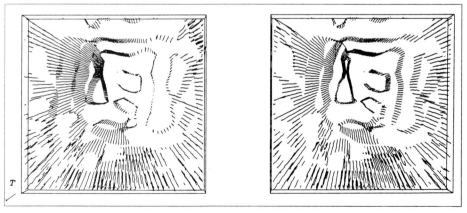

Figure 18. Epipolar-plane surface representation of image evolution.

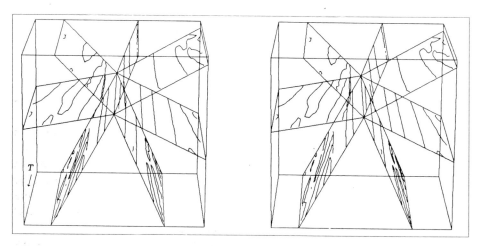

Figure 19. Intersection of seven epipolar planes (as shown in Figure 8) with the spatio-temporal surfaces (taken over 30 frames).

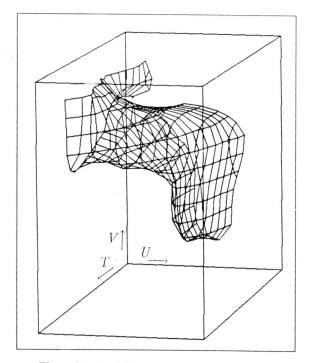

Figure 20. Individual spatiotemporal surface.

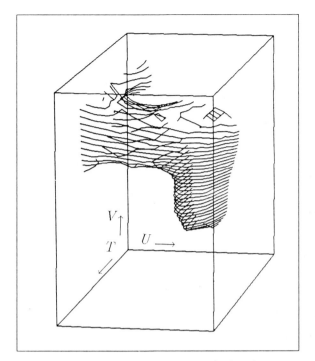

Figure 21.   Surface structured as epipolar planes.

example, the work reported in Waxman & Wohn (1985), Hildreth & Grzywacz (1986) and elsewhere, which does not utilize this particular mathematics. Tracking systems built using estimation theory include those described by Gennery (1982) and Broida & Chellappa (1986), as mentioned, as well as those of Hallam (1983), Dickmanns (1988) and Matthies *et al.* (1988). The former two describe vehicle navigation controllers that work sequentially (as does ours), utilizing Kalman and other filters for estimating motion parameters. Our tracker is a sequential linear estimator, and is implemented as a Kalman filter without the extrapolation phase. Extrapolation is unnecessary since the camera constraints and the space–time surface tell us where each feature will move from frame to frame—there is no need to extrapolate and verify this. The work of Matthies *et al.* has similarities to ours in its pursuit of scene depth from the analysis of image sequences, but lacks several important elements. These include the generality with respect to view angle that comes with our use of the line-of-sight formulation, and the explicit use of spatial connectivity—they obtain only scene point estimates (as we had with our earlier approach), rather than higher-level descriptors such as scene contours. Furthermore, they must establish feature correspondence via correlation between frames, and this is not necessary with the spatiotemporal surface. On the other hand, we do not aim currently at producing the dense depth maps that they do. Their depth maps are obtained through a combination of tracking and regularization: when we attempt full-surface reconstruction we will do so with analysis over scale (as discussed later), and through the use of inference on the computed free space (the determination of scene free space was shown by Bolles et al., 1987).

Figure 22 shows the tracking of scene features on the spatiotemporal surfaces in the vicinity of the surface of Figure 20. The tracking occurs along paths such as those shown in Figure 21. The final pair shows, in crossed-eye stereo form, the result of the tracking after ten frames. The coding is as follows: initiation of a feature tracking is marked by a circle; the leading observation of a feature (active front) is shown as a cross; lines join feature observations; five observations (an arbitrary number, two may be sufficient) must be acquired before an estimate is made of the feature's position—at that point an initial batch estimate is made, and a Kalman filter (discussed in Gelb, 1974, and Mikhail, 1976) is turned on and associated with the feature—this initiation of a Kalman filter is coded by a square; where two observations merge, the tracking is stopped and the features are entered into the database—this is coded by a diamond.

As mentioned earlier, observations are expressed as line-of-sight vectors, and these are represented in the epipolar plane by the homogeneous line equation $ax + by - c = 0$ [its dual is the point (a, b, c)—see the description of duality in the section on "Keeping the Problem Linear"]. For the initial batch estimation, the coordinates (X) of the feature are the solution of the normal equations for the weighted least squares system: $X = (H^TWH)^{-1}H^TWC$. H is the $m \times 2$ matrix of (a_i, b_i) observations; C is the vector of c_i; and W is the diagonal matrix of observation weights, determined by σ of the Gaussian, the distance from the camera to the observed feature at observation position i, and the focal distance. We estimate X first without weights, then compute the weighted solution and the desired covariance matrix, V. Given a current estimate X_{i-1} and covariance V_{i-1}, the Kalman filter at observation i updates these as:

$$K_i = V_{i-1}H_i^T/[H_iV_{i-1}H_i^T + w_i]$$
$$V_i = [I - K_iH_i]V_{i-1}$$
$$X_i = X_{i-1} + K_i[c_i - H_iX_{i-1}],$$

where K_i is the 2×1 Kalman gain matrix, and w_i is the observation weight, a scalar, dependent on the distance from the camera at observation position i to the estimate X_{i-1}.

The tracking of an individual feature is depicted in Figure 23. The camera path runs across the figures from the lower left. Lines of sight are shown from the camera path through the observations of the feature at the upper right. As the Kalman filter is begun (T_4), an estimate (marked by a cross) and confidence interval (the ellipse) are produced. As further observations are acquired, the estimate and confidence interval are refined. Tracking continues until either the feature is lost, or the error terms begins to increase—suggesting that observations not related to the tracked feature are beginning to be included. This could arise because, among other reasons, the zero crossing is erroneous, the feature is not stationary, or the feature is on a contour rather than being a single point in space. Note that although a single feature is presented in this tracking depiction, it is part of a spatiotemporal surface.

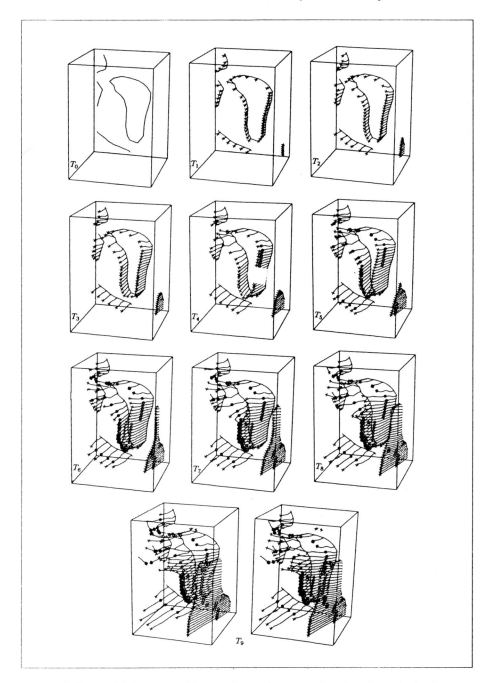

Figure 22. Sequential feature tracking on the spatiotemporal surface through nine images: each growing line indicates an individual feature being tracked through time; a cross indicates the current observation of a feature; some batch estimates are made with image T_4; initiation of a sequential filter is coded by a square (as at T_4); termination of a tracker is marked by a diamond.

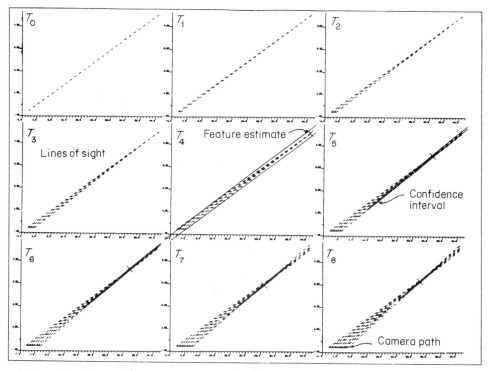

Figure 23. Sequential feature tracking on the spatiotemporal surface through nine images: the vertical axis is radial distance from the camera path, and the horizontal axis is distance along the camera path from the origin (the camera's position at T_0). Camera path moves along the bottom of each frame; dashed lines are line-of-sight vectors to the observed feature; the cross marks the estimate of feature position, and the ellipse indicates the confidence interval. Notice that the first batch estimate is made at image T_4, and that the estimate and confidence interval refine with each subsequent image.

This means that we have explicit knowledge of those other features to which this is spatially adjacent. Figure 24 shows a contour—a connected set of features on such a surface—observed over time as its shape evolves. Such contours are being constructed and refined over the entire image as the analysis progresses. Our current representation of scene structure is based on these evolving contours.

Path Generality on the Spatiotemporal Surface

A crucial constraint of the current epipolar-plane image analysis is that having a camera moving along a linear path enables us to divide the analysis into planes, in fact, the pencil of planes of Figure 8 passing through the camera path. With this, we assured that a feature will be viewed in just a single one of these planes, and its motion over time will be confined to that plane. Another crucial constraint is the one we generalized from the orthogonal viewing case—we know that the set of line-of-sight vectors from camera to feature over time will all intersect at that feature,

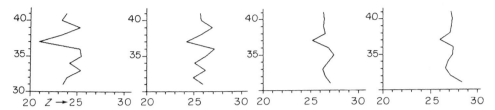

Figure 24. 3D contour evolving over time: the vertical axis is epipolar-plane number, and the horizontal axis is distance from the origin (the camera's position at T_0). The left frame shows a contour formed by 11 connected features (seen connected spatially in the images, and therefore represented as connected on the spatiotemporal surface). The jags in the contour arise from the differing estimates of the features' positions. As time progresses (the following three frames), the individual estimates and their implied contour refine to more consistent positions.

and determining that feature's position is a linear problem. As Figure 12 shows, the linearity of the estimator does not depend upon the linearity of the camera path—the problem would remain linear even if the camera meandered in three dimensions all over the scene.

This knowledge gives us a possibility of removing the restriction that limits us to a linear camera path. All that the linear path guarantees is that the problem is divisible into epipolar planes. If we lose this constraint, then we cannot restrict our feature tracking to separate planes. The observations will, however, still form linear paths in the space of line-of-sight vectors [not to be confused with the (u, v, t) observation space]: this is because the lines of sight will all pass through the single feature point. The motion of these observations will give us *ruled* surfaces in this space—visualize pick-up-sticks jammed in a box, with the sticks being the rules. The rules can be used in the same way they have been with the linear path constraint, to determine the positions of features in the scene. The difference is that the linearities must be located—and the spatiotemporal surface is just the place for doing this. It would also be possible here to track using the epipolar constraints that apply pairwise between images—that the constraints are limited to pairwise use arises because, for a non-linear path, the images will not have the transitivity property we cited earlier.

It is equally worth noting that, when the camera attitude and position parameters are not provided, the spatiotemporal surface contains everything that is necessary for determining them. This is, of course, another problem, but one that must be addressed for a realistic vision system. Our initial work in this involves locating distinctive projective features on the spatiotemporal surface—dihedrals selected using Förstner's measure (Förstner, 1986)—and tracking them. Depending upon knowledge of the features chosen, these can permit estimation of both relative and absolute camera parameters (Förstner, 1987).

This generality suggests there is even broader application for the technique than we had initially thought—it seems quite adaptable to non-linear camera paths, and should be usable equally in refining the camera model, or solving for its unknown parameters.

Figure 25.   First image in scale-space hierarchy: box on a table, shirt draped over chair in the foreground.

Scale Generality on Four-dimensional Surfaces

One of the unresolved issues in motion sequence analysis work, and in computer vision in general, is the selection of a Gaussian to be the basis for detection operations; in effect, selecting the scale of analysis. If one wants to detect blades of grass, elephant-sized filters will not work; equally, small filters will miss large coarser features. In researching this issue, we have done some limited experimentation with surface building where the third dimension is Gaussian scale (σ). Building a surface of the evolution of an image as its resolution varies provides a vivid picture of how Witkin's 1D scale-space studies (Witkin, 1983) can extend to images. Figure 27 shows a surface constructed at the 3D Laplacian zeros obtained battery of increasingly larger Gaussians to the image of Figure 25. This depiction

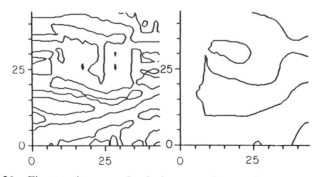

Figure 26.   Finest and coarsest Laplacian zeros: intermediates are not shown.

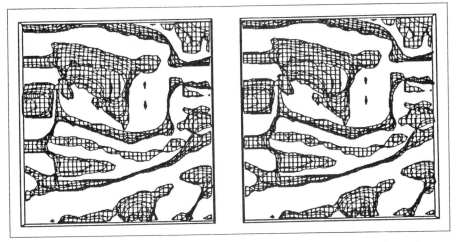

Figure 27. Surfaces defined by the evolution of the image as it blurs: the scale-space surface.

was produced from a series of eight images, each differing in σ by 0.5 from the one before. Figure 26 left shows the zero-crossings of the smallest Gaussian, and its right shows the zero-crossings of the largest Gaussian—these are the extremes of which Figure 27 represents the continuum. The most stable representation of a feature in this space may be at that part of its evolution exhibiting minimum spatial velocity with respect to $\Delta\sigma$—if the feature moves a lot with a small change in σ, then it is sensitive to and not stable at that σ. The connected scale-space surface makes this stability explicit. These, and other gradient measures (see, for example, Clark, 1989) will be used in distinguishing signal from noise, and in selecting the most appropriate scale for tracking operations.

We will soon be modifying the Weaving Wall to produce four-dimensional surfaces, where the first three are the spatial and temporal as before, and the fourth is Gaussian scale. Our intention is to use the most stable representation of a feature as its instantiation to be tracked. The linear estimators will then use these more appropriate σ values in determining observation weights and in estimating the resulting spatial precisions. Tracking will be occurring at all scales at once. At the moment this is speculative, but the possibility of using feature stability as a measure in tracking seems quite promising.

CONCLUSIONS

In rounding up the contribution of this chapter, it is important to return to the points expressed in the introduction: our goal has been to develop a capability for constructing descriptions of three-dimensional world objects, and to do this by exploiting the dimensionality and redundancy presented to the human processor as it would move about the same environment. Our focus has been on building up and encoding our visual experience, and the research described here has made large advances toward this goal. Only when this is accomplished will we feel it appropriate to turn to the multitude of other issues relating to the *use* of these descriptions.

In our earlier work we showed the feasibility of extracting scene depth information through a unified spatiotemporal processing of image sequences. The generalizations obtained through the major contribution of our current work— spatiotemporal-surface analysis—bring us the advantages of:

Incremental analysis.
Unrestricted viewing direction (including direction varying along the path).
Spatial coherence in our results, providing connected surface information for scene objects rather than point estimates structured by epipolar plane.
The possibility of removing the restrictions that fix us to a known linear path.
A capability of dealing with feature stability in a quantitative manner.
The warm feeling that we are doing it right.

Certain elements of our theory have been initially implemented to exploit special-case geometric considerations; overall, the approach has the generality to permit unrestricted motions through (probably) unrestricted scenes. Ahead lies the prospect of integrating color, scale, free-space and full-surface reconstruction, and the analysis of moving and dynamic objects, all within a robust framework. Interestingly, we have discovered that as more information is brought into a unified analysis—for example, space, time, scale, and other parameters which can be treated in a coherent and continuous framework—our problems have become less rather than more difficult, and our results have become more accurate and more reliable.

The current implementation of the space–time surface builder, running on a Symbolics 3600, processes the spatiotemporal surfaces at a 1 kHz voxel rate. The associated intersecting, tracking, and estimation procedures bring this rate down to about 150 Hz, 75 % of which is consumed in the surface intersection (recall that the surface intersection would not be required if we have a sensor of the appropriate geometry). Both the feature tracking and the surface-construction computations are well suited to MIMD (perhaps SIMD) parallel implementation, and we are investigating some of these now. With these computational considerations and the process's inherent precision and robustness, we feel spatiotemporal-surface-based epipolar-plane image analysis shows great promise for the complex task of scene modeling and mapping—building descriptions of our three-dimensional world —and for real-time control of an autonomous visual processor making his way around and interacting with his environment.

ACKNOWLEDGEMENTS

This research has been supported by DARPA Contracts MDA 903-86-C-0084 and DACA 76-85-C-0004. The early part of this work owes much to the collaboration and insights of Bob Bolles. David Marimont, currently with Xerox PARC, was crucial in the development, providing advice on both the geometry and mathematics of the tracking process and the design of the surface builder. Lynn Quam has provided excellent image manipulation and graphics tools and, whenever required, thoughtful assistance.

REFERENCES

Baker, H. H. (1989). Building surfaces of evolution: the Weaving Wall. *International Journal of Computer Vision*, **3**(1).

Baker, H. H. & Bolles, R. C. (1989). Generalizing epipolar-plane image analysis on the spatiotemporal surface. *International Journal of Computer Vision*, **3**(1), 33–49.

Baker, H. H., Binford, T. O., Malik, J. & Meller, J.-F. (1983). Progress in stereo mapping. In *Proceedings DARPA Image Understanding Workshop, Arlington, Virginia*. Morgan Kaufman, San Mateo, CA, pp. 327–335.

Bolles, R. C., Baker, H. H. & Marimont, D. H. (1987). Epipolar-plane image analysis: an approach to determining structure from motion. *International Journal of Computer Vision*, **1**(1), 7–55.

Broida, T. J. & Chellappa R. (1986). Kinematics and structure of a rigid object from a sequence of noisy images. In *Proceedings of the Workshop on Motion: Representation and Analysis*, IEEE Computer Society, Kiawah Island, South Carolina, pp. 95–100.

Buxton, B. F. & Buxton, H. (1983). Monocular depth perception from optical flow by space time signal processing. *Proceedings of the Royal Society (London), Series B*, **218**, 27–47.

Clark, J. J. (1989). Authenticating edges produced by zero-crossing algorithms. *IEEE Transactions: Pattern Analysis and Machine Intelligence*, **11**, 43–57.

Dickmanns, E. D. (1988). An integrated approach to feature based dynamic vision. *Proceedings of the Conference on Computer Vision and Pattern Recognition*, IEEE Computer Society, Ann Arbor, Michigan, pp. 820–825.

Förstner, W. (1986). A feature based correspondence algorithm for image matching. In Proceedings of the Symposium *From Analytical to Digital. International Archives of Photogrammetry and Remote Sensing*, Vol. 26-III. Rovaniemi, Finland.

Förstner, W. (1987). Reliability analysis of parameter estimation in linear models with applications to mensuration problems in computer vision. *Computer Vision, Graphics and Image Processing*, **40**, 273–310.

Gelb, A. (1974). *Applied Optimal Estimation*. The Analytic Sciences Corporation, MIT Press, Cambridge, MA.

Gennery, D. B. (1982). Tracking known three-dimensional objects. In *Proceedings of the National Conference on Artificial Intelligence (AAAI-82), Carnegie-Mellon University, Pittsburgh*. Morgan Kaufman, San Mateo, CA, pp. 13–17.

Gibson, J. J. (1950). *The Perception of the Visual World*. Houghton Mifflin, Boston.

Hallam, J. (1983). Resolving observer motion by object tracking. In *Proceedings of the Eighth International Joint Conference on Artificial Intelligence, Karlsruhe, West Germany*. Morgan Kaufman, San Mateo, CA, pp. 792–798.

Heeger, D. J. (1986). Depth and flow from motion energy. In *Proceedings of the Fifth National Conference on Artificial Intelligence (AAAI-86), Philadelphia, Pennsylvania*. Morgan Kaufman, San Mateo, CA, pp. 657–663.

Hildreth, E. C. & Grzywacz, N. M. (1986). The incremental recovery of structure from motion: position vs velocity based formulations. In *Proceedings of the Workshop on Motion: Representation and Analysis*, IEEE Computer Society, Kiawah Island, South Carolina, pp. 137–143.

Jain, R., Bartlett, S. L. & O'Brien, N. (1987). Motion stereo using ego-motion complex logarithmic mapping. *IEEE Transactions: Pattern Analysis and Machine Intelligence*, **9**, 356–369.

Marimont, D. H. (1986). Projective duality and the analysis of image sequences. In *Proceedings of the Workshop on Motion: Representation and Analysis*, IEEE Computer Society, Kiawah Island, South Carolina, pp. 7–14.

Matthies, L., Szeliski, R. & Kanade, T. (1988). Incremental estimation of dense depth maps from image sequences. In *Proceedings of the Conference on Computer Vision and Pattern Recognition*, IEEE Computer Society, Ann Arbor, Michigan, pp. 366–374.

Mikhail, E. M. (with Ackerman, F.) (1976). *Observations and Least Squares*. University Press of America, Lanham, MD.

Negahdaripour, S. & Horn, B. K. P. (1987). Direct passive navigation. *IEEE Transactions: Pattern Analysis and Machine Intelligence*, 9, 168–176.

Subbarao, M. (1986). Interpretation of image motion fields: a spatio-temporal approach. In *Proceedings of the Workshop on Motion: Representation and Analysis*, IEEE Computer Society, Kiawah Island, South Carolina, pp. 157–165.

Waxman, A. M. (1984). An image flow paradigm. In *Proceedings of the Workshop on Computer Vision: Representation and Control*, IEEE Computer Society, Annapolis, MD, pp. 49–57.

Waxman, A. M. & Wohn, K. (1985). Contour evolution, neighborhood deformation, and global image flow: planar surfaces in motion. *International Journal of Robotics Research*, 4(3), 95–108.

Waxman, A. M., Kamgar-Parsi, B. & Subbarao, M. (1987). Closed-form solutions to image flow equations for 3D structure and motion. *International Journal of Computer Vision*, 1, 239–258.

Waxman, A. M., Wu, J. & Bergholm, F. (1988). Convected activation profiles and the measurement of visual motion. In *Proceedings of the Conference on Computer Vision and Pattern Recognition*, IEEE Computer Society, Ann Arbor, Michigan, pp. 717–723.

Witkin, A. P. (1983). Scale space filtering. In *Proceedings of the Eighth International Joint Conference on Artificial Intelligence*. Morgan Kaufman, San Mateo, CA, pp. 1019–1021.

11 Visual Recognition as Probabilistic Inference from Spatial Relations

David G. Lowe

Computer Science Department, University of British Columbia, Vancouver, BC, Canada V6T 1W5

INTRODUCTION

Although the study of computer-based vision has often proceeded independently from the study of biological vision, there are reasons for believing that there will be an increasing convergence of these fields in the future. The essential reason for this convergence, as enunciated by Marr (1982), is that if we believe that biological vision is highly optimized to perform its tasks and that neural hardware is flexible enough to perform any necessary computations, then the computational structure of vision will be determined by intrinsic properties of the task rather than by accidents of biology. Given a similar flexibility in electronic computation, it follows that any system optimized to perform visual inference, whether based on neurons or transistors, will likely be based on the same computational principles. This is particularly true of a data interpretation task such as vision, in which much of the apparent difficulty arises from ambiguities in the data itself, which must be faced by any system for interpreting the data. While the relationship between biological and computer vision has been obscured in the past by a lack of understanding of the biology and by the limitation of many computer systems to artificial visual situations, we can expect that progress in understanding biological vision and attempts to generalize computer vision will lead to a continuing convergence of many of the underlying principles in the two fields.

In this chapter, I will examine the computational structure of the specific task of visual recognition by first defining the goal of recognition and then proposing various computational strategies for achieving that goal. If these proposals correctly incorporate the important computational constraints on recognition,

AI and the Eye   Edited by A. Blake and T. Troscianko
© 1990 John Wiley & Sons Ltd.

then they will serve both as a theory of biological vision and a design for computer vision. To support these claims, a functioning computer implementation for performing visual recognition will be described and various parallels will be shown between aspects of these proposals and properties of biological visual systems.

THE GOAL OF VISUAL RECOGNITION

We use the term recognition to mean that an equivalence has been identified between a certain subset of the input data and a previously known visual category. The capability for recognition implies the existence of some previous form of learning, in which the various potential categories are created and defined, but we will be examining only the recognition stage along with any implications for the form of the visual categories. The goal of recognition is to perform these identifications correctly, in the sense that an identification reflects a meaningful property of the world that is independent of the particular image data that is being interpreted. This can be tested, for example, by showing different images of the same scene and seeing whether the same identifications are made. This goal follows from the fact that the survival of an animal depends very much on its responses to its environment, but not at all on responses to the visual data itself, which are independent of the environment.

If visual identification were always correct, then the problem of recognition could be limited to those aspects of the data and computation that were necessary to achieve correctness. However, we will argue that recognition is very often often incorrect, and all that can be hoped for is to improve the probability of correctness. This means that every available independent source of information about the contents of a scene must be incorporated into a recognition system to achieve optimal performance, and that there is little opportunity to simplify the problem by looking at only a subset of the data without sacrificing performance.

The claim that visual recognition by humans is often incorrect may find disagreement among certain researchers. However, we are all familiar with the fact that identification is difficult when objects are distant or partially hidden, or illumination is poor. Given the prevalence of camouflage and visual deception in the animal world, it must be the case that identification is often incorrect and that improving the probability of correctness has a high survival value. Every time we move our eyes to obtain a clearer image of an object in the peripheral visual field, or when we change our viewpoint to get a better view, it is an acknowledgement that our identification is uncertain. In fact, the possibility of misidentification is so commonplace that it is only when we assign a very high confidence to an interpretation which is subsequently found to be incorrect that the error is given conscious attention.

If we assume that recognition is inherently difficult and unreliable, then it is no longer sufficient to define the goal of recognition as finding the correct or even the best match between image data and prior knowledge. In order to select the most appropriate response to visual input, it is necessary to treat recognition as a form of probabilistic inference, in which various conclusions are assigned subjective probabilities of correctness on the basis of the given evidence. These probabilities can be used to infer the most appropriate action, which may not even be based on the highest probability. For example, we may see an animal moving in the bushes that appears to be a harmless deer (probability 0.7) or a dangerous tiger (0.2), but the action with the highest survival value may be based on the possibility of it being a tiger. The same goals hold for a computer vision system in an industrial setting, where the probability of correctness and the importance of the task could be used to determine when it is worthwhile to obtain further image data. Many implications follow from these assumptions, such as the fact that an optimized vision system must take account of the prior probabilities of occurrence for each interpretation, as otherwise its performance would suffer in comparison with a system that did bias its results in favor of interpretations with higher prior probabilities.

To summarize, if we accept the fact that recognition can never be made absolutely reliable, it is necessary to describe the goal of recognition as maximizing the probabilities of a correct identification and also providing a confidence measure for each identification. This implies that an optimized system will incorporate every independent source of information available to improve these estimates, as no subset of the data is sufficient to achieve certainty. It further implies that it is necessary to maintain a confidence measure for each step of the inference process leading to identification, as any thresholding of confidence measures at earlier stages will discard information that could be used to improve the final probability.

THEORY OF PERCEPTUAL ORGANIZATION

If we assume that the goal of recognition is to maximize the probability of correct identification, then it follows that the goal for each intermediate inference on the path to the final result must also be to maximize the probability of correctly identifying some property of the scene. If an intermediate inference were to be formed on the basis of a different principle which did not maximize this probability, then it would contribute nothing to the final identification in those situations in which it did not correctly identify a property of the scene. Therefore, its contribution to the final result could be improved by modifying it to increase its correlation with the occurrence of the scene property, implying that the original system is less than optimal.

One well-studied form of intermediate visual inference is perceptual organization. The human visual system strongly favors the formation of certain groupings and spatial structures over others, even when there is no higher level identification. Many theories have been proposed to account for the formation of these groupings, including the Gestalt law of *Prägnanz* (Koffka, 1935), the simplicity or minimum principle (Hochberg, 1957; Hatfield & Epstein, 1985; Leeuwenberg & Boselie, 1988) and the likelihood principle (Helmholtz, 1962; Rock, 1983). Out of these various possibilities, the arguments given above support a strong form of the likelihood principle, which is that an optimal recognition system will assign significance (probabilities) to groupings according to the likelihood that they reflect some property of the scene that is independent of the particular image. This is somewhat stronger than the traditional statement of the likelihood principle, in that it does not simply select the most likely interpretation, but requires assigning probabilities to all possible interpretations which have a reasonable likelihood (could contribute significantly to the final interpretation) and provides a measure to determine the extent to which any interpretation is likely at all. It also emphasizes the fact that groupings are selected according to whether they correlate with a property of the scene, which is the only way in which they will be useful for higher-level recognition.

In fact, the available psychophysical evidence on perceptual organization in human vision strongly supports the likelihood principle, as summarized in detail by Rock (1983). For example, Kanizsa (1979) has shown that when people make figure–ground distinctions, they assign priority to convexity over symmetry as a property to be used in making the distinction. This is strong evidence against the simplicity principle, since a symmetric figure can be represented with only about half the information required for a non-symmetric one, and there is no representational saving from convexity. However, from the probabilistic viewpoint, it is true that object boundaries are substantially more likely to be convex than concave, and that therefore this is a useful source of evidence for assigning figure–ground probabilities. Since many objects have symmetric cutouts as well as symmetric outlines, symmetry does not carry an overwhelming weight.

There continues to be debate within the psychology community on this question, with some researchers (Leeuwenberg & Boselie, 1988) arguing that likelihood provides a circular definition for perception, in that it selects interpretations according to likelihood of the interpretation itself. However, this ignores the fact that vision is situated in a particular world, in which properties of the world determine the appropriate response of the visual system. Theories of vision will not be like theories of physics, in which the functioning of a complex system is explained in terms of theories for the detailed interaction of individual components. Vision does not arise from principles underlying individual neurons or components, but instead is the result of a complex system optimization process to achieve certain goals in our particular world. The explanation for vision will consist of how useful results are derived from images, and the details of the mechanisms which implement this computation will be incidental, in the sense that many potential mechanisms may be used in different biological or computer systems to achieve the identical visual behavior. The extent to which the underlying components adhere to pre-defined principles (such as simplicity) rather than goal-defined behavior will detract from overall performance rather than enhance it.

GROUPING OF LINE SEGMENTS

The principles described above have been used to derive specific probability measures for judging the significance of groupings of line segments. These in turn have been used to implement a working computer vision system for recognizing three-dimensional objects from any viewpoint in single two-dimensional images. This not only provides a detailed example and test of these principles of organization, but also a practical and efficient method for achieving recognition in computer vision.

We assume that the purpose of grouping is to identify features that are likely to have arisen from some scene property rather than reflecting some accidental arrangement in the image. Given that the viewpoint from which a scene is projected to form an image is in most cases independent of the scene, all perceptual grouping operations must satisfy the following condition:

The viewpoint invariance condition: Perceptual features must remain stable over a wide range of viewpoints of some corresponding three-dimensional structure.

There are only a few spatial properties which satisfy this condition across projection from three dimensions to a two-dimensional image, but they include proximity, connectivity, collinearity, parallelism, repetitive textures and rotational symmetry. The precise sense in which these remain stable under projection will be described below. However, it is interesting to note that there is a very close match between these properties and those of the original Gestalt laws of organization.

Most classes of spatial relations between image features do not satisfy the viewpoint invariance condition and are therefore not suitable as a basis for perceptual organization. For example, it would be pointless to look for lines that form a right-angle in the image, since even if it is common to find lines at right-angles in the three-dimensional scene they will project to right-angles in the image only from highly restricted viewpoints. Therefore, even if an approximate right-angle were detected in the image, there would be little basis to expect that it came from a right-angle in the scene as opposed to lines at any other three-dimensional angle. Compare this to finding lines at a 180° angle to one another (i.e. that are collinear). Since non-collinear lines in the scene will project to non-collinear lines in the image from virtually all viewpoints, we can expect instances of collinearity in the image to be due to collinearity in three dimensions. Likewise, proximity and parallelism are both preserved over wide ranges of viewpoint. It is true that parallel lines in the scene may converge in the image due to perspective, but many instances of parallelism occupy small visual angles so that the incidence of approximate parallelism in the image can be expected to be much higher than simply those instances that arise accidentally.

If we were to detect a perfectly precise instance of, say, collinearity in the image, we could infer with complete confidence that it arose from an instance of collinearity in the scene. That is because the chance of perfect collinearity arising due to an accident of viewpoint would be vanishingly small. However, real image measurements include many sources of uncertainty, so our estimate of significance must be based on the degree to which the ideal relation is achieved. The quantitative goal of perceptual organization is to calculate the probability that an image relation is due to actual structure in the scene. We can estimate this by calculating the probability of the relation arising to within the given degree of accuracy due to an accident of viewpoint or random positioning, and assuming that otherwise the relation is due to structure in the scene. An extensive discussion of these issues has been presented by the author in previous work (Lowe, 1985), but here we will examine the more detailed question of applying these methods to particular grouping problems that can be used in the development of a practical vision system. We will simplify the problem by looking only at groupings of straight line segments detected in an image and by considering only those groupings that are based upon the properties of proximity, parallelism and collinearity.

Grouping on the Basis of Proximity

We will begin the analysis of perceptual organization by looking at the fundamental image relation of proximity. If two points are close together in the scene, then they will project to points that are close together in the image from all viewpoints. However, it is also possible that points that are widely separated in the scene will project to points arbitrarily close together in the image due to an accident of viewpoint. Therefore, as with all of the cases in which we attempt to judge the significance of perceptual groupings, we will consider a grouping to be significant only to the extent that it is unlikely to have arisen by accident.

An important example of the need to evaluate proximity is when attempting to form connectivity relations between line segments detected in an image. The proximity of the endpoints of two line segments may be due to the fact that they are connected or close together in the three-dimensional scene, or it may be due to a simple accident of viewpoint. We must calculate for each instance of proximity between two endpoints the probability that it could have arisen from unrelated lines through an accident of viewpoint. Since we often have no prior knowledge regarding the scene and since the viewpoint is typically unrelated to the structure of the three-dimensional objects, there is little basis for picking a biased background distribution of image features against which to judge significance. Therefore, this calculation will be based upon the assumption of a background of line segments that is uniformly distributed in the image with respect to orientation, position and scale.

Given these assumptions, the expected number of endpoints, N, within a radius r of a given endpoint is equal to the average density of endpoints per unit area, d, multiplied by the area of a circle with radius r (see Figure 1):

$$N = d\pi r^2.$$

For values of N much less than 1, the expected number is approximately equal to the probability of the relation arising accidentally. Therefore, significance varies inversely with N. It also follows that significance is inversely proportional to the square of the separation between the two endpoints.

However, the density of endpoints, d, is not independent of the length of the line segments that are being considered. Assuming that the image is uniform with respect to scale, changing the size of the image by some arbitrary scale factor should have no influence on our evaluation of the density of line segments of a

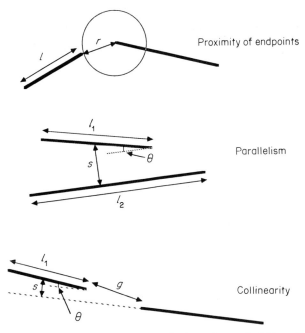

Proximity of endpoints

Parallelism

Collinearity

Figure 1. Measurements that are used to calculate the probability that instances of proximity, parallelism or collinearity could arise by accident from randomly distributed line segments.

given length. This scale independence requires that the density of lines of a given length vary inversely according to the square of their length, since halving the size of an image will decrease its area by a factor of four and decrease the lengths of each segment by a factor of two. The same result can be achieved by simply measuring the proximity r between two endpoints as proportional to the length of the line segments which participate in the relation. If the two line segments are of different lengths, the higher expected density of the shorter segment will dominate that of the longer segment, so we will base the calculation on the minimum of the two lengths. The combination of these results leads to the following evaluation metric. Given a separation r between two endpoints belonging to line segments of minimum length l:

$$N = \frac{2D\pi r^2}{l^2}.$$

We are still left with a unitless constant, D, specifying the scale-independent density of line segments (the factor 2 accounts for the fact that there are two endpoints for each line segment). This constant could either be assigned the same value in all images (as was done for our computer implementation) or could be based on an actual measurement of feature densities in the local image region.

When applied in our model-based vision system, this formula does an excellent job of selecting instances of endpoint proximity that correspond to three-dimensional connectivity in the scene. The incorporation of an assumption of uniformity across changes in scale has had an important practical impact on the algorithm. It means that the algorithm will correctly pick out large-scale instances of connectivity between long segments, even if there are many short segments nearby which would otherwise mask the instance of endpoint proximity.

Grouping on the Basis of Parallelism

A similar measure can be used to decide whether an approximate instance of parallelism between two lines in the image is likely to be non-accidental in origin. Let l_1 be the length of the shorter line and l_2 be the length of the longer line. In order to measure the average separation s between the two lines, we calculate the perpendicular distance from the longer line to the midpoint of the shorter line. As in the case for evaluating proximity, we assume that the density of line segments of length greater than l_1 is $d = D/l_1^2$, for a scale-independent constant D. Then, the expected number of lines within the given separation of the longer line will be the area of a rectangle of length l_2 and width $2s$ multiplied by the density of lines of length at least l_1. Let θ be the magnitude of the angular difference in radians between the orientations of the two lines. Assuming a uniform distribution of orientations, only $2\theta/\pi$ of a set of lines will be within orientation θ of a given line. Therefore, the expected number of lines within the given separation and angular difference will be:

$$E = \left(\frac{2sl_2 D}{l_1^2}\right)\left(\frac{2\theta}{\pi}\right) = \frac{4D\theta sl_2}{\pi l_1^2}.$$

As in the previous case, we assume that significance is inversely proportional to E.

Grouping on the Basis of Collinearity

Measuring the probability that an instance of collinearity has arisen by accident shares many features in common with the case of parallelism. In both cases, the ideal relation would involve two line segments with the same orientation and with zero separation perpendicular to the shared orientation. However, in the case of parallelism the line segments are presumed to overlap in the direction parallel to their orientation, whereas in collinearity the segments are expected to be separated along the direction of their orientation with an intervening gap. Let g be the size of this gap (the separation of the endpoints). As in the case of parallelism, let s be the perpendicular distance from the midpoint of the shorter line segment, l_1, to the extension of the longer line segment, l_2. These bounds determine a rectangular region of length $g + l_1$ and width $2s$ within which other lines would have at least the same degree of proximity. Therefore, by analogy in other respects with the case of parallelism, we get

$$E = \frac{4D\theta s(g + l_1)}{\pi l_1^2}.$$

Notice that this measure is independent of the length of the longer line segment, which seems intuitively correct when dealing with collinearity.

Implementation of the Grouping Operations

The subsections above have presented methods for calculating the significance of selected relationships between given pairs of straight line segments. The most obvious way to use these to detect all significant groupings in the image would be to test every pair of line segments and retain only those pairs which have high levels of significance. However, the complexity of this process would be $O(n^2)$ for n line segments, which is too high for practical use in complex scenes.

One method for limiting the complexity of this process is to realize that proximity is an important variable in all of the significance measures. Since significance decreases with the square of separation, two small segments that are widely separated in the image are unlikely to produce significant groupings regardless of their other characteristics (constraints on measurement accuracy limit the contribution that orientation or other measurements can make to judging significance). Therefore, complexity can be limited by searching only a relatively small region surrounding each segment for candidates for grouping. Since proximity is judged relative to the size of the component features, the size of the region that must be searched is proportional to the length of the line segment from which we are initiating the search. In order to make efficient use of these restrictions in a computer implementation, all segments in the image are indexed in a grid-like data structure according to the position of each endpoint. For further efficiency, the segments in each element of this position matrix can be further indexed according to orientation and length. The use of this index allows all groupings with interesting levels of significance to be detected in time that is essentially linear in the number of features. The representation of features in primate vision according to retinotopic position, orientation, and scale (Van Essen, 1985) would allow for a similar reduction in the computational complexity of grouping operations.

THE ROLE OF DEPTH RECONSTRUCTION IN RECOGNITION

The grouping methods outlined above are all based on two-dimensional properties of the image, rather than three-dimensional measurements such as may be derived from stereo vision. In addition, we will also be basing the later stages of our model of recognition on the analysis of only a single two-dimensional image. This deviates from a widespread assumption in both the computer vision (Marr, 1982) and psychology (Gibson, 1979) communities that the recognition of three-dimensional objects is based on an initial derivation of depth measurements from the two-dimensional image. However, this assumption seems to be based more upon the perceived difficulty of achieving recognition from a two-dimensional projection than from any convincing psychological data. In fact, human vision appears to be much more powerful than this standard model suggests, and shows little evidence of requiring the derivation of three-dimensional representations prior to recognition of familiar objects. It is certainly true that human vision contains a number of capabilities for the bottom-up derivation of depth measurements, such as stereo and motion interpretation, and these presumably have important functions. However, biological visual systems have many objectives in addition to recognition, so it does not follow that these components are central to the specific problem of visual recognition of familiar objects.

One difficulty with these methods for depth reconstruction is that the required inputs are often unavailable or require an unacceptably long interval of time to obtain. Stereo vision is only useful for objects within a restricted portion of the visual field and range of depths for any given degree of eye vergence, and is never useful for distant objects. At any moment, most parts of a scene will be outside of the limited fusional area. Motion information is available only when there is sufficient relative motion between observer and object, which in practice is also usually limited to nearby objects. Recognition times are usually so short that it seems unlikely that the appropriate eye vergence movements or elapsed time measurements could be taken prior to recognition even for those cases in which they may be useful. Depth measurements from shading or texture are apparently restricted to special cases such as regions of approximately uniform reflectance or regular texture, and they lack the quantitative accuracy or completeness of stereo or motion.

Secondly, human vision exhibits an excellent level of performance in recognizing images—such as simple line drawings—in which there is very little potential for the bottom-up derivation of depth information. Biederman (1985) describes an experiment in which almost identical reaction times (about 800 ms) and error rates were obtained for recognition of line drawings as compared with full-color slides of the same objects from the same viewpoints. Whatever mechanisms are being used for line-drawing recognition have presumably developed from their use in recognizing three-dimensional scenes. The common assumption that line-drawing recognition is a learned or cultural phenomenon is not supported by the evidence. In a convincing test of this conjecture, Hochberg & Brooks (1962) describe the case of a 19-month-old human baby who had had no previous exposure to any kinds of two-dimensional images, yet was immediately able to recognize ordinary line drawings of known objects. It is true that there has been some research on the bottom-up derivation of depth directly from line drawings or the edges detected in a single image (Barrow & Tenenbaum, 1981; Stevens, 1981), including previous research by the author (Lowe & Binford, 1985). However, these methods usually lead to sparse, under-constrained relationships in depth rather than to something resembling Marr's $2 + \frac{1}{2}$D sketch. In addition, these methods apply only to special cases and it is often not possible to tell which particular inference applies to a particular case. For example, one often-discussed inference is the use of perspective convergence to derive the orientation of lines that are parallel in three dimensions; however, given a number of lines in the image that are converging to a common point, there is usually no effective way to distinguish convergence due to perspective effects from the equally common case of lines that are converging to a common point in three dimensions.

Finally, recent neurophysiological data (Ungerleider & Mishkin, 1982; Van Essen, 1985) indicate that most forms of depth reconstruction are carried out on a different visual pathway from recognition, and that recognition remains functional even when this reconstruction and locational pathway is destroyed. Given the value of being able to perform recognition directly from the two-dimensional input image and the importance of speed in identification, it would be natural to separate these functions into different pathways. Of course, there will always be a few cases in which discriminations important to identification require precise depth measurements, and in those cases we can expect interaction between the two pathways at some cost in speed.

None of the above is meant to imply that depth recovery is an unimportant problem or lacks a significant role in human vision. Depth information may be essential for the initial stages of visual learning or for acquiring certain types of knowledge about unfamiliar structures. It is also clearly useful for making precise measurements as an aid to manipulation or obstacle avoidance. Recognition will sometimes leave the position in depth undetermined if the absolute size of an object is unknown. Human stereo vision, with its narrow fusional range for a given degree of eye vergence, seems to be particularly suited to making these precise depth measurements for selected nearby objects as an aid to manipulation and bodily interaction.

THE SCERPO VISION SYSTEM

The techniques of perceptual organization described above have been used as a central component in the implementation of a functioning computer vision system for recognizing known three-dimensional objects in single gray-scale images. In order to produce a complete system, other components must also be included to perform low-level edge detection, object modeling, matching, viewpoint determination and control functions. Figure 2 illustrates the various components and the sequence of information flow. The system is named SCERPO after its three central methodologies (Spatial Correspondence, Evidential Reasoning and Perceptual Organization). This work builds upon a number of previous attempts in the computer vision field to achieve reliable recognition from single 2D images (Roberts, 1965; Brooks, 1981; Goad, 1986).

In order to provide the initial image features for input to the perceptual grouping process, the first few levels of image analysis in SCERPO use established methods of edge detection. The 512 × 512 pixel image shown in Figure 3 was digitized from the output of an inexpensive vidicon television camera. This is an image of a jumbled bin of disposable razors in which no prior information is known regarding their location, orientation or scale (however, the focal length of the camera is specified). Intensity discontinuities (edges) are identified by convolving the image with a Laplacian of Gaussian function ($\sigma = 1.8$ pixels) as suggested by the Marr–Hildreth theory of edge detection (Marr & Hildreth, 1980). Edges in the image should give rise to zero-crossings in this convolution, but where the intensity gradient is low there will also be many other zero-crossings that do not correspond

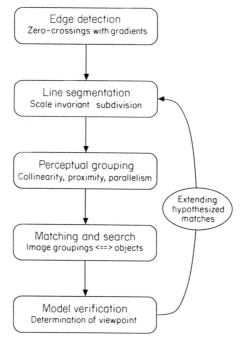

Figure 2. The components of the SCERPO vision system and the sequence of computation.

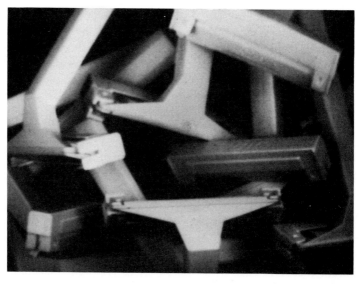

Figure 3. The input image of a bin of disposable razors, taken at a resolution of 512 × 512 pixels.

to significant intensity changes in the image. Therefore, the Sobel gradient operator was used to measure the gradient of the image following the $\nabla^2 G$ convolution, and this gradient value was retained for each point along a zero-crossing as an estimate of the signal-to-noise ratio.

The zero-crossing points were linked together and then broken into straight line segments, producing the set of about 350 line segments shown in Figure 4(a). The straight line segments are indexed according to endpoint locations and orientation. Then a sequence of procedures is executed to detect significant instances of collinearity, endpoint proximity (connectivity) and parallelism. Each instance of these relations is assigned a level of significance using the formulas given above in the section on perceptual organization. Pointers are maintained from each image segment to each of the other segments with which it forms a significant grouping. These primitive relations could be matched directly against corresponding structures on the three-dimensional object models, but the search space for this matching would be large due to the substantial remaining level of ambiguity. The size of the search space can be reduced by first combining the primitive relations into larger, more complex structures.

The larger structures are found by searching among the graph of primitive relations for specific combinations of relations which share some of the same line segments. For example, trapezoid shapes are detected by examining each pair of parallel segments for proximity relations to other segments which have both endpoints in close proximity to the endpoints of the two parallel segments. Parallel segments are also examined to detect other segments with proximity relations to their endpoints which were themselves parallel. Another higher-level grouping is formed by checking pairs of proximity relations that are close to one another to see whether the four segments satisfy Kanade's (1981) skewed symmetry relation (i.e. whether the segments could be the projection of segments that are bilaterally symmetric in three-space). Since each of these compound structures is built from primitive relations that are themselves viewpoint-invariant, the larger groupings also reflect properties of a three-dimensional object that are invariant over a wide range of viewpoints and are unlikely to have arisen by accident. The results of these grouping processes are shown in the various parts of Figure 4.

Even after this higher-level grouping process, the SCERPO system clearly makes use of simpler groupings than would be needed by a system that contained large numbers of object models. When only a few models are being considered for matching, it is possible to use simple groupings because even with the resulting ambiguity there are only a relatively small number of potential matches to examine. However, with large numbers of object models, it would be important to find more complex viewpoint-invariant structures that could be used to index into the database of models.

All processing to this point has been performed in a bottom-up manner that is independent of the objects that might be present. For this example, the high level processing is performed by matching to only a single potential object model, as shown in Figure 5. The model is represented as simply a set of three-dimensional line segments, with attached specifications of the directions from which they are visible. In order to speed the runtime performance of the matching process, the

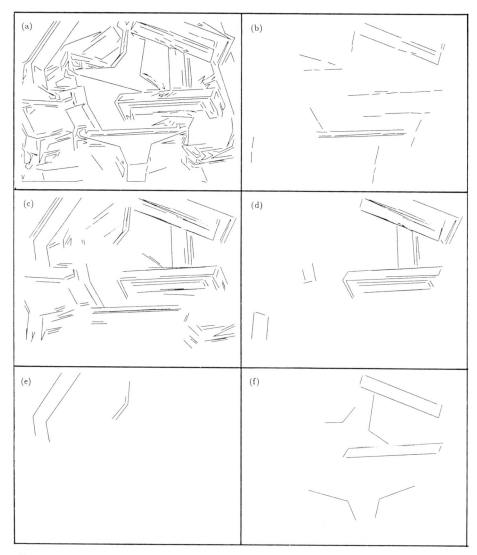

Figure 4.   The extraction of perceptual groupings from the image shown in Figure 3. Frame (a) shows an initial set of 350 straight line segments detected in the original gray-scale image. The segments are first grouped on the basis of collinearity. Each segment in (b) has been found to be significantly collinear with another nearby segment, and a new segment is created joining each of these pairs. Segments are further grouped on the basis of parallelism (c) and then as sets of parallel segments with a connecting segment in close proximity to their endpoints (d). Finally, higher-level pairs of connecting parallels (e) and trapezoid or skewed-symmetry groupings (f) are formed.

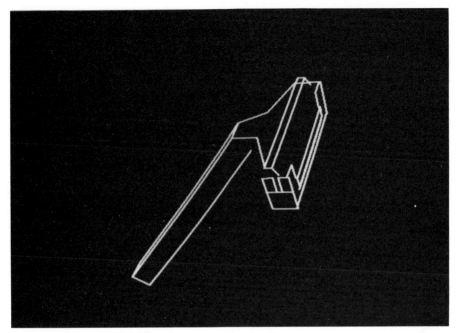

Figure 5. The three-dimensional wire-frame model of the razor shown from a single viewpoint. This model can be translated or rotated through six degrees of freedom, including changing apparent size as it moves toward or away from the camera.

viewpoint-invariant groupings that each model can produce in the image are precomputed off-line. The model is simply checked for three-dimensional instances of the three primitive image relations that are detected during the perceptual grouping process: i.e. connectivity, collinearity and parallelism. These relations are then grouped into the same types of larger structures that are created during the perceptual grouping process, and are stored in separate lists according to the type of the grouping. Any rotational symmetries or other ambiguities simply create new elements in the list of possible matches.

The matching process consists of individually comparing each of the perceptual groupings in the image against each of the precomputed structures of the object model that are likely to give rise to that form of grouping. Obviously, many of these potential matches will be incorrect. Therefore, for each of these matches a verification procedure is executed to solve for the relative viewpoint between the model and image, extend the match to new image segments, and return an answer as to whether the original match was correct. The viewpoint-solving and verification process is itself a major component of the system and is described in detail in other papers (Lowe, 1987a, b). Briefly, the viewpoint determination is done using Newton–Raphson iteration to solve for the values of the six viewpoint parameters that minimize the perpendicular distance between projected model segments and matching image segments. The initial match can then be extended by looking for image segments near the projected positions of model segments from this calculated viewpoint. A probabilistic model similar to that used for grouping is used to select the matching image segments that are least likely to have matched by accident. After a few new matches have been selected, the viewpoint solution is updated to improve the accuracy for the more difficult cases. The final decision regarding the presence of the object is straightforward in these examples, as any mistakes at the initial stage of matching will find very few plausible image segments to extend the match, whereas correct matches will typically find 20 or more matching image segments at the predicted locations. Obviously, a detailed decision criterion would need to be developed for a more general vision system. The verification component is the most robust and reliable component of the system, and its high level of performance in extending and verifying a match can compensate for many weaknesses at the earlier stages. The low probability of false positives in this component means that failure at the earlier levels tends to result simply in an increased search space rather than incorrect matches.

Since the final viewpoint estimate is performed by a least-squares fit to greatly over-constrained data, its accuracy can be quite high. Figure 6 shows the results following recognition, with the model projected from the final calculated viewpoints. The model edges in this image are drawn with solid lines where there is a matching image segment and with dotted lines over intervals where no correspond-

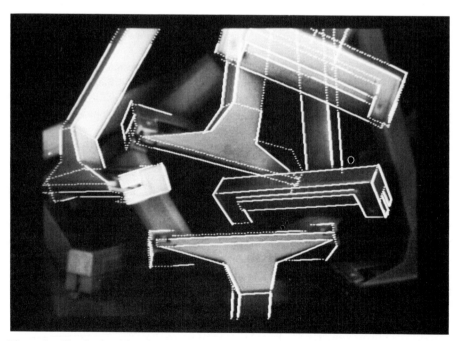

Figure 6. The final results of recognition, with the model projected onto the image from the identified viewpoints. Model edges are shown solid where there was a matching image segment and are shown dotted elsewhere.

ing image segment could be found. The accuracy of the final viewpoint estimates could be further improved by returning to the original zero-crossing data or even the original image for accurate measurement of particular edge locations. The total computation time for these examples included a few seconds of computation on a VICOM image processor to extract the edges, and about 3 minutes for all other stages running under Franz Lisp on a VAX 11/785. There are numerous ways in which the code could be improved to reduce the required amount of computation time if this were a major goal.

FUTURE DIRECTIONS

At first sight, the performance of the computer vision system described here may seem limited enough that it would have little relevance as a model of the vastly more general capabilities of human visual recognition. However, many of these limitations are not inherent in the underlying model. For example, the fact that only one object model is used in the example is entirely arbitrary. Any number of models could be added with at most a linear increase in computation time. Of course, for very large databases of visual knowledge, it would be important to have better than linear performance, which could be achieved by incorporating better grouping techniques (as shown by Jacobs, 1987). Similarly, the fact that the model and image features are composed of only straight line segments is due more to the fact that it simplifies implementation than to an underlying difficulty in incorporating arbitrary curves. Work is currently underway to extend all levels of the system to work with arbitrary curves represented at multiple scales (Lowe, 1989). In fact, curves contain much more information than line segments and therefore provide richer descriptions for perceptual grouping and indexing into the model database.

Clearly, most visual knowledge used by human visual recognition is not limited to rigid objects but can encompass large classes of related objects that vary along multiple dimensions. One way to approach this problem in the computer implementation is to allow for the incorporation of multiple free parameters in addition to viewpoint (Brooks, 1981). Those parameters that are least constrained, such as viewpoint, would be solved for first during the matching process, and then other parameters could be incorporated into the solution as further image data was matched. Even more flexible models could be specified by allowing families of deformations that could be applied to all parts of the model. These techniques would raise many new issues, such as the relative weighting of the various parameters, but they do suggest that very general visual categories could be identified by a process that is similar to the one used for rigid objects.

The assumption stated at the beginning of this chapter was that the goal of recognition is to maximize the probabilities of identifying stable properties of the scene and that the same assumption must therefore hold for each intermediate property derived from the image. For those familiar with recent work on recognition learning in artificial neural networks, this may seem to be very similar to the goals of many neural network models. Indeed, many of the neural network learning algorithms, such as back-propagation (Rumelhart *et al.*, 1986), can be interpreted as maximizing similar probabilistic goals. However, the existing learning algorithms are far too slow to apply to a network of the size and generality necessary to model three-dimensional visual recognition. Therefore, it will still be necessary to examine individual components of vision, such as perceptual organization or viewpoint determination, to model the appropriate computational constraints on their solution. An example of this approach within the neural net framework is Hinton's (1981) model of enforcing consistent viewpoint interpretations during shape recognition from isolated features.

ACKNOWLEDGEMENTS

I would like to thank Bob Hummel, Alan Mackworth, Bob Woodham and Jim Little for valuable discussions and assistance with this work. The author is supported as a Scholar of the Canadian Institute for Advanced Research. This work was also supported by the Natural Sciences and Engineering Research Council and by the National Science Foundation.

REFERENCES

Barrow, H. G. & Tenenbaum, J. M. (1981). Interpreting line drawings as three-dimensional surfaces. *Artificial Intelligence*, **17**, 75–116.

Biederman, I. (1985). Human image understanding: recent research and a theory. *Computer Vision, Graphics and Image Processing*, **32**, 29–73.

Brooks, R. A. (1981). Symbolic reasoning among 3-D models and 2-D images. *Artificial Intelligence*, **17**, 285–348.

Gibson, J. J. (1979). *The Ecological Approach to Visual Perception.* Houghton Mifflin, Boston.

Goad, C. (1986). Special purpose automatic programming for 3D model-based vision. In Alex Pentland (Ed.) *From Pixels to Predicates.* Ablex, Norwood, NJ, pp. 371–391.

Hatfield, G. & Epstein, W. (1985). The status of the minimum principle in the theoretical analysis of visual perception. *Psychological Bulletin*, **97**, 155–186.

Helmholtz, H. (1962). *Treatise on Physiological Optics.* Dover, New York (first published 1867).

Hinton, G. E. (1981). A parallel computation that assigns canonical object-based frames of reference. In *Proceedings of the 7th International Joint Conference on Artificial Intelligence*, pp. 683–685.

Hochberg, J. E. (1957). Effects of the Gestalt revolution: the Cornell symposium on perception. *Psychological Review*, **64**(2), 73–84.

Hochberg, J. E. & Brooks, V. (1962). Pictorial recognition as an unlearned ability: a study of one child's performance. *American Journal of Psychology*, **75**, 624–628.

Jacobs, D. W. (1987). GROPER: a grouping-based recognition system for two-dimensional objects. In *IEEE Workshop on Computer Vision*, Miami, pp. 164–169.

Kanade, T. (1981). Recovery of the three-dimensional shape of an object from a single view. *Artificial Intelligence*, **17**, 409–460.

Kanizsa, G. (1979). *Organization in Vision.* Praeger, New York.

Koffka, K. (1935). *Principles of Gestalt Psychology.* Harcourt Brace, New York.

Leeuwenberg, E. & Boselie, F. (1988). Against the likelihood principle in visual form perception. *Psychological Review*, **95**, 485–491.

Lowe, D. G. (1985). *Perceptual Organization and Visual Recognition.* Kluwer, Boston.

Lowe, D. G. (1987a). Three-dimensional object recognition from single two-dimensional images. *Artificial Intelligence,* **31,** 355–395.

Lowe, D. G. (1987b). The viewpoint consistency constraint. *International Journal of Computer Vision,* **1**(1), 57–72.

Lowe, D. G. (1989). Organization of smooth image curves at multiple scales. *International Journal of Computer Vision,* in press.

Lowe, D. G. & Binford, T. O. (1985). The recovery of three-dimensional structure from image curves. *IEEE Transactions: Pattern Analysis and Machine Intelligence,* **7,** 320–326.

Marr, D. (1982). *Vision.* W. H. Freeman, San Francisco.

Marr, D. & Hildreth, E. (1980). Theory of edge detection. *Proceedings of the Royal Society (London), Series B,* **207,** 187–217.

Roberts, L. G., (1965). Machine perception of three-dimensional solids. In J. Tippet *et al.* (Eds) *Optical and Electro-optical Information Processing,* pp. 159–197. MIT Press, Cambridge, MA.

Rock, I. (1983). *The Logic of Perception.* MIT Press, Cambridge, MA.

Rumelhart, D. E., Hinton, G. E. & Williams, R. J. (1986). Learning internal representations by error propagation. In D. E. Rumelhart and J. L. McClelland (Eds) *Parallel Distributed Processing,* Vol. 1, pp. 318–362. MIT Press, Cambridge, MA.

Stevens, K. A. (1981). The visual interpretation of surface contours. *Artificial Intelligence,* **17,** 47–73.

Ungerleider, L. & Mishkin, M. (1982). Two cortical visual systems. In D. Ingle *et al.* (Eds) *Analysis of Visual Behavior.* MIT Press, Cambridge, MA.

Van Essen, D. C. (1985). Functional organization of primate visual cortex. In A. Peters & E. Jones (Eds) *Cerebral Cortex,* Vol. III. Plenum Press, New York.

Author Index

281

Subject Index

3D descriptor 121, 123
activation
   bottom-up 92, 94
   top-down 93
acuity
   peripheral 115
   spatial 218
adaptation 108, 202
afterimage 60
algorithm 4, 80
aliasing 242
ambiguity 53, 58
   of motion 38, 106
Ames room 21
aperture problem 52, 58–59, 105–106
apparent motion 62
articulation
   non-rigid 187–188
   of body 190
assimilation 48
attention
   parallel guidance of 93
   serial 79–80, 89, 100
   spotlight of 27

bag of tricks 4–5, 24
barber-pole 60
basis Fourier 204, 207
basis function 204
binocular disparity 16
binocular matching 12
biological stimulus
   dynamic 183
   static 183
bistability 58
blob 115
border
   chromatic 25, 27, 34, 36
   luminance 34
   texture 65
bottom-up processing 192
boundary
   salient 82
   segmentation 71–72

camouflage 9, 11, 187, 261
canonical illuminant 221
cast shadow 125
cell
   body-motion sensitive 184
   broad stripe 25
   motion-sensitive 184
   view-selective 183
cells 73
   disparity tuned 27
   double opponent 73
   tuned 25
centroid 157–159
channel, spatial-frequency 106
cinematograms 15
circle, illusory 60
closure 10
code, error-correcting 171
coefficient rule 203, 209, 212
collinearity 264, 272, 274
   accidental 267
color 10
   absolute 204
   surface 202–203, 206, 218–219
color constancy 73, 201–209, 218–219, 224
color constancy equation 222
color descriptor 203, 207, 210–211
color vision 50, 73
colorimetry 203
common fate 186
compression, signal 137
computation, natural 22
computational theory 2–3, 119, 148–149
confidence intervals 232
conjunction 81, 85, 87, 90, 93
   search 81
   triple 90
conjunctive targets 82
connectivity 274
   spatial 243
   temporal 243
constancy algorithm 217
constraint 23, 34
   natural 38

NATIONAL UNIVERSITY
LIBRARY SAN DIEGO c 1